THE MAN IN THE BROWN SUIT

MI5, Edward VIII and an Irish Assassin

THE MAN IN THE BROWN SUIT

MI5, Edward VIII and an Irish Assassin

JAMES PARRIS

First published 2019

The History Press
97 St George's Place, Cheltenham,
Gloucestershire, GL50 3QB
www.thehistorypress.co.uk

British Library Cataloguing in Publication Data.
A catalogue record for this book is available from the British Library.

ISBN 978 0 7509 9064 6

Typesetting and origination by The History Press
Printed and bound in Great Britain by TJ International Ltd

Contents

Contents

Prologue

'Thou shalt not kill; but needst not strive
Officiously to keep alive.'[1]

At 12.30 p.m. on 16 July 1936, as the massed bands of the Brigade of Guards had passed and King Edward VIII was following on horseback, a limping man in a shabby brown three-piece suit pressed his way through the crowd lining the pavement along Constitution Hill and drew a loaded revolver from his pocket. Edward was a few yards and seconds from death. In a flurry of panic and confusion, the gun left the man's hand, skidding across the road, coming to rest between the hind legs of the king's horse. The *Annual Register* for 1936 recorded that this 'alarming incident created a momentary panic throughout the country'.[2]

The man with the gun was George Andrew Campbell McMahon, a 32-year-old Irishman. At his Old Bailey trial in September he was dismissed by the Attorney General Sir Donald Somervell as an attention-seeking eccentric acting in pursuit of a petty grievance against the police. Pronounced guilty by the jury of unlawfully and wilfully producing a pistol with intent to alarm the king, McMahon was sentenced to twelve months in prison with hard labour.

So far, so simple.

But MI5, the British security service, had been aware since April 1936 that there was a plot to assassinate Edward: McMahon himself had told them. He informed an MI5 officer with whom he was in regular contact that the attack was planned for June or July and that he was involved. He had even shown the agent the revolver he said he always carried. Interviewed by Special Branch, McMahon told the same story. When McMahon met his MI5 handler on 13 July he named the day and place that the attempt would be made. MI5's chief, Sir Vernon Kell, discussed the threat with the Metropolitan Police assistant commissioner, Norman Kendal.

Despite knowing what was coming – where, when, how – MI5 and Special Branch did nothing: they neither placed McMahon under close observation nor tailed him as he set out from home on 16 July carrying a .36 calibre revolver loaded with four bullets, with more ammunition in his pocket. McMahon had the nerve to ask a mounted policeman to shift out of his line of vision and took the gun from his pocket, yards from the king. Why were MI5 and Special Branch paralysed? Crass bungling, or was something more sinister involved? Were they intentionally standing aside, allowing an attempt on the king's life to proceed?

Edward had no doubt that the threat to his life had been real, masking his concern with an attempt at a joke. His courage in the circumstances was admirable. 'We have to thank the Almighty for two things,' he later wrote to the general who had been accompanying him on horseback from the ceremony in Hyde Park. 'Firstly, that it did not rain, and secondly that the man in the brown suit's gun did not go off!!'[3] The king's mistress and future wife Wallis Simpson wrote after the incident, 'The shot at HM and the upset summer plans have all been very disturbing ... No place seems very safe for kings.'[4]

Assassination was certainly in the European air. On 6 May 1932 Paul Gorguloff, a Russian refugee from the 1917 revolution, fired three pistol shots at the French president, Paul Doumer, at the opening of a Paris book fair. Two bullets hit the 75-year-old Doumer, one in the right armpit, the other his head. He died in a hospital bed the following day. Gorguloff, a convicted abortionist, had been angered by what he saw as the French government's weak attitude towards Communists. In court Gorguloff's lawyer claimed his client was insane, a plea the jury rejected. Gorguloff was condemned to death and despatched by guillotine on 14 September.

Two years later, on 25 July 1934, a squad of Austrian Nazis gunned down Chancellor Engelbert Dollfuss in a failed coup attempt. The plotters were tried and hanged. Not long after, on 9 October, King Alexander I of Yugoslavia was shot, along with his chauffeur and the French foreign minister, Louis Barthou, while driving through the streets of Marseilles at the opening of a state visit. Both the king and the minister died. The assassin, Vlado Chernozemski, a Bulgarian separatist, was slashed by a cavalry sabre, trampled by the crowd and shot by a police officer, dying the same evening.

In 1929 the French writer André Breton proposed in his *Second Manifesto of Surrealism*: 'The simplest Surrealist act consists of dashing down into the street, pistols in hand, and firing blindly, as fast as you can pull the trigger, into the crowd.'[5] Breton intended no such thing and this display of intellectual terrorism was merely an attempt to shock the bourgeoisie. By coincidence, an International Surrealist Exhibition opened in London in the summer of 1936, with Breton – the 'Pope of Surrealism' – a dominating presence. The exhibition catalogue claimed for the movement: 'It is defiant – the desperate act of men too profoundly convinced of the rottenness of our civilisation to want to save a shred of its respectability.'[6]

A few weeks later, McMahon stood on Constitution Hill brandishing a loaded revolver. Cold and efficient, the weapon – even in the hands of an inexperienced gunman – was capable of unleashing five bullets in two seconds. His exploit appeared as senseless as Breton's projected *acte gratuit*, an empty gesture. When he came to trial, the prosecution seemed determined to convince an Old Bailey jury that this was indeed the case, minimising the deadly implications of McMahon's action. The essential difference was that he carried a real weapon, with real bullets, in the presence of a living king.

Was McMahon acting out his own surreal fantasy, or had MI5 and Special Branch allowed or perhaps even colluded in something far graver and far more disturbing? There were many in the political establishment and in the royal family itself who had long believed Edward was not fit to be king, even that he represented a danger to national security.

King Edward VIII did not die as some may have wished in the summer of 1936. The problem of removing an unsuitable monarch found its resolution a few months later with Edward's self-inflicted social death, his act of abdication. He and Wallis Simpson – the twice-wed and twice-divorced 'woman I love' – went into exile, married and measured out the decades that followed in an idle faux-aristocratic charade as the 'Duke and Duchess of Windsor'.

His conversations often began, 'When I was king …' The couple's associates were seedy, moneyed Americans, minor European nobility of dubious provenance, and – with an all-too-apt irony – their near neighbours the fascist Mosleys, Oswald and Diana. The duke died in 1972, aged 77, followed fourteen years later by his widow. But Edward had faced the possibility of his actual demise, his physical death, much earlier, while the forces of law and order stood by with arms folded.

I

Two Men:
Edward and George

1

At first glance, the contrast between the two men whose paths crossed so dramatically on Constitution Hill on 16 July 1936 – Edward Windsor and George McMahon – could not have been greater: the invisible man emerging from the crowd to confront the all-too-visible man, history from below clashing with history from above. But what they had in common would have surprised them. Both were estranged from their families, having broken painfully and irrevocably. Both had brothers who outshone them in managing the business of everyday life. Both took pains with their appearance, anxious to present a stylish image to the world. Both flirted with the politics of the right. Above all, both sought to escape the constricted and unsatisfying existences to which they felt themselves condemned. Their shared unwillingness to accept the parts birth intended them to play made them, despite the vastly different arenas in which they performed, companions in subversion.

2

Unlike the ever-obscure George McMahon, every fact is known about Edward Windsor, every detail set out, scrutinised, analysed, fictionalised. A glance each morning at the Court Circular in *The Times*, *Daily Telegraph* or *Morning Post* in the 1920s or '30s would tell the reader where Edward had been and was due to go, though not what he was thinking. Blessed, or cursed, with a sensitivity that heightened an awareness of his position, Edward recognised early on the essential emptiness of the public role to which he was destined. A fellow European royal, Victor Emmanuel III of Italy, had been advised by his father Umberto, 'Remember: to be a king, all you need to know is how to sign your name, read a newspaper, and mount a horse.' Victor Emmanuel, like Edward, eventually abandoned his throne. At the age of 25 the Prince of Wales bemoaned to his private secretary, 'Christ, how I loathe my job now and the press "puffed" empty "succés". I feel I am through with it and long to die.'[1]

Edward Albert Christian George Andrew Patrick David Saxe-Coburg und Gotha was born on 23 June 1894 at White Lodge, Richmond, the first son of the Duke and Duchess of York. Four names – George, Andrew, Patrick, David – were intended to represent in his person the unity of the nations making up the kingdom. The Independent Labour Party Member of Parliament for West Ham South, Keir Hardie, outraged the House of Commons a few days after the birth by telling them, presciently:

> From his childhood onward this lord will be surrounded by sycophants and flatterers by the score (*Cries of 'Oh, oh!'*) and will be taught to believe himself as of a superior creation. (*Renewed cries of 'Oh, oh!'*) A line will be drawn between him and the people whom he might be called upon some day to reign over. In due course, following the precedent which has already been set, he will be sent on a tour round the world, and probably rumours of a morganatic alliance follow (*Loud cries of 'Oh, oh!' and 'Order!' and 'Question'*), and the end of it all will be that the country will be called upon to pay the bill.[2]

Half a century later Edward, now Duke of Windsor, would write of Hardie that, 'as a prophet of Royal destiny he has proved uncannily clairvoyant.'[3]

The roll of the child's godparents at his christening in July showed the wide reach of the family's European network, a Monarchic International: Queen Victoria (great-grandmother), King Christian IX and Queen Louise of Denmark (great grandparents), the Prince and Princess of Wales (grandparents), the Duke and Duchess of Teck (grandparents), the Duke of Cambridge (grand-uncle), the Duke of Saxe-Coburg und Gotha (grand-uncle), Queen Olga of Greece (grand-aunt), Prince Adolphus of Teck (uncle), the Tsarevitch Nicholas of Russia (father's cousin), and King William II of Württemberg (mother's cousin).

Within two decades many of the titles had gone, the emperors, kings and nobles banished, leaving Britain one of the few countries maintaining the institution of monarchy. Tsar Nicholas II of Russia, left to the mercy of the Bolsheviks by his fearful cousin George V (Edward's father), was driven from the throne in 1917 and then a year later executed, wife and children perishing with him in a Yekaterinburg cellar. All the German princes and dukes lost their crowns in 1918, and Kaiser Wilhelm, another of George's cousins, scuttled off to exile in the Netherlands as his country went down to defeat and revolution. In total, five emperors, eight kings and eighteen minor dynasties were stripped of their crowns during George V's reign.

How long would the British monarchy survive? Even before the First World War Edward's grandfather, Edward VII, was bleakly pessimistic about the Crown's prospects, as the former Grand Duke Alexander of Russia recalled in 1932:

> I shall never forget the reconciled irony of Edward VII's voice when, as he sat on the terrace of his summer palace and looking at his then very youthful grandson, the present Prince of Wales, playing in the garden below, he nudged me and said with the air of an astrologist reading the future: 'You see that boy – the last King of England!'[4]

In 1917 Edward's family began adjusting to what already promised to be a new and, for them, alarming state of affairs. In February cousin Nicky had been toppled from the Russian throne. In July, with no end in sight to the war and the embarrassing paradox of the Saxe-Coburg und Gotha clan leading the nation against the Hohenzollern house in Germany impossible to ignore (particularly when Gotha bombers appeared over London), the royal family adopted a fresh, more English guise. Summoned by the king to Buckingham Palace on his appointment as prime minister in December 1916, the relatively lowly born David Lloyd George had asked, 'I wonder what my little German friend has got to say to me?' Older members of the family had been so at ease with their Teutonic roots, Edward recalled in later life, that they relaxed into German once the English servants were safely out of the room.[5]

'We,' George proclaimed on 17 July 1917, 'having taken into consideration the Name and Title of Our Royal House and Family, have determined henceforth Our House and Family shall be styled and known as the House and Family of Windsor.' Hearing the news, the German Kaiser – Queen Victoria's grandson, Edward's first cousin removed – laughed and said he was off to the theatre to see a performance of Shakespeare's *Merry Wives of Saxe-Coburg-Gotha*. The household of one of Edward's cousins and future close friend Louis made the equally hasty transition from Battenberg to Mountbatten.

As well as undergoing this change of surname at the age of 23, Edward would pass through a succession of titles: Prince Edward, Duke of Cornwall and Duke of Rothesay; Prince of Wales and Earl of Chester; King and Emperor of India; finally coming to rest as Duke of Windsor. To family and close friends he was David, not Edward. His early formation had all the casualness of preparation for an insubstantial, if not inconsequential, life: a man born to what he had no choice but to become. Reared with the emotional neglect common to the contemporary upper classes, tormented physically and psychologically by his nanny, Edward was barely educated by a private tutor chosen for sporting rather than academic ability. 'He never taught us anything at all,' Edward recalled to a friend half a century on, adding in an almost word-for-word echo of something George McMahon would say, 'I am completely self-educated.'[6]

Edward often complained in later life that he had felt unloved as a child. 'I had a wretched childhood,' he was quoted as saying. 'Of course, there were short periods of happiness but I remember it chiefly for the miserableness I had to keep to myself.'[7] Whether George V actually made the terrible promise, 'My father was frightened of his mother; I was frightened of my father, and I am damned well going to make sure that my children are frightened of me,' and it is disputed, he certainly gave the impression this was the child-rearing philosophy he felt happiest with. A family acquaintance once remarked that Edward's father enjoyed setting ambushes for his children on trivial points of etiquette or dress so he could then berate and humiliate them, his booming voice taking a sarcastic edge. The outcome for his sons was hardly surprising: Edward, a fashion-obsessed playboy with an inability to concentrate; Albert (Duke of York, later George VI), who suffered from a stutter, a ferocious temper, lifelong gastric problems and an obsession with uniforms; George (Duke of Kent), a sexually ambivalent drug addict.

When Edward's emotionally inhibited mother, Queen Mary, died in 1953 he observed to his wife, 'I somehow feel that the fluids in her veins must always have been as icy cold as they are now in death.'[8] The Liberal Chancellor of the Exchequer Lloyd George, who organised Edward's investiture as Prince of Wales in 1911, underlined this feeling about Queen Mary's distance from her son, telling his private secretary, 'She was always against the little fellow.'[9] Mary herself was once heard describing Edward as 'my poor silly son'.[10] As if this sense of a dearth of affection were not enough, Edward had little contact with children of his own age, playtime confined to his brothers and carefully selected companions.

In 1907 Edward followed in his father's steps as a cadet at Osborne, the naval college on the Isle of Wight, despite failing the entrance exam. This was a necessary emblematic move in a Britain that 'ruled the waves'. Tearful on arrival, he was the only boy never to have been away from home before. Asked his name – an obvious provocation, as no one could be in doubt – he replied, 'Edward'. 'Edward what?' – 'Just Edward, that is all.' Shy and small for his age, he was stamped with the nickname 'Sardine'. Thrust into the company of thirty strangers in a dormitory, Edward was bullied and given a reminder one afternoon that England had executed a monarch. A group of cadets seized him, raised a sash window, slowly lowered the frame until he was held by the neck, and ran off. This symbolic acting out of the axe that had decapitated Charles Stuart, and of the French revolutionary guillotine, continued until the boy's cries brought release.

The Royal Naval College at Dartmouth was the next destination for a young man intended for a career as a sea-going officer. Edward went on to Dartmouth in 1909 but it soon became obvious that a naval life was out of the question and that his future would be purely ceremonial. On the death of Edward VII in May 1910 and his father George's accession to the throne, Edward became heir, taking the title Duke of Cornwall and the duchy's revenues of £90,000 a year, largely held in trust until he reached 21. His grandfather's funeral at the end of the month represented the last unified parade of European monarchy, with Kaiser Wilhelm of Germany, the kings of Spain, Portugal, Denmark, Greece, Norway, Belgium and Bulgaria, together with representatives of Emperor Franz Joseph of Austria, Tsar Nicholas of Russia and the King of Italy.

A year later, on his sixteenth birthday, Edward was invested as the nineteenth Prince of Wales at Caernarfon Castle in an 'invention of tradition' ceremony mocked up by Lloyd George – Constable of the Castle, as well as Chancellor of the Exchequer. He primed the prince with a few rudimentary Welsh phrases. Against a background of suffragette 'outrages', bitter class war in Britain's industrial areas, and intensifying strife over Irish home rule, Edward and his family were called upon – not for the last time – to provide a colourful diversion from reality.

At the conclusion of his course at Dartmouth, Edward went briefly to sea, spending three months as midshipman on the battleship HMS *Hindustan*, never leaving British waters, hardly more than a lengthy cruise. Nevertheless, it was the taste of a career Edward might have enjoyed had he been free to choose. A letter from the ship's captain to Queen Mary praised her son's zeal. But George called Edward to Sandringham, the family home, and told him he would have to leave the navy, which he said was 'too specialised' an activity for the heir to the throne. The adult Edward understood all too well the irony of his pretend life, joking that though he was now entitled to wear an admiral's uniform he pitied anyone having to rely on his navigational ability.

The pattern of Edward's existence now seemed determined – shifting from one activity to another, with no opportunity to focus or concentrate on an occupation or endeavour that might satisfy him. In October 1912, after spending four months in France with the Marquis de Breteuil to develop his French, Edward registered as an undergraduate at Magdalen College, Oxford. His stay at the university had originally been intended to last for one year, but he stayed for two. Though accompanied by an equerry, his childhood tutor and a valet, Edward enjoyed greater freedom than he had previously known, living and mixing with a wider range of men – though obviously still within a narrow class band – hunting, playing tennis, golf and polo, turning out for the college football 2nd XI, and parading with the Officers' Training Corps. He was also celebrated for annoying his neighbours with incessant strumming of the ukulele. Naturally, he was elected to the Bullingdon, the socially exclusive dining club, but was forced to resign by his mother, Queen Mary, when she had reports of a particularly raucous evening.

Edward took little if any interest in what Oxford had to offer academically. His tutors cobbled together a special course in history and modern languages, but there was never any intention he should take a degree. He passed the Easter and summer vacations in the palaces of a string of his German relations. Kaiser Wilhelm, with whom Edward stayed in Berlin, described him as 'A most charming, unassuming young man ... a young eagle, likely to play a big part in European affairs because he is far from being a pacifist'.[11] Edward later wrote of how the Germany he knew at this time impressed him. 'I admired the industry, the perseverance, the discipline, the thoroughness, and the love of the Fatherland so typical of the German people, qualities that were to be found in every calling ...'[12]

Wealthy and with no encouragement to take up interests that could in any way be described as cultural or intellectual – 'Bookish he will never be,' his Oxford tutor blurted out to *The Times* in 1914 – Edward became devoted to fashion. This was understandable given that the role to which he was born involved turning up at the right place at the right time in the right outfit. Appearance was everything. For Edward as Prince of

Wales and as king the cut and pattern of trousers (from Foster & Son) and jackets (from Frederick Scholte of Savile Row) took on an absolute importance. He single-handedly created a new vogue by defying his father and wearing brown shoes with a navy blue suit. In later life he described himself, with no hint of irony, as a 'true British dandy'. In 1934, as Prince of Wales, Edward could claim to have been the first man in England to replace the conventional button fly in trousers with the zip, a move followed by his brother, the Duke of York, and his cousin Lord Louis 'Dickie' Mountbatten.

George V had developed the solid and unostentatious respectability of a country squire during his reign, marking out the contrast with his own father, the rakish Edward VII. George's son, whose manner of life would make him increasingly vain, selfish and extravagant, found this a difficult part to play. 'We have come to regard the Crown as the head of our morality,' Walter Bagehot had written in *The English Constitution* in the reign of Edward's great-grandmother, Victoria. George understood that; Edward could not or preferred not to. The danger for Edward lay in continuing to play the eternal pretty youth, slim, slight and irresponsible, into adulthood. In 1916 Lord Edward Cecil would describe to his wife how the 21-year-old prince had struck him: 'He is a nice boy of fifteen, rather immature for that age … I hope he will grow up, but he is leaving it till late.'[13]

Two decades later Wallis Simpson, the double divorcée Edward abandoned his throne and country to marry, called him 'Peter Pan' when writing to a previous husband, in what had been a long-standing private joke between them. As Peter says in J.M. Barrie's play, 'I just want always to be a little boy and have fun.'[14]

3

Two days after Britain declared war on Germany on 4 August 1914, Edward was commissioned and drafted into the 1st Battalion Grenadier Guards. His first hope had been to rejoin the navy, where he had trained to be an officer. His pleas in October to be allowed to accompany his regiment to the battlefront in France were rejected. He told the War Secretary, Lord Kitchener, that with four brothers in line to replace him as heir to the throne his death would hardly be a disaster. Kitchener's response was that he was less concerned with Edward being killed than with the possibility of his being taken prisoner. To Edward's disappointment he was transferred to the 3rd Grenadier Battalion at Wellington Barracks and then attached to the staff of the commander-in-chief, Sir John French. A general promised the king in November he would keep his son well occupied and as far from gunfire as possible.

Edward was deployed on morale-boosting visits to the armies in France, generating what appeared to be a genuine and long-lasting affection for him among the troops who, despite the extra bull and cleaning his appearances demanded, perhaps instinctively recognised – albeit from a distance – his genuine and sympathetic humanity. But he complained to a family friend in March 1915, seven months into the war, 'I hold commissions in both services and yet I'm not allowed to fight. Of course, I haven't got a proper job, which is very painful to me and I feel I am left too much in a glass case.'[15]

In Autumn 1915 Edward conducted a tour of inspection of the front line with the Guards Division commander, the Earl of Cavan, during a lull in the Battle of Loos. Waves of men had advanced earlier across open ground towards enemy trenches and many of Edward's Grenadier comrades were lying where German machine guns had cut them down. This was his first real encounter with the carnage of battle. As he returned to the royal Daimler with Cavan the area came under shell fire, forcing them to take shelter. When the bombardment ceased and they emerged into the open, Edward found his car riddled with shrapnel, his driver killed. He wrote in his diary, 'I can't yet realise that it has happened!! ... This push is a failure ... I have seen & learnt a lot about war today.' The impact of all this remained in his mind and he was to write thirty years later, 'The battle of Loos was one of the great military fiascos of the war.'[16]

Edward was distressed by his recognition of the essentially make-believe nature of his role. He slept comfortably in chateaux in France, never in a trench or dug-out under shell fire, plagued by rats and the ever-present fear of death. He was to write bitterly forty years later,

'It took me a long time to become reconciled to the policy of keeping me away from the front line. Manifestly I was being kept, so to speak, on ice, against the day that death should claim my father.'[17] His frequent periods of leave in London and the frustration of his position encouraged a taste for drinking and lounging in nightclubs he was never to lose.

In the June 1916 King's Birthday Honours list Edward was awarded the Military Cross. The medal had been instituted in 1914 as a decoration for officers carrying out 'acts of exemplary gallantry during active operations against the enemy'. He was aware of the contempt fighting troops felt for staff officers sporting decorations intended to commend acts of exceptional bravery. He tried to reject the award, just as he had earlier attempted to decline the presentation of the *Croix de Guerre* from France and the Order of St George from Russia. Edward wrote to his father, 'I think you know how distasteful it is for me to wear these two war decorations having never done any fighting & having always been kept well out of danger!!' He continued, 'I feel ashamed to wear medals which I only have because of my position ...'[18] His father ordered him to have the medal ribbons sewn onto his uniform tunic at once. Edward went on to protest at the absurdity of his promotion from lieutenant to captain when he held no position of command over troops and was never likely to.

The pressure of war was teaching Edward a lesson about the nature of monarchy. What he saw as undeserved medals and unmerited promotion symbolised an existence he found humiliating: never really a sailor, a student, a fighting soldier or an officer with responsibility for the lives and welfare of his men; always the pretender. Edward's war continued uneventfully with six weeks in Egypt, ostensibly inspecting and reporting on transport and supply organisation in the Canal Zone, but mainly devoted to visiting Australian and New Zealand troops recently withdrawn from the Dardanelles debacle, and sightseeing along the Nile. He interrupted his journey home to pass a few days near the front against the Austrians with Victor Emmanuel of Italy, whose father had tutored him in the minimal demands made on kings; he returned to France in September 1918, attached to the Canadian army staff until the Armistice ended the war in November.

In 1919 Edward described his wartime experience to a City of London audience: 'The part I played was, I fear, a very insignificant one, but from one point of view I shall never regret my periods of service overseas. In those four years I mixed with men. In those four years I found my manhood.'[19] This was an honest, if touchingly immature, estimation of the part he had played. But a manufactured myth that Edward had endured the danger and squalor of the trenches was encouraged to take root in the popular imagination. *The Times* once described King Edward as 'a soldier proven in war'.[20] The fascist William Joyce – who as 'Lord Haw-Haw' would go on to broadcast Nazi propaganda from Berlin in the Second World War – exaggerated even more in an article praising Edward, describing him as 'a soldier, who possesses actual fighting experience'.[21]

Edward would surely have shown himself to be as brave and dogged as the millions of men in every army thrown into battle as volunteers or conscripts. As a steeplechase rider in the 1920s his nerve would border on the reckless. But fate denied him the chance to test himself under fire. Though he certainly suffered the distress of hearing that friends and army comrades had been killed, Edward did not experience the trauma of their dying beside him. On 1 April 1918, as the German Spring Offensive on the Western Front was breaking through the Allied lines, he wrote to his new mistress Freda Dudley Ward: 'How kind fate is to have sent me back to Italy, so that I am escaping that fearful battle!! It's very unpatriotic of me to say this but still these are my genuine feelings …'[22] It was only to Freda that he could reveal these kinds of emotions and thoughts.

An official photograph of Edward taken shortly after the war shows him dressed as the recently appointed colonel-in-chief of the Welsh Guards, a lavish display of medal ribbons over his left breast pocket, three lines in all, not a single one earned under fire, much to his regret. There is another side to this, a spontaneous display of immense compassion. Following the Armistice in November 1918 Edward visited a Belgian military hospital and was taken to a ward where twenty-eight horrifically wounded men were being cared for. He greeted and exchanged a few words with twenty-seven and then asked where the final man was:

They explained that this case was too ghastly a wreck of humanity. He was no more than a breathing lump of ruined flesh. None knew even his nationality. The Prince demanded to see him, and against what was left of that face he put his cheek.[23]

The war had given Edward a ringside seat at the fracturing of the old order throughout Europe. It was inconceivable that, as for many of his generation, this would not have an impact on his attitude to life and his response to what the world expected of him.

4

At Buckingham Palace, Edward's post-war role as Prince of Wales was already being mapped out behind his back. As early as April 1917 – when Tsar Nicholas had lately been deposed by his subjects and the word 'revolution' was beginning to ring out across Europe – the Bishop of Chelmsford, John Watts-Ditchfield, suggested to the king's private secretary, Lord Stamfordham, that 'the stability of the Throne would be strengthened if the Prince of Wales married an English lady,' adding that she must be 'intelligent and above all full of sympathy'.[24] After the embarrassment of a war fought out by the subjects of inter-married royal cousins, making the farcical name change from Saxe-Coburg und Gotha to Windsor an urgent necessity, the future monarchy must be fully English, with no European influences there to provoke awkward questions about the meaning of 'patriotism'. The *Daily Express*, though, thought it might be an idea for Edward to marry an American.

A new face of monarchy was being prepared, one that left the palaces and showed itself to the public. One, in Stamfordham's words, that demonstrated that the Crown was 'a living power for good'.[25] An early signal was the appointment in 1918 of a full-time Buckingham Palace press officer. Next, there were plans to deploy royal patronage of charities and voluntary social services to make the monarchy appear relevant to people's everyday lives. An occasional wave from the fairy-tale coach was no longer seen as enough. This would, the feeling was, justify the institution's continuing existence at a time when, as Lloyd George put it at the London Guildhall the day the war ended, 'Emperors and Kingdoms and Kings and Crowns are falling like withered leaves before a gale.'[26]

The part Edward personally was to play was outlined in October 1918 by Clifford Woodward, soon to be appointed as the king's chaplain and future Canon of Westminster Abbey. He recommended to the influential Stamfordham that in view of the Labour Party's growing strength, and the threat of a levelling revolution, the Prince of Wales should engage himself with social problems to consolidate working-class loyalty to the Crown. 'It would, I suppose, be far easier for him than for the King and it might lead to very big results.' Woodward submitted that Edward night even set up home for a time in one of Britain's major industrial centres.[27]

Edward was never forced to make that always-unlikely move to the provinces, but his parents and their advisers encouraged him to present himself over the next decade or so as 'the people's friend' to further the Windsor survival strategy. A deferential and compliant media – the press, the cinema newsreel corporations and BBC radio – bolstered him in this until the very moment of his abdication in 1936. He eventually became patron of over 750 charitable and welfare organisations.

But first came the Empire, as Edward was despatched to reinforce imperial unity, 'a family of nations bound together', as *The Times* was to put it, 'by the golden link of the Crown'. It had, of course, been Queen Victoria's assumption of the title 'Empress of India' in 1876 that re-injected popular enthusiasm into a faltering monarchy. A parallel role was to drum up trade for British goods – one newspaper described him as the 'Empire's star salesman'. Edward's next few years were taken up with a run of visits to Britain's overseas possessions, confirming the forecast Keir Hardie had made in 1894. From August to November 1919 Edward toured Canada (also taking in the United States), cheered by rapturous crowds, eulogised by the press in every city as a royal for the modern age (as every young royal invariably is), descending into the multitude to bestow the princely touch. When the prince's arrival in Basutoland (now Lesotho) coincided with the end of a long drought, he was eulogised for his supposed supernatural powers.

In almost daily letters to his mistress Freda Dudley Ward, the estranged wife of a Liberal MP sixteen years her senior, Edward revealed the self-doubt and sense of entrapment plaguing him behind the smiling mask. A month into the tour he complained about the pressure of maintaining the 'P. of W. stunt' and doubted his fitness for kingship. 'I feel I am through, & realise as I have so often told you sweetheart that I'm not ½ big enough man to take on what I consider is about the biggest job in the world.' Two weeks later he complained, 'I feel like a caged animal.'[28]

When he came to write his autobiography *A King's Story* after the Second World War Edward described what his father had said to him in 1918, and would often repeat: '*Remember your position and who you are* – in the years that were to come that injunction was to be dinned into my ears many, many times. But who exactly was I?'[29] Edward knew the crowds flocking to greet him did not see an individual, a man, but a walking symbol. 'I am not so foolish as to think that the wonderful welcome given me in Canada and again today are mere tributes to myself,' he said on his return to England from North America. 'I realise that they are given to me as the King's son and heir.'[30]

What followed from this for Edward was whether he could feel confident anyone at all would like, love, admire or respect him for the person he was rather than the title he carried, or, as he had said, whether they saw only the fiction the press created. Every prince is handsome, every princess is beautiful, every king dutiful and wise. The prison in which he believed himself trapped could drive him to an agony of despair and self-loathing. In a Christmas 1919 letter to his private secretary, Edward wrote, 'No one else must know how I feel about my life, and everything ... I do feel such a bloody little shit.'[31]

Edward felt no enthusiasm for what he described to Freda as the 'next fucking trip', to Australia and New Zealand in 1920. His companion – cousin, and at the time his closest friend, 'Dickie' Mountbatten – calculated that the 210-day round of charming strangers, delivering speeches and dancing with smitten women ate up 45,000 miles, taking in 208 cities and towns. Being in such intimate confinement for such a length of time gave Mountbatten insight into Edward's moods. He wrote to his mother, 'At times he gets so depressed, and says he'd give anything to change places with me.'[32]

In one letter to Freda during the long Pacific crossing Edward wrote that he longed to marry her, that he could marry no other woman, but that it would be cruel to ask her to take on the job of wife to the Prince of Wales. 'It just would not be fair on you sweetheart though who knows how much longer this monarchy stunt is going to last or how much longer I'll be P. of W.'[33]

In March 1920 the anguished prince confessed, 'I'm not strong by nature & so have to rely on other people for help in my work & have to be bolstered up though I know it's silly and unnecessary; if only I had some guts.'[34] Two years later his mood had not altered: 'What I wouldn't give to chuck this P. of W. job. I'm so fed up with it you know & don't fit in.'[35] He was a man trapped, self-destructive, self-pitying, already desperate to cast off the role he was born to, sixteen years before his eventual abdication. Freda recalled a fraught conversation in which Edward asked why he could not live an ordinary life. 'You were born to be king,' she told him,

> It's there waiting for you, and you can't escape it.
> Again and again I heard him grumble, 'What does it take to be a good king? You must be a figurehead, a wooden man! Do nothing to upset the Prime Minister or the Court or the Archbishop of Canterbury! Show yourself to the people! Mind your manners! Go to church! What modern man wants *that* sort of life?'[36]

The years 1921 and 1922 found Edward representing his father the king-emperor in India, Ceylon and Malaya. India he felt was the most dispiriting destination of all. The tour of these imperial possessions came not long after the Amritsar massacre, when Indian troops under British command killed over 300 unarmed civilians protesting peacefully against the deportation of two nationalist leaders. The atmosphere was bitter.

Edward had tried to persuade Prime Minister Lloyd George to talk the king into sending his younger brother Albert instead.

Despite his self-image as 'progressive' and a 'democrat' to whom the experience of army life had given the common touch, Edward seemed to have no comprehension of the widespread resentment Indians had towards alien British rule. He was critical of even the most limited moves towards self-government, denouncing them as 'pandering to the natives'. As Edward's official biographer tactfully put it, 'He had no doubt that the Indians and Burmese were wholly incompetent to run their own affairs and would be lost without the benevolent supervision of their colonial masters.'[37]

Agitation by Mahatma Gandhi and the pro-independence Congress Party ensured, despite mass arrests of activists, that the crowds greeting Edward were meagre compared to those he had grown accustomed to in North America and Australia. Security was tight as plans were uncovered to bomb Edward's party. He wrote to his father on 16 December 1921, 'Well I must tell you that I'm very depressed about my work in British India as I don't feel I am doing a scrap of good; in fact I can say that I am not.'[38]

Edward boasted in his autobiography, *A King's Story*, that he was a rebel, scorning the outdated values of his father's generation, and in some minor ways he was and did. But one value he did share was their deeply rooted sense of white superiority, a prejudice he was to maintain all his life and took no trouble to hide from his peers. He wrote to Freda from Barbados in March 1920, 'I didn't take much to the coloured population, who are revolting.' In July he wrote excitedly from Australia:

Oh, I forgot to tell you that they showed us some of the native aborigines ... they are the most revolting form of living creatures I've ever seen!! They are the lowest known form of human beings & are the nearest thing to monkeys I've ever seen ... these filthy nauseating creatures ...[39]

Stopping briefly in Mexico during the cruise home from Australia and New Zealand, Edward gave Freda his impression of the town of Acapulco. 'The people are too revolting for words, sweetheart,' he wrote, 'super dagoes & some of them are quite black as a result of Spaniards inter-breeding with the Indians; & of course they only talk Spanish so that i couldn't make myself understood even in my bad Italian ...'[40]

5

Edward's expeditions to Britain's industrial and mining areas through the 1920s followed a similar pattern to his Empire tours and were undertaken for similar reasons – an attempt to bind together an economically fragile nation, one still psychologically traumatised by war, through the magic of monarchy. In post-First World War Britain, the fear that discontent could lead to revolution, though exaggerated, remained in the minds of the authorities. Returning from Glasgow, the city of the radical Clydesiders, Edward wrote to Freda, 'I do feel I've been able to do just a little good propaganda up there and given Communism a knock.'[41] He would later say in his memoirs, 'These provincial forays were miniatures of my Imperial tours.'[42] The left-wing Labour MP Aneurin Bevan spotted the inference of this *de haut en bas* attitude on one of Edward's visits to South Wales, organised, Bevan commented angrily, in 'much the same way as you might go to the Congo'.[43]

In July 1922 Edward came closer to danger than he realised when two Irish Republican Army volunteers contrived an audacious plan to kidnap him at the Cowes Regatta. On 22 June two IRA gunmen – both former British soldiers – murdered the Chief of the Imperial General Staff, Sir Henry Wilson, outside his London home, firing six bullets into him. Surrounded by a crowd and captured, the men were tried and sentenced to death. A London-born Republican activist, John Carr, persuaded Dublin IRA command that their lives could be saved by taking the Prince of Wales hostage, holding him to force the British authorities into granting a reprieve. Carr and a Republican volunteer named Denis Kelleher made their way to the Isle of Wight, close to the house where Edward was staying with the Barings, the Anglo-German banking family. But when an alert constable began to take an interest in Kelleher's strong Irish accent the pair were scared off and abandoned the attempt.

It takes only a small leap of the imagination to see the dire possibilities had the Republican exploit gone any further. A bungled attack could have seen Edward shot. Had the kidnapping succeeded, he might have died in a subsequent botched rescue attempt or been murdered by the IRA men out of desperation. Edward would never have become king and the succession would have passed to his younger brother, Albert, the future George VI. The plan itself was patently amateurish and absurd, the work of two not-very-bright pawns in a wider struggle. But the same could have been said of a plot to murder the Chief of the Imperial General Staff in a London street in broad daylight. That had succeeded.

In England, Wales and Scotland, as in Canada, Australia and India, Edward stood before audiences grinding out the platitudinous speeches written by his private secretaries Godfrey Thomas and Alan Lascelles, affecting knowledge and experience he had never achieved.[44] The comic Charlie Chaplin performed an impression among friends of Edward addressing a crowd that captured the vulnerability of his style. 'Chaplin tugged at non-existent cuffs, acknowledged the thunder of the mob, licked a lip and bobbed his head in nervous modesty from side to side: almost a prevision of the melancholy future King.'[45]

In May 1926 Edward addressed the annual pageant of the Boys' Brigade in the tone of confident faux-wisdom common to royal speeches. 'It has been stated, and it most certainly is not exaggerated, that the most important members of the community are the boys, not only for the future of this nation, but for the future of the British Empire.'[46] The man who would never spend a moment of his life in productive work or knowingly risk a penny of his unearned wealth in any kind of useful enterprise instructed an audience of hard-headed Birmingham business-men in January 1927 to visit Canada, where he owned a 4,000-acre dude ranch. 'Canada and the Canadians are a real tonic. They sharpen one up, and they provide, on the serious side, a widened outlook in business ideas which will compensate for any apparent loss of time in work over here.'[47] Edward's problem was that while he could rustle up a convincing performance, he understood the absurdity of what he was doing only too plainly.

Despite the Bishop of Chelmsford's hope in 1917 that Edward would eventually marry 'an English lady', Edward's preference for relationships with already married women suggested he was reluctant to adopt the ostensibly settled domestic life the public had been led to expect from the heir to the crown. His father, George, had married at 28, and his grandfather – the philandering Edward VII – even earlier at 21. Edward remained a bachelor when he came to the throne at the age of 41, his lustre already showing signs of fading. 'I have an inordinate dislike for weddings,' he wrote to his mother, Queen Mary, in 1922. 'I always feel so sorry for the couple concerned.'[48]

Why was he loath to marry? There were rumours, impossible to substantiate, of gay flings with his cousin 'Dickie' Mountbatten during their Empire tours together, with his equerry Major Edward 'Fruity' Metcalfe, and earlier, at Oxford, with his private tutor Henry Hansell. But Lady Diana Cooper, at the heart of the prince's circle in the 1920s and 1930s laughed at the idea when it was put to her. 'Don't be ridiculous. He was never out of a woman's legs.'[49]

In 1916 Edward's fellow officers had taken him to a brothel in Calais, where he was entertained by some kind of sexual performance. 'A perfectly filthy and revolting sight, but interesting for me as it was my first insight into these things,'[50] he recorded in his diary. His first heterosexual experience was orchestrated in the same year by two Guards officers, who introduced him to a prostitute in Amiens named Paulette. In April 1917 he began an intense liaison lasting some months with an up-market prostitute Marguerite Alibert, four years his senior.

Edward's next physically and emotionally significant relationship was with Freda, wife of the Liberal MP William Dudley Ward and mother of two daughters. It was to her – as his many letters showed – he could openly express his unhappiness about his role as heir to the throne. The affair was at its most fervid from 1918 to 1923, when Freda cooled, but she remained his closest confidant until the mid-1930s. In the early years, one biographer observes, Edward was 'madly, passionately, *abjectly* in love with her'.[51] Edward's affairs, while enthusiastically gossiped about in high society (to the embarrassment and anger of his parents), were kept from the public by an obsequious press absorbed in projecting him as the eternally eligible bachelor.

His final mistress before Wallis Simpson made her appearance, was Thelma, wife of Viscount Furness. From early 1930 Thelma and Edward, whom she called the 'Little Man', were regular weekend companions at his home, Fort Belvedere, and at her houses in London and Leicestershire. In January 1931 she introduced Edward to her friend Wallis, unwittingly bringing forward the woman who would turn out to be her replacement.

In one aspect of his life, Edward gave every appearance of feeling comfortable with established practice – Freemasonry – though he makes no mention of this enthusiasm in *A King's Story*. As Prince of Wales he restored the convention broken briefly by his father, George V, of members of the royal family joining the 'Craft'. He was initiated into the Household Brigade Lodge No. 2614 in March 1919 and elected master of the lodge by fellow members in 1921. He was additionally a member of the St Mary Magdalen Lodge No. 1523 (master in 1925), the Lodge of Friendship and Harmony No. 1616 (master in 1935), and the Royal Alpha Lodge, No. 16.

Edward rose through Masonry's perhaps intentionally comic-sounding hierarchy until in June 1936, five months after succeeding to the throne, he broke his formal connection and took the title 'past grand master'. Not before, however, exerting his influential position to ease the passage of Wallis Simpson's husband Ernest into his lodge, angering fellow masons who were convinced that by doing so Edward had broken his masonic oath.

In his private moments, Edward knew that for much of the time he was living a charade, aware how out of kilter he felt in the role to which birth had condemned him. Not only was there the existence that convention expected him to lead, there was the life the people – for all their enjoyment of his apparent informality – had been conditioned to anticipate. 'How shall I behave here?' Edward once asked an American as he walked into a Paris club. 'Like a human being,' the

American replied, just as another English visitor bowed to the prince. Edward sighed, 'How can I?'[52] What could he have become had he been free to follow his inclinations, to find and develop his own talents? He least of all knew. 'I am a misfit,' he told his private secretary in 1927.[53] George McMahon, despite the gulf in their circumstances, would, if he were being honest, have echoed Edward's words exactly.

6

Jerome Bannigan, there can be no doubt, was in revolt against the narrowness of the life to which he seemed destined. His brother Patrick, seizing one opportunity open to a bright young Roman Catholic, trained for the priesthood, while another held 'a fairly responsible position' in a Clyde shipyard office. Jerome left school at 14 to work as a barboy. In his late twenties he changed his name to George Andrew Campbell McMahon, perhaps hoping that a new identity would open up fresh prospects. He remained in the world's eyes a loser, thwarted in his aspirations, an unstable drunk, always on the look-out for a financial opportunity, a chronic – though at first hearing plausible – liar. He was even untruthful about his father's occupation when he came to marry, trying to elevate himself a notch or two up the class hierarchy.

But McMahon was also a complex man, risking his liberty to expose corruption among Metropolitan Police officers, spying on refugees from Fascism and Nazism, consorting with the intelligence agencies of three European powers, and confronting the King-Emperor with a loaded revolver. There was more to him than the 'ordinary' man with a petty grievance that the police, press and courts worked in concert to persuade the public he was in 1936.

'I should think that he is the sort of man who is perpetually thinking out magnificent schemes, but who has very little ability to execute them,' an MI5 officer would note.[54] 'Since a child I never had a chance,' McMahon complained in a petition to Edward VIII in February 1936.[55] The following year he wrote to Lieutenant Colonel Cecil Bevis, a justice of the peace and regular visitor to Wandsworth Prison who had befriended him, 'My career has been a varied one in retrospection. I have very little to enthuse over.'[56]

McMahon sometimes seems a figment of his own imagination. His history is fragmented to the extent that even the vividly dramatic moment in the summer of 1936, at which he was the centre, remains a puzzle. An account of his life has to be weaved together from reports and memoranda in MI5 and police files, from responses his father and friends gave to journalists' questions, and from the sketches McMahon made of himself in letters, petitions and court testimony, rarely reliable and sometimes contradictory. The expression 'unreliable narrator' might have been invented for him. An editorial in *The Times* wrote him off as a sociological and psychological cliché, though one requiring punishment:

> McMahon is evidently part of the economic wreckage of the day, an intellectual and moral weakling broken by unemployment and poverty, nursing his grievances until they become a blind rancour against society ... But, however pitiable, such men are dangerous and it is necessary to remove them to a place where they can do no harm.[57]

There was more to him than a piece of economic wreckage, though he was sometimes that. But if this was all he amounted to he would have lived and died an alcoholic petty criminal in Glasgow, never leaving, never heard of. What was consistent was the way McMahon slid easily into a world of exaggeration and make-believe, one in which everyday reality was fashioned into a shape more closely resembling his dreams. He had, out of context, the contorted sensibility of the spy, the urge to shuffle identities, to contrive situations, to see how far the game could be taken.

When war broke out in 1939 a drifting McMahon wrote to MI5 applying for employment – ludicrously, given his personal history and his recent chequered relationship with the security service, but apparently seriously. 'I can prove useful if given a chance, and would if given a trial be found tactful and silent.' An officer commented in disbelief to a colleague, 'This man is slightly insane. He should not be employed in any confidential capacity.'[58] Had McMahon been making a private joke? It was sometimes hard to tell. The head of the Criminal Investigation Department at Scotland Yard was just as dismissive, writing around the same time, 'Everybody who knows McMahon is satisfied that he is a border line mental case and a born liar.'[59] Nobody used the word 'misfit', but the implication was always there.

One thing is certain: McMahon perhaps was Jerome Bannigan. Jerome, for Roman Catholics – as the Bannigan family were – is the patron saint of people with 'difficult personalities'. Why he should have chosen the particular alias George Andrew Campbell McMahon he never explained, though it must have been when he was fleeing Glasgow, the place of his childhood and youth. Five members of a Belfast family named McMahon had been murdered by police in a revenge shooting in 1922, killed for being readily available Catholic victims. McMahon is of ancient Irish origin and Bannigan may have adopted the family's name as a token of Irish Republican sympathies, but this is conjecture. George, of course, was the name of the man on the British throne when McMahon took on his new identity.

Though he continued to sign himself 'Jerry' in letters to his wife and family, and was known as 'Mac' to acquaintances (and his MI5 handler) in London, 'George' served as a stage name, a *nom de plume* or *nom de guerre*. Like the existential hero he imagined himself to be, McMahon strained to throw off the burden of a troubled past, struggling to create fresh identities and opportunities by an act of will.

When McMahon became a figure of notoriety in 1936 in Britain and beyond, the press and public found the man as baffling as the action that brought him to their notice. He gave his age in court as 34, though newspaper reports ranged from 32 to 38. And on his death in 1970 he was assumed to have been born in 1900, which would have made him 36 at the time of the incident. Was he a Scot or Irish? *The Scotsman* was sure he had been born in Govan, the heart of Clyde shipbuilding, and the *Mid-Ulster Mail* agreed: 'He is not an Irishman … He first saw the light in Glasgow.' The *Daily Mirror* and the *Yorkshire Post* both said he was a Scotsman. Scotland Yard's assessment was that McMahon was 'an Irishman and was taken to Glasgow as a baby'.[60]

A *Mid-Ulster Mail* reader – Patrick M'Guckin of Cookstown – wrote to the editor to clarify matters. 'He was born in Coagh Street, Cookstown, the son of Patrick Bannigan, a breadserver, and Eileen Bannigan (*née* Darragh).' The father had delivered bread for Malone the baker by horse-drawn van and relatives on both sides of the family were still living in the area. 'There were three children of the family, including Jerome,' M'Guckin went on, 'and parents and children left Cookstown for Govan when the family were very young.'[61]

At Bow Street Police Court in July 1936, McMahon told the magistrate, 'I am a natural born British subject and so were my ancestors so far as I can trace.' At the Old Bailey in September that year he replied to the question 'You are an Irishman, are you not?' – 'Irish by birth'. McMahon had been born in the north of Ireland when the entire island was part of the United Kingdom. When the south gained independence in 1921 and Northern Ireland retained the connection, he remained a British subject, though feeling himself to be an Irishman.

Newspapers at the popular end of the market made much of the fact that McMahon was 'club-footed', with the none too subtle implication that the personality of a man who could threaten the life of the king must surely be as malformed and sinister as his body. The disability came as the result of a childhood accident. The boy slipped playing football and dislocated a hip. When he recovered, McMahon's left leg was markedly shorter than the right, giving him a limp for the rest of his days.

'I was only a few weeks at school throughout my life so that I am entirely self-educated,' McMahon wrote in 1937.[62] Given the limitations of early twentieth-century elementary school education, he may have felt that to be the case, but the fact was that he remained at school until he was 14. Nevertheless, his writing style, clumsily pompous and anxious to impress, has all the marks of the autodidact. He was educated at St Anthony's Roman Catholic school, a three-storey Victorian building in Harmony Row, Govan. A former friend told a reporter he and the boy he knew as Jerome met at the school gates every morning and played until they were called into lessons by the bell. 'He left school when I did. We were both fourteen, but his reading had taken him far ahead of me in education.'[63]

McMahon's father Patrick and his Govan acquaintances agreed that the young Jerome – pale and fair-haired – had been a compulsive reader, losing himself in any book that came into his hands. His father told a reporter, 'He seldom mixed with other youngsters, and that, I think, had the effect of giving him an unusual outlook on life ... He read a lot, too much, I think.'[64] Journalistic licence and the tendency to fit the character into a prefabricated category aside, there was some truth to this, at least as far as the post-accident Jerome was concerned. A friend recalled, 'He did not take part in the rough-and-tumble of school life, spoke quietly even as a boy, and impressed us all by his cultured speech.' With one brother training for the priesthood, there would have been ambition in the family, encouraging McMahon to strive to learn more than St Anthony's could teach, to better himself, to escape the confines of Glasgow working-class life, its limitations and deprivations.

'He was just a serious-minded boy,' the friend previously quoted said. How did this serious boy, with his cultured speech and his quiet voice, become a petty criminal and find himself pointing a loaded gun at the king? The story of the course McMahon's life took after leaving school relies almost entirely on his own testimony and in particular the letter he wrote from Wandsworth Prison to retired Lieutenant Colonel Cecil Bevis on 1 April 1937. The letter is long – a copy in his MI5 file runs to six closely-typed pages, hundreds of words – artfully constructed, and described by McMahon as 'a synopsis of my career'.[65]

The letter reads like an intricate blend of fact and fantasy, McMahon working on the raw material of his life to achieve a particular effect, the creation – in its own way – of an artist, a confidence trickster able to convince even himself. His progress after leaving school, as he describes it, was marked by small successes, sudden failures and lost opportunities, with alcohol playing a catastrophic part at crucial moments. 'He has drinking bouts, which send him crazy,' an acquaintance said as the world began to take an interest in McMahon. 'When he drinks – that is, when he has money – he drinks neat whisky mostly.'[66]

What McMahon does not mention is also revealing. The deeply rooted religious sectarianism of Glasgow, the often violent antagonism between Protestants and Catholics, a Northern Ireland in miniature, plays no part in the story McMahon tells of his Scottish childhood and youth. The bitter class struggle on Red Clydeside, the near revolutionary situation in early 1919, when 10,000 troops and a rumoured half a dozen tanks were deployed in the streets of Glasgow to counter what the Scottish Secretary called 'a Bolshevist rising', seems to have passed McMahon by. As did the rent strikes and the anti-eviction battles fought against landlords and the police. Perhaps this forgetting is tied up with his desire for respectability. Poor but decent – not like those people down the street.

McMahon remained unknown beyond his family, friends and acquaintances, and even in their eyes there would be a large element of mystery. But what one section of the wider world knew was that by his mid-twenties, McMahon had served time in prison. A Scotland Yard report set out the facts starkly: 'Jerome Bannigan (his true name) C.R.O. No. 119814-27, upon whom sentence was deferred at Govan Police Court on 7th August 1927, for obtaining money by fraud. Subsequently, he was sentenced to 60 days' imprisonment at Glasgow Sheriff Summary Court, 29th November 1927, on further charges of fraud and embezzlement.'[67]

A convicted felon, with a record that would track him down the years, marked for life as untrustworthy, with little hope of respectable work. The serious boy, the disabled boy, the reader who avoided the rough-and-tumble, the brother of a priest, had become an ex-prisoner, with the bleakest of prospects. What had brought him to this?

From the vantage point of his mid-thirties, McMahon sees a pattern to his life, which he describes in his April 1937 letter to Colonel Bevis. Leaving St Anthony's, he is taken on as a barboy in a Glasgow pub, keeping the bars supplied with glasses and bottles, at general beck and call. His ability is recognised and in a few years he rises to the position of assistant manager, overseeing the work of a staff of twenty. A former friend in Glasgow later recalled: 'His dress when he started to work was a cut above those of his friends. He was, in fact, always stylishly dressed.'[68]

But it does not last. 'I became addicted to drink at this early age and was dismissed, through this weakness or foolishness.'[69] Alcohol, McMahon knew and probably feared, would be the end of him.

Perhaps it was his parents' decision to remove him from the temptations of Glasgow, from the company he kept, to enable him to become, as he put it to Bevis, 'free from the desire for drink'. McMahon took the ferry to Ireland to labour on his uncle's farm in County Tyrone, where his mother and father had their roots. A local newspaper, the *Mid-Ulster Mail*, confirmed in 1936 that he had indeed been to Northern Ireland. 'A resident of the district informs us that Jerome paid a visit to this country about fourteen years ago, and enjoyed the hospitality of many of his parents' neighbours.' But having been sacked from his first job for drunkenness, the stay could very well have been a ploy to enable McMahon to pretend, on his return to Scotland, that he had never worked in Glasgow.

Back in Scotland, cured – as he claimed – of his addiction to alcohol, McMahon said he found work as a conductor on the cable-operated Glasgow Subway Railway and, his ability once again recognised, he was soon promoted to driver. Working as many as eighteen hours some days, McMahon was able to save enough to buy his parents a home. Was he going in for wishful thinking here? His parents had been living in a tenement at 13 Roseneath Street when he was a child, were living there when, after a long interval, he wrote to them from prison in 1936, and remained at that address until they died. Buying them a home feels like the gift of security he would like to have made and by 1937 he believed, or wanted to convince Colonel Bevis, he had, that he was the kind of man who would.

Not just a house, he also bought a small shop. McMahon did not say in the letter what he dealt in, but the business prospered and expanded. He opened more shops, engaged staff, and was eventually making enough to stop working as a tram driver. But – as in the best morality tale, on which the letter gave every impression of being modelled – fate was waiting to strike. Having made sufficient money to enable him to leave the railway, and the quiet boy, the loner, blossomed into an organiser of sports clubs, entertainments and weekend dances. 'Through my many activities, football clubs, etc., I acquired a large circle of "pals" and once more gave way to drink. I neglected my business, and soon lost all.'[70] A theme of triumph and disaster is emerging. What is revealing of McMahon's character is that he places himself at the centre of the drama but rarely blames anyone but himself for the apparently inevitable debacle. There is hardly a trace of self-pity.

Once more out on the street, though probably living with his parents, McMahon first becomes secretary of an ex-servicemen's club, but then has to leave when it is discovered he was never in the armed forces. He takes on the last resort of the desperate – unpaid, commission-only work, insecure and uncertain, the between-the-wars equivalent to the twenty-first-century zero-hours contract. His version of events is that while working as an agent for a drapery warehouse he embezzled 'less than £1', was charged and placed on probation. Engaged next as a travelling salesman for a firm of printers, again on commission rather than a wage, he repeats the crime. 'I was charged with embezzling £1.4.0, and after over a month in custody awaiting trial was given a further 60 days' sentence.'[71]

Why had McMahon turned to crime, relatively petty though it was? He gives no explanation in his letter, nor does he make any excuse. He records the event as a simple fact of life. Had he found it impossible to survive on what he earned, or more likely did not earn? Was he afraid he was adding to the burden his already impoverished family carried? Did drink, as in the past, play a part? Whatever the reason, McMahon was convicted and sent by the sheriff court to the bleak and brutal Barlinnie Prison in the east of Glasgow. Released at the end of his sentence, McMahon left Scotland, never to return. 'We corresponded for a time,' his father later said, 'but things happened which had the effect of breaking this link of communication.'[72]

McMahon's story now takes flight, perhaps because he feels safe in the knowledge there is nobody to contradict what he is saying. He becomes a 'wanderer', stowing away on a ship, allowed to work his passage when he is discovered, roaming the seas, a boy's comic adventure come to life. He is a man with a rich imagination, building on a well of disappointment, carried away with his own ingenuity, the careful placing of details giving an apparent authenticity to the portrayal of his life. One person remained unimpressed, the recipient, for whom McMahon had gone to so much effort. 'There is nothing much in his letter,' Bevis told the head of MI5. 'But I think it should be, or a copy of it, attached to his dossier.'[73]

McMahon's travels bring him to Dublin where, 'down and out', he scrubs floors for bed and board at the Peter Street Salvation Army hostel. As always in McMahon's story, his abilities are recognised and rewarded, this time by 'a grand man, Commandant Mahaffey'. He first becomes cook and then cashier, the latter a risky move on the commandant's part had he been aware of McMahon's record in Glasgow. In McMahon's telling, he becomes a local Salvation Army officer, assistant manager of various hostels, converts numerous patrons to the army's brand of Christianity – 'I honestly feel this was my proper sphere' – and forms bands of musicians from among the residents that win acclaim as far afield as London. So popular is he among the 'lodgers' that when he moves on from one hostel they – pensioners, seamen, homeless, unemployed – present him with a 'little wallet of notes', which, unfortunately, army regulations forbid him from accepting.[74]

McMahon is then 'persuaded' – his word – to sit the examination for entry to the Irish Church Missions College, which he passes. What drove his transition from Roman Catholicism to Protestantism he never explains. The Irish Church Missions had been established in 1849 as an 'Anglican evangelical mission', to persuade Roman Catholics to abandon their faith and to embrace a rigid Protestantism. McMahon begins his studies at the college but is disappointed to find his fellow students – graduates from Trinity College, Dublin, and the sons of 'well-to-do parents' – are 'snobs' and, worse, not 'real Christians'. He had no choice, he told Colonel Bevis, but to abandon the course. The mirroring of his brother Patrick's career – St Patrick's College in Dublin, followed by ordination in 1926 – suggests McMahon is, as in the story of the house he bought his parents, carrying out an exercise in wish-fulfilment, perhaps jealous of the way his brother had been able to seize an opportunity.

It may have been the ICM's link with the ultra-Protestant Orange Order that enabled McMahon to make his next move, a curious one for a man born to an Irish Catholic family. He takes passage to Liverpool, where, according to the summary of his life, he becomes attached to a virulently anti-Irish Protestant Reform Church pastor, Harry Longbottom. McMahon sold sixpenny religious books door to door for Longbottom, earning three halfpence a copy commission. Longbottom doubled as leader of the anti-Catholic Protestant Party, and, from 1930, held a seat on the city council. The party had been founded in 1903 at the height of sectarian conflict in Liverpool, with local Orange Order members prominent among activists.

McMahon's association with Longbottom and his party may have given him the introduction to the eccentric form of right-wing politics he adopted in later life. Meanwhile, he 'assisted' (once again, his word) Longbottom at the 1931 general election, when he stood as Protestant Party candidate in Kirkdale in Liverpool, coming bottom of the poll with a quarter of the vote. Longbottom had run a campaign heavy with bitter anti-Irish and anti-Catholic invective. Irish immigrants, he told large crowds, were entirely responsible for Liverpool's chronically high unemployment, for the slums blighting the city, and for the high rates levied to support them on poor assistance. What McMahon made of this rabble-rousing he never revealed in his letter to Bevis.

McMahon's final destination was London, where he lived for the remainder of his life. He gave no reason for moving south, although – and he does not mention this in his letter – his brother Patrick also moved to London in 1931 to become assistant priest at the Church of the Sacred Heart, Mill Hill. The brothers appear to have long been estranged, but their arrival in the capital at about the same time is an interesting coincidence.

McMahon would have reached London late in 1931, probably November. He knew nobody. It could hardly have been a worse time, with the Depression at its most intense and unemployment continuing to climb by the month, even in the relatively prosperous capital. He told Bevis that he first slept on the Embankment and then found work as a kitchen porter, presumably living-in. From here he was taken on as a salesman at a 'small drug or herbal store' in Notting Hill, and in no time took over the shop and was managing it with two assistants. How he did this he does not say, but it is likely the business fell into his hands when the owner was arrested, tried and imprisoned for conducting 'an illegal operation', an obvious euphemism for abortion. At a time when terminations were illegal, herbal remedies were known abortifacients – pennyroyal, rue and tansy in particular. Herbalism was unregulated and encompassed a range of so-called remedies and 'cures'. There had been a revival of interest in 1930s London, making the business a useful opening for a man with few prospects. McMahon went on to trade in nearby Westbourne Grove and then, for a time in 1935, Lower Regent Street according to later newspaper reports.

McMahon became a familiar figure around Notting Hill through his business, which, if the fate of the previous owner is any guide, would have had a shady reputation and been of interest to the police. 'I placed free advertisements outside my shop door for widows and unemployed men,' he told Bevis, describing this as the 'social work' he always claimed to undertake. He went on, 'I was also able to help divers other persons, policemen, doctors, and still have a letter of appreciation for a little service which I rendered to a certain member of the Duke of York's (now H.M.) household.'[75] The latter is pure McMahon: a carefully dropped reference to an unspecified favour rendered to an unnamed person of implied importance – 'I could say more, but ...' Was McMahon, like his predecessor as a herbalist, an abortionist? He was certainly sometimes in the company of a doctor struck from the register for terminating pregnancies. And was the woman he married, an experienced nurse, also involved in this?

The present now seemed stable, the future possibly secure. As an independent trader McMahon was obliged to nobody, his past life and record irrelevant. But following the epic he saw his life to be, destiny working itself out inexorably, he set off a chain of events that were to bring him once more into the hands of the police, to the Old Bailey and, by a roundabout route, MI5, and, finally, to be brandishing a revolver on Constitution Hill.

7

On 22 October 1932 a letter reached the desk at Scotland Yard of the Metropolitan Police chief constable, Maurice Drummond. As Colonel Drummond had been in the post no more than a fortnight, the writer must have been a close observer of movements in the police hierarchy. The letter, which was unsigned, made serious allegations against two West London division officers based in Notting Hill. 'Sergeants Tracey and Dennis are carrying out a system of blackmail. One bookmaker pays £3 5s weekly and a publican £2. Even I have been tapped by these rotters.' The accuser asked for the sergeants' corruption to be investigated.[76]

The authorities took no action until the arrival of a second letter at Scotland Yard on 11 February 1933. This was addressed to the head of the Criminal Investigation Department, Chief Superintendent Norman Kendal, and repeated the allegations. 'They have carried on their rotten games for years,' the anonymous informant said,

> One can get a drink any hour from 7 a.m. to midnight. Tracey gets £2 from this shop, and all policemen 5s and drinks. A number of persons, businessmen in a small way, have been blackmailed by these men. Clubs, billiard halls, quack doctors all pay up.

If what the writer was saying were true, he was exposing a deeply rooted culture of corruption at Notting Hill police station, with the two sergeants at the centre. These particular officers, he went on, protected dealers in stolen property, allowed a bookmaker to work the streets unhindered, and turned a blind eye to a man 'guilty of improper conduct with little girls', all in return for regular cash. The mother of two thieves, herself an illegal moneylender, had paid up for a year: 'A few weeks ago she refused to pay her regular payment. She was shown what would happen and was fined. Now she pays up.'

It was hardly a revelation that police corruption was rife, not just in London but in forces throughout the country. Examples were regular features in the popular press. In Sheffield twenty-two members of the city force were tried at West Riding Assizes and all were convicted.

When a Metropolitan Police sergeant, George Goddard, was caught pocketing bribes from West End club owners, he was found on arrest to have £12,471 in bank notes squirrelled away in a safe deposit box. He was given eighteen months. Bookmakers who worked the streets illegally were the easiest prey for bent officers, second only to prostitutes.

The Old Bailey judge, Sir Ernest Wild, sentenced another Metropolitan Police sergeant, Malcolm Jones, to eighteen months in 1932 for extracting regular bungs from one bookmaker, and probably more. Jones was six months from retirement and forfeited his pension. No fewer than forty officers had lately resigned from the force across London in the face of bribery allegations and though none were brought to court they all lost their pensions.

McMahon's dealings with the authorities over his allegations followed a similar pattern to those he would have with MI5 in 1935 and 1936. Was he telling the truth, or did he have some other motive for what he was saying? If what he said was true, would he be believed? And if he were believed, would those with the power to act wish to do so?

Divisional Detective Inspector Young, himself based at Notting Hill, had been given the letters to investigate and, alerted by the writer's use in one of them of the word 'resetter' – the Scottish expression for a receiver of stolen goods – he questioned McMahon, a familiar figure to the local police it appeared. McMahon may even have been one of the businessmen 'in a small way' that he said the officers had been tapping for money. Or perhaps, given his trade as a herbalist, he was the 'quack doctor'. He initially denied any knowledge of the letters but then, according to Young, changed his mind, admitted he was the writer and signed a full statement.

McMahon's story differed markedly from Young's. After writing the two letters to Scotland Yard he claimed he sold his business in Notting Hill and took a job as secretary of a social club owned by 'a well known Harley Street doctor, Dr Longinotto'. Shortly after he started work, two CID officers – including one of the sergeants he had alleged was corrupt – came to the club and asked him to go to Notting Hill police station, where their 'chief' wanted to speak to him. Arriving at the station,

McMahon was taken to an interview room where he found two inspectors, Young and Fairweather, waiting. They told him they knew he had written both the letters. They suggested he would be wise to withdraw his allegations 'otherwise I would be, to use their own words, "running my head against a stone wall"'. They told him to 'forget everything' and, he recalled, the meeting ended 'with handshakes all round'.

After leaving the station, McMahon believed the purpose of the meeting had just been to warn him off. He had accepted this and considered the matter closed. But then the social club manager called him into his office and said, 'Mac, I have been told by the police that unless you leave the club they will cause trouble, and I was told by a CID officer to advise you to leave London.' McMahon went directly to Scotland Yard to complain to the Chief Constable, Colonel Drummond.

Young, in the meantime, had been making what he described as 'exhaustive' enquiries into the allegations, including questioning the two officers, both of whom were his colleagues at Notting Hill police station. Eleven days after the discussion with McMahon, Inspector Young arrested him at his home in St James's Square, Notting Hill, taking his prisoner to Canon Row police station, where he charged him with defamatory libel. Young told the Bow Street magistrate on 30 March that McMahon said when he was arrested, 'I am not surprised. I have been expecting this. I have got some good people behind me.'

McMahon refused to be fingerprinted, presumably hoping to avoid revealing his previous convictions in Glasgow under the name Jerome Bannigan, and the magistrate remanded him to Brixton Prison. But on 6 April he relented, gave his prints, and was released on £200 bail to await trial at the Central Criminal Court, the Old Bailey, on 12 May. He had good reason to want to leave Brixton: in the course of that month of freedom, he became a husband.

McMahon married Rose Meeres, 34 according to her declaration, and four years his senior. 'Poor girl!' he later wrote. 'She has suffered much since having the misfortune to be my wife, which she did to try to make me a better man.'[77] Rose McMahon – sometimes called 'May' by McMahon – was the daughter of a Lincolnshire farmer and had served in the last years of the First World War with Queen Mary's Army Auxiliary Corps in France. She had enlisted following her brother's death in the trenches, was awarded service medals, and McMahon was unaffectedly proud of her. She was, he told one friend, 'the most wonderful woman in the world, May'.[78]

The couple were married at Kensington Register Office on 25 April. McMahon gave his name as 'Jerome Bannigan otherwise George Andrew McMahon' and his profession as 'Journalist'. His father, he declared, was a retired solicitor. Patrick Bannigan had been a bread deliveryman in Ireland and it was unlikely he had qualified and worked as a solicitor in Glasgow. Had McMahon – with a Roman Catholic priest as a brother and his father a solicitor – been trying to impress Rose Meeres, claiming a respectable background?

McMahon's wife remained with him through the troubles of the 1930s and beyond, working as a shop assistant to keep the home going while he indulged himself in a series of rackety schemes. 'She adored him,' a friend of McMahon's told one newspaper. And to the *Daily Mirror*, Mrs McMahon would say, '"Whatever it means to me, I shall stick by my husband." With that resolution helping her to fight back the tears from her eyes …'[79] What did she know about his activities outside the home? Apparently little. On one occasion he wrote from Brixton Prison begging her to forgive his behaviour: 'I really regret that I never availed myself of your valuable help, had I only done so, I may never have got into this awful mess, because I know you would have kept my secrets …'[80]

When McMahon came up for trial at the Old Bailey on 12 May there were clear conflicts over what had passed between him and the Notting Hill police. Sir Ernest Wild, the Recorder of London, the judge in the 1932 Jones corruption case, presided over the trial. Equally coincidentally, Eustace Fulton, prosecuting barrister in the Jones trial, presented the Crown case against McMahon. Fulton and McMahon were to meet again in three years in even more dramatic circumstances, once more at the Old Bailey.

Inspector Young told the court that when he questioned McMahon on 18 March that McMahon at first denied writing the two letters. But then McMahon had explained he was persuaded that the officers were corrupt by a neighbour whose sons they had arrested on, alleg-edly, a trumped-up charge. But, Young went on, he then admitted, 'All the matter I said, I wish to retract, as I cannot prove it.' Questioned by McMahon's barrister, D.C. Rosenberg, Young denied he offered to drop the charge if McMahon withdrew his allegations. He said it was untrue that McMahon had responded, 'I prefer not to withdraw any-thing, because I want justice done.' When Rosenberg persisted with this line of questioning, the judge stopped him speaking and ordered the jury to leave the court.

In the jury's absence Rosenberg accused Young of fabricating his client's statement, tricking him into signing blank sheets of paper and then concocting a story afterwards, in short that he had 'verballed' him. Young denied this. When the jury were back in their places, the judge instructed them to ignore what they had heard about Young making an offer and said they should disregard the written statement Young had presented as coming from McMahon, adding this was not in any way to be seen as a criticism of the police. Round one to McMahon and Rosenberg.

It now turned out there was a history of bad blood between McMahon and one of the sergeants he had accused, Dennis. McMahon said, 'People have told me Sergeant Dennis and Tracey were getting a lot of money.' But he revealed the particular personal grievance against Dennis, who, he said, had told him in late March to close down his herbalist shop because the previous owner had been imprisoned for per-forming what must be assumed to be an abortion. McMahon said that he thought he was doing his duty in making the corruption allegations and that he believed them to be true when he wrote the letters. The judge accepted the claim of McMahon's barrister that the statements were 'privileged' because they were contained in letters to the police, but said what remained to be decided was whether McMahon had been motivated by malice.

When the prosecution and defence barristers had presented their cases, the judge took the unusual step of calling witnesses on his own account, including the two sergeants whom McMahon had accused. In addition he called a builder, the landlord of the pub McMahon had said served drinks at all hours, and a street bookmaker – all denied giving money to the police. The pub landlord said he knew the sergeants as regular patrons, that he had never 'squared' them and that they always paid for their drinks. Sergeant Tracey told the judge he had been in the force for nineteen years, Sergeant Dennis for twelve years, and both strenuously denied ever taking a bribe in all their years of service.

The absurdity of the judge's questioning was obvious: if the witnesses agreed they had paid bribes, each would be admitting he had committed offences that made him vulnerable to police pressure. They also had to consider the reaction of officers at Notting Hill station, who would not take kindly to individuals blowing the whistle on their colleagues in court. The two sergeants, of course, were not prepared to admit to corruption unless they were caught with the money in their hands.

In his summing up Judge Wild cautioned the jury that if what McMahon was saying in his letters were true then Notting Hill would be a 'leper spot' where every form of vice and crime could flourish as long as the police were 'squared'. Obviously, he implied, this was a ridiculous proposition. The jury found McMahon guilty without leaving the box. Inspector Young detailed McMahon's convictions in Scotland. 'He is known to the Glasgow police as a person of deceitful character, imaginative, and a person who says things which would not be relied upon.' By contrast the two sergeants, Young said, had a string of commendations for their past work and had lately been engaged in cracking a criminal gang plaguing Notting Hill, some of whose members – he added significantly – McMahon knew personally.

Asked if he had anything to say, McMahon protested that he had been denied a fair trial. 'I have been baulked in my efforts to get witnesses. The police have gone to great lengths to stop me from getting them. Had they been called, they would have put a different complexion on my case.' McMahon enlarged on this later. 'Witnesses whom I called were visited at their homes a day prior to my trial and virtually intimidated by the two CID officers. Therefore the trial became a farce.'[81]

Judge Wild gave McMahon twelve months, regretting he had no power to impose a harsher sentence. 'It is perfectly intolerable that two respectable policemen, doing their duty among a gang of criminals, with whom you resort, should be stabbed in the back in this way. The whole of your defence is simply riddled with malice.' McMahon was taken from the Old Bailey to Wandsworth Prison to begin his second term inside. But before two months were up he was free, his conviction overturned.

At the Court of Criminal Appeal on 3 July 1933, Lord Chief Justice Hewart criticised Judge Wild for taking McMahon's trial in May on what he called 'a peculiar course'. The jury's function, he declared, had been to determine whether McMahon's allegations were motivated by malice, not whether they were true. But by calling six witnesses, including the officers concerned, after the prosecution and defence had put their cases, and by questioning them in the way he had, Judge Wild may very well have given the jury the impression that their role was to decide on the veracity of the accusations. The Lord Chief Justice said Wild had acted 'improperly'. Hewart allowed McMahon's appeal, quashed the conviction and ordered the prisoner's immediate release.[82]

Having endured seven weeks in Wandsworth Prison for exposing what he genuinely believed was police corruption of an extensive and systemic kind, and having been in his own eyes vindicated by the Appeal Court's decision, McMahon was now determined the authorities had an obligation to pay for the distress and discomfort their actions had caused him.

II

Prelude to Assassination

1

MI5 (dealing with domestic counter-espionage) and MI6 (responsible for espionage overseas) evolved from the Secret Service Bureau, which was formed in 1909 to co-ordinate intelligence as Germany was seen to pose a greater threat as an imperial rival.[1] MI5's role was to investigate and combat the activities of what was feared might be an army of spies and possible saboteurs among the 50,000 German nationals known to be living in the United Kingdom. Spy and invasion fears were widespread, thanks in part to a spate of sensationalist novels. The most influential were *The Invasion of 1910* by William Le Queux and H.H. Munro's *When William Came: A Story of London under the Hohenzollerns*. Against a background of manufactured anxiety, the *Daily Mail* advised readers to refuse service from any German waiter. If the cunning foreigner claimed to be a Swiss citizen, he should be made to show his passport. But as one writer on British intelligence put it, the spy network:

> … was a figment of the imagination. We now know that Germany military intelligence ignored Britain before the Great War. The German Army had no plans to invade the island and, indeed, believed the British Army would play no part in the coming European War.[2]

A 36-year-old army captain, Vernon Kell, was appointed director of MI5, which initially came under the War Office and would always maintain a quasi-military tone. An active soldier, Kell had fought in the Boxer Rebellion in China in 1900. On Britain's declaration of war against Germany in August 1914, Kell headed a staff of sixteen, including the former chief of the Metropolitan Police Special Branch, William Melville, who became MI5's main 'detective'. In 1892, the then Inspector Melville of Special Branch had engineered the use of a half-Irish, half-French agent provocateur to frame anarchists in a spurious 'Walsall bomb plot', conspiring with Pyotr Rachovsky, head of the Okhrana, the Tsarist secret police, to discredit left-wing dissidents.

MI5's relations with Special Branch – effectively the 'political' police – would necessarily be close, if sometimes problematic. In the early days of the First World War, Kell claimed to have masterminded the seizure of twenty-one of twenty-two German agents believed to be operating in Britain, supposedly breaking the back of the enemy's intelligence network. One historian has subsequently revealed that the extent and significance of the operation was a 'complete fabrication', placing responsibility for the lie at Kell's door as he sought to secure for MI5 a reputation for effectiveness.[3] The unfortunate irony for Kell and for MI5 was that, as the service's officers had no power of arrest, Special Branch's head, Basil Thomson, secured the credit and the praise when it was his men who were deployed to conduct the round-up.

During the course of the war, MI5 extended its remit from an interest in German spies to broader counter-subversion, encompassing the surveillance of pacifists, anti-war activists, militant trade unionists and anti-capitalist revolutionaries. The bulk of MI5 recruits over the long period when Kell was director came – as he had – from the military, and certainly possessed what was seen as a 'good background'. As they were relatively poorly paid, Kell believed a private income was helpful. Selection largely through personal recommendation on the old-boy network ensured a comfortable *esprit de corps*. A former member of Kell's staff said, 'Working in the office then was like being in a family firm, one felt secure.'[4] An obvious drawback was that this narrowed the range of outlook and experience available to the organisation. But, it goes almost without saying, MI5 saw itself as existing to defend a particular way of life.

The pressure of war encouraged rapid growth in numbers and by 1918 total MI5 personnel amounted to almost 850, 130 of these operational officers, with an annual budget of £100,000. At the core was Central Registry, with a 250,000-card general index of aliens, and almost 30,000 personal files on individuals of particular interest. But victory in 1918 and the government's post-war austerity policy brought a drastic budget cut to £35,000, with staff numbers plummeting in 1920. At various points, the struggle for resources and inter-agency jostling for survival threatened MI5's existence, first from Special Branch's head, Sir Basil Thomson, when he was briefly director of intelligence with overall responsibility for countering domestic subversion. Kell commissioned a historian working for MI5, Lucy Farrer, to write an exaggerated description of the organisation's wartime accomplishments, *MI5 in the Great War*, as part of his battle for survival.

The next effort at undermining MI5 came from MI6, whose head, Rear Admiral Hugh Sinclair, argued unsuccessfully that the distinction between counter-espionage and espionage was anomalous and that the two bodies should be amalgamated, preferably under his leadership. By the mid-1920s MI5 had survived as a separate body, but much weakened. Kell complained to the Secret Service Committee in 1925 that he was unable to afford to run a network of agents, relying on casual *ad hoc* informants for intelligence. Through these he was able to maintain a 'precautionary index', 25,000 files on individuals who, according to MI5, represented a potential danger to national security, often on the flimsiest evidence.

MI5 had a working connection with the Metropolitan Police Special Branch, which had been established in 1883 to deal with the threat from Irish Republican terrorists, gradually expanding its remit to monitoring the activities of political dissidents, predominantly left-wing, overlapping MI5 territory. Special Branch officers operated as the 'arms and legs' of MI5, arresting individuals the service had identified as a threat to national security. The relationship between the two was delicately balanced, weight shifting towards MI5 with the discovery in 1929 that Special Branch had been penetrated by Soviet agents. In the wake of this debacle, absolute responsibility for combatting domestic subversion passed to MI5 in 1931.

After 1931 MI5 had two divisions: A Division, dealing with administration, personnel and Registry (where information on individuals and organisations of interest was collated, indexed and filed); B Division, whose officers were actively engaged in counter-espionage and counter-subversion. Attention was devoted for much of the inter-war period on the Soviet Union's use of British Communist Party members and sympathisers for espionage, the 'Red Menace'. Invariably starved of personnel, MI5 found the interception of a suspect's post via the GPO Investigation Branch a valuable source of intelligence. This was authorised by a Home Office Warrant (HOW), normally signed by the Home Secretary. As use of the telephone spread, tapping calls became another fruitful – if time-consuming – source.

Kell, who had fought so effectively in the early 1920s to ward off the threats from rival agencies, remained MI5 director until 1940, with the army rank of major general. An accomplished linguist, discreet and reserved, Kell was short-sighted and asthmatic. His management style was paternalistic, cordial but distant. A former MI5 officer wrote of him, 'Sir Vernon Kell was a small quiet man rarely seen by us.' Another recalled that at her initial interview for a post he asked only two questions: what school she had been to and the games she had played. Kell's wife later summed up his character, carried over into his home life: 'I asked little, and was told little.'[5]

One historian has identified a central problem with the director's mode of work, one permeating the organisation: 'Vernon Kell had built MI5 from a staff of one, and tradecraft and agent operations reflected this personal, pragmatic and historically amateur culture; recruitment was informal, and training was on the job.'[6] When the intense pressure of war in 1940 exposed the weaknesses in Kell's inward-looking and unimaginative approach, the head of the civil service abruptly dismissed him on the orders of newly installed prime minister Winston Churchill.

The head of MI5's B Division, which conducted investigations and enquiries and was to have the closest dealings with McMahon in 1935 and 1936, was Brigadier Oswald Harker, commonly known as Jasper. Harker had served in the Indian police for fourteen years, rising to the position of deputy commissioner in Bombay before being invalided home in 1919. He joined MI5 in 1920, giving his recreations on recruitment as big-game hunting, fishing and riding, a not-unusual clutch of hobbies among his peers. He was described variously as 'good looking but not clever' and 'a fearsome character'.[7] More bluntly, a fellow officer recalled 'a sort of highly-polished barrel which, if tapped, would sound hollow (because it was).'[8] Harker would become director of MI5 briefly after Kell's dismissal.

An irony in all this was that behind MI5's back in 1934 and 1935 Soviet intelligence was quietly and efficiently recruiting young Communists and sympathisers from the very heart of the establishment as prized long-term agents. The 'Cambridge Five' – named after the university from which they were enlisted – would spend the following decades working their way up the British power hierarchy in the service of the Soviet Union, passing a string of secrets as they rose: Kim Philby (Westminster and Cambridge; MI6), Guy Burgess (Eton and Cambridge; MI5, MI6 and the Foreign Office), Donald Maclean (Gresham's and Cambridge; the Foreign Office), Anthony Blunt (Marlborough and Cambridge; MI5) and John Cairncross (Hamilton Academy and Cambridge; MI6, HM Treasury).

History revealed MI5 and MI6 to have been pitifully incompetent when it came to protecting their own ranks from infiltration. This was based, as one writer on security put it, on a 'false belief, which was to cost MI5 and the country dear ... the assumption that no well-educated Briton from a good family could possibly be a traitor'.[9]

2

McMahon's successful appeal against his conviction for criminal libel and his release from Wandsworth Prison on 3 July 1933 not only failed to end his troubles but marked the beginning of a new phase. He and his wife were evicted from their home by an unsympathetic landlord. The couple then struggled to secure alternative accommodation because of police pressure on landlords and estate agents. McMahon was to complain, 'On three occasions when we had been accepted by landlords as suitable tenants the C.I.D. officers prevented our getting these apartments.'[10] Finding work became difficult and a further problem for McMahon was that he was ineligible for unemployment benefit because he had been self-employed.

He was taken on as a barman at a Tottenham Court Road public house, only to be dismissed when the landlord heard about his recent dealings with the police and courts. This was presumably more interference by the police themselves. He eventually found casual work addressing envelopes for a charity at five shillings a day. Then, as in the past, the clouds parted. Based on a loan of £2 and the use of a free office in Holborn, McMahon started a business – dealing in what is not clear, possibly a return to herbalism – and he was soon thriving, turning, he claimed, the £2 into £600.

But his grievance with the authorities still rankled. As he explained in a petition to King George in August 1934, his requests to the Home Office 'on numerous occasions' for compensation for wrongful imprisonment had been at first ignored and then rejected. Solicitors told him he had an arguable claim, but he could not afford the fees they demanded to pursue it. The Law Society's Poor Persons Commission refused to take up his case because it was precluded from funding actions against the government.

McMahon opened his three-page typed petition to the King with the words 'May it please your Majesty, as a loyal subject of your Majesty I claim your kind condescension to this appeal for justice' and ended 'I therefore appeal to your Majesty in person for a full inquiry into the disgraceful treatment of one of your subjects by your Majesty's Home Office.' Describing himself as a young and disabled married man, McMahon said he had devoted his life 'to assist in my humble way my fellow citizens and have suffered not a little inconvenience in this direction'. In his business in West London he had been, he said, 'the confidant of many troubles, and endeavoured to see that justice was meted out to all'.[11] Buckingham Palace ignored his petition, the first of a number McMahon sent.

'I now attempted to realise my greatest ambition, my own newspaper,' he later wrote, 'and on the promise of financial backing from certain gentlemen launched my "Human Gazette".'[12] Only one edition of what seemed more a magazine appeared, dated February 1935, and McMahon was seen hawking copies along Fleet Street and in Piccadilly in the build-up to George V's Silver Jubilee in May 1935. The *Gazette* described itself as 'Britain's Premier New Non-Sectarian & Non-Political Journal', sold for two pence, and had a photograph of a studious-looking McMahon, the 'Managing Editor', on the front cover. A list of contents included articles on 'Wandsworth Prison', 'Is Nudism Immoral', 'How to Land a Job' and 'Why I Shall Not Marry'. The next issue promised 'Full Particulars of Several Original Competitions'.

McMahon claimed the paper sold well on bookstalls in Britain, abroad and in the 'Colonies', both its content and tone being praised by 'highly placed persons', though he gives no evidence. One thing the *Gazette* did not do was turn a profit and McMahon remained in dire financial straits. 'Then I started to drink and the usual happened.' He lost the office, abandoned his business, and was reduced to canvassing for a Sunday newspaper, uncertain commission-only work trying to recruit new readers. 'I lost even this, then sank into debt so that still drunk most of my waking hours, I soon fell in with the wishes of my "alien" friends ... undertaking apparently harmless work for the German and Italian Embassy ...'[13] Witnesses, later questioned by the police probing McMahon's recent background, described him as living a hand-to-mouth existence, always trying to borrow money or passing cheques that were more often than not returned marked 'Refer to Drawer'.

McMahon's sense that he was a victim of injustice drew him – at first without his knowledge – into the orbit of MI5, the domestic security service. In August 1933 he wrote to the Communist newspaper, the *Daily Worker*, requesting the editor to pass his letter to the 'chairman of the Communist Party'. McMahon asked for support for a £4,000 compensation claim he intended to make against the Metropolitan Police for wrongful arrest and imprisonment. All letters to the Communist Party and to its newspaper were routinely intercepted by the postal authorities and copied before they arrived at their destination. McMahon would probably not have been aware of this, though officials of the tiny party would have assumed every move they made was watched in one way or another.

A photocopy of McMahon's letter went to Oswald 'Jasper' Harker, head of MI5's B Division, on 16 August 1933 and – trivial though the content was – he brought this to the attention of the director, Vernon Kell, on his return from leave a few days later. Concluding it had no security interest in itself, Kell sent a copy on to the Metropolitan Police commissioner, Lord Trenchard. Despite this, and against the possibility that McMahon's involvement with the Communists might develop, MI5 opened a personal file on him – PF 42090. McMahon had become – he would have been flattered to realise – a person of interest.

This overreaction by MI5 to what was a trifling matter in intelligence terms was not unusual. Some years later a letter from a schoolboy writing to Communist Party headquarters seeking information for a school project was intercepted, the boy was categorised as a 'sympathiser' and MI5 opened a file on him. But, for the moment, that was the extent of MI5's relationship with McMahon – a letter in a buff paper file – and they would hear no more of him for two years. That would be in connection with a woman called Mrs Violet Van der Elst.

3

It was written in the stars that McMahon and Violet Van der Elst would at some point be brought together: two eccentric exhibitionists, both suffering from what an amateur psychologist would be tempted to call 'histrionic personality disorder'. Born in Middlesex in 1882, the daughter of a coal porter and a washerwoman, Violet Dodge was a scullery maid who went on to make a fortune through her invention, production and astute marketing of Shavex, the first brushless shaving cream, and a range of cosmetics. She married twice. Her first husband, a civil engineer, died in 1927. A few months later she wed a Belgian, Julien Van der Elst, her factory manager. Following the sudden and unexpected death of her second husband at Ostend in August 1934, the widow threw her energies into a campaign against capital punishment.

The by-now-wealthy Mrs Van der Elst was already a familiar figure on the ostentatious do-gooding circuit, enabling her to move in circles far beyond those into which she had been born. In November 1931 *The Times* noted her presence at 'The Best of Everything, and Buy British' dinner in aid of a hospital for consumptives, presided over by the Marchioness of Carisbrooke, wife of a Mountbatten. In March 1932 she donated two paintings to be given as prizes at an anti-Communist bridge tournament at the Park Lane home of the wife of a former foreign secretary and chancellor of the exchequer. And so Mrs Van der Elst progressed through the early 1930s, brushing shoulders at balls, dinners and gala evenings with, as *The Times* reported, the Duke and Duchess of York (the Prince of Wales's brother and sister-in-law) the Duchess of Portland, the Countess of Cromer, and Princess Marie Louise (formerly of Schleswig-Holstein), one of Queen Victoria's granddaughters.

But Mrs Van der Elst's main, even obsessive, interest was her crusade to secure the abolition of hanging in the United Kingdom, a cause on which she spent much of her fortune and reputation. It was this that attracted McMahon's attention. As her commitment to the fight grew, she placed an advertisement in *The Times* in March 1935 seeking volunteers willing to work alongside her, asking them to 'write, call, or 'phone at once'. She gave her London address, 4 Palace Gate, and her telephone number, Western 5737. McMahon, a diligent newspaper scanner and collector of 'names', was alerted.

He turned up at Mrs Van der Elst's front door in Palace Gate one evening in what she would describe as 'a distressed condition. We gave this man a couple of pounds. The butler said he had been drinking.' McMahon later claimed she had sought his help in writing a book on capital punishment, a story she angrily denied. 'This man is not an educated man, and I am a writer,' she told the police. 'Why should I have this class of man when I could get real writers?'[14] McMahon's version of events was that he helped her in 1935 for over three months, having to work from 9 p.m. to 7 a.m. at her house because of her irregular hours, sleeping briefly, going to the British Museum to carry out research. Then, he claimed, one of the CID officers he had accused of corruption visited Mrs Van der Elst and warned her against associating with him. 'As a result I did not get the promised amount for my labour.'[15]

Mrs Van der Elst gave a vivid display of her campaigning style at Wandsworth Prison on 2 April 1935 as she led a protest against the hanging of a naval stoker for the Chatham murder of a petty officer. An hour before the prisoner was due to be despatched she arrived in her yellow Rolls-Royce, chauffeur driven, leading a convoy of cars, a loudspeaker van bringing up the rear. Mrs Van der Elst addressed the waiting crowd, crying the word 'murder' repeatedly as the moment of execution approached. Meanwhile, the loudspeaker broadcast hymns until the police ordered an end to the playing. Two weeks later she was again outside Wandsworth, though this time a heavy police cordon surrounded the prison in expectation of her arrival, preventing her leading her followers to the gates.

Mrs Van der Elst announced at the end of April 1935 that she would raise the temperature of the campaign by flying a black aircraft over London, her name painted in white on the sides. The plane, she told the *Daily Mirror*, would be 'a big one, more like an R.A.F bomber.'[16] At Durham in May a line of police cars blockaded her approach to the prison and in July she was fined £3 with five guineas costs for driving at a police officer outside Wandsworth Prison, having first ordered her chauffeur to vacate his seat so she could take the wheel.

When the prime minister, Stanley Baldwin, called a general election in the autumn of 1935, Mrs Van der Elst – having already spent £50,000 on her crusade over the past two years – prepared to move more directly into the political arena, putting herself forward as Independent Conservative candidate for the Putney constituency. It was here that McMahon renewed his contact with her, this time in the guise of a benefactor. As the election campaign took off, McMahon visited Mrs Van der Elst to offer his services. According to McMahon, she asked him to hire a fleet of cars for her. He assumed these were for publicity purposes and set about making the arrangements.

A little later McMahon – for no apparent reason, though drink would surely have played a part – made a nuisance of himself at the Van der Elst campaign office in Putney, turning up with two men, who he introduced as Dr Starkie and Colonel Matthews. Richard Starkie had been struck off the medical register in 1921 for illegally terminating pregnancies, an interesting friend for McMahon to have, considering the connection between abortion and the herbalist's trade. Starkie was then imprisoned in 1929 after being found guilty of writing heroin prescriptions for a bogus British Army major and an Italian princess. An 'F. Matthews' was linked with McMahon in a Special Branch report attached to McMahon's MI5 file on 25 September 1935, a month before McMahon had his first direct dealings with MI5.[17] His name would crop up together with McMahon's a number of times over the next few years.

McMahon, now unmistakably drunk as he roamed around the constituency office, drew a typed page of poetry from his pocket, an obscene skit on Mrs Van der Elst, and announced, 'Unless I receive £50 this will be printed and published and given to everyone in Putney.' Helpers in the office were able to forcibly eject McMahon, Starkie and Matthews from the building. But later that evening McMahon, arriving by taxi and recognised immediately as a troublemaker, tried to force his way into an election meeting at Earlsfield School.

In a confused mêlée, McMahon accused the steward on the door of threatening to slash him with a razor and produced a small nickel-plated revolver, which he said he was prepared to use to defend himself. McMahon was persuaded to accompany a few of Mrs Van der Elst's supporters to a pub across the road. Having calmed down, he told them the Home Office had given him permission to carry a weapon because Italians had threatened him over activities he had been involved in that were connected to Italy's dispute with Ethiopia.[18]

Despite this bizarre behaviour, seven cars did turn up to Putney on election day, 14 November 1935, as McMahon had promised, rented from the American Car Company of Vauxhall Bridge Road. He claimed that Mrs Van der Elst had said she would reimburse him and presented her with a bill for £19 for petrol and £67 10s cost of the hire, insisting he had supplied the cars at her request. He repeatedly telephoned her demanding payment and, according to Mrs Van der Elst in a statement to police, threatened to shoot her. When she asked why, McMahon replied, 'You are too well known, and also I feel I would like to.'[19]

Rather than murdering Mrs Van der Elst, McMahon sued her in April 1936 at Marylebone County Court for the money he claimed she owed. The judge accepted her version of events and dismissed McMahon's claim. McMahon shouted, 'This is not justice', but was told by the judge to be quiet or he would be charged with contempt of court. At one point in the proceedings McMahon was asked if he had ever appeared at the Old Bailey. He became angry and at first refused to answer, but finally admitted he had been tried for criminal libel, adding that he had successfully appealed against his conviction. 'At present the case is before the Home Secretary,' he told the court.[20] Mrs Van der Elst was not elected, losing her deposit, but more would soon be heard of her in connection with McMahon.

4

Edward's obvious reluctance as Prince of Wales to marry had not in itself presented an immediate problem, though his father George had set a new standard of respectability, with the *family* aspect of 'royal family' taking on an emphasis not seen since the time of Queen Victoria and her consort Albert. An underlying nagging issue was the constant need to dissemble, to erect a facade of propriety behind which Edward could amuse himself sexually. As one cynical writer was to put it:

Prince Charming had had a normal number of mistresses: sufficient certainly to calm the nervous spasms of those who feared he might cause embarrassment by preferring homosexuality like so many of his

Oxford contemporaries and his German cousins. As things were, it was assumed that at least his sex life was not going to prove troublesome. Little did they know.[21]

The press barons loyally played their part, boosting the 'eligible and desirable bachelor' pretence in much the same way that rock stars would later be presented as distant but attainable to adolescent fans. The result is a particular form of infantile silliness that recurs decade after decade, typified by the fashion journalist Diana Vreeland in her memoirs: 'You must understand that to be a woman of my generation in London – *any* woman – was to be in love with the Prince of Wales.'[22] Meanwhile, Edward was engaging in serial relationships with married women, snapping up other opportunities as they presented themselves in nightclubs and at balls, with occasional one-night stands on overseas tours with celebrity-struck wives of colonial district commissioners.[23] This was all a secret about which Edward's subjects were kept safely in the dark.

Edward understood all too well the lie he was living. He wrote at one point, 'If only the British public really knew what a weak, powerless misery their press-made national hero was, they would have a nasty shock and be not only disappointed but d---- angry too.'[24] It was the arrival on the scene in 1931 of the twice-married and once-divorced American Wallis Simpson, and Edward's growing infatuation, that threatened to expose finally the extent of the charade. A well-informed contemporary commentator, one generally sympathetic to Edward, noted:

> The impression gained growth that he did not take his duties with adequate seriousness, and it was this apparent absence of responsibility, apart altogether from his friendship with Mrs Simpson, that worried Mr Baldwin and others of his advisers.[25]

The chickens were gathering and something would have to be done.

Edward remained emotionally close to his first serious long-term lover, Freda Dudley Ward, but had shifted his main physical interest to Thelma, the elegantly frivolous wife of Viscount Furness, mother of a son and, like Freda, half-American. The couple consummated their relationship on safari in Kenya in 1930. They became constant week-end companions at Edward's newly acquired home, Fort Belvedere in Windsor Great Park, or her country house in Melton Mowbray, Leicestershire. It was here in 1931 that Furness introduced Edward to her close friend Wallis Simpson, together with her second husband, the American-born but naturalised British businessman Ernest.

Bessie Wallis Warfield was born in 1896 in Blue Ridge Summit, Pennsylvania, into an old and once well-off Southern family, now living in relatively reduced circumstances following her father's death. Growing up in Baltimore, she married a naval aviator, Earl Winfield Spencer Jr, in 1916. Their relationship soon degenerated, became chaotic and sporadic, the couple often separating. This enabled Wallis to enjoy a series of affairs, including with an Argentine diplomat in Washington and, it was rumoured, with Count Galeazzo Ciano, Mussolini's future foreign minister and son-in-law. There was even a story that she had worked briefly for American intelligence while in China with her husband. The Spencers divorced in 1927 and in the following year Wallis married the shipping broker Ernest Simpson. They settled in London and enjoyed a smart Mayfair life of dancing, cocktails and relaxed sexuality. The witty and unpretentious Mrs Simpson, far removed from the upper-class English women a prince was expected to cultivate relationships with, soon caught Edward's eye.

By 1933, with Edward regularly entertaining the Simpsons at Fort Belvedere and he a frequent visitor at their London flat, rumours had begun. In 1934 both the long-term Freda and the more recent Thelma were dropped as the 37-year-old Wallis edged herself into place beside Edward, her husband looking on acquiescently and not entirely reluctantly. He had romantic interests of his own and saw possible social advantages in being close to the heir to the throne. 'I must in all fairness to Ernest say this,' Wallis later wrote, 'whatever he may have been thinking or feeling, he loyally played his part.'[26]

In August 1934 Wallis accompanied a small party of Edward's friends and cronies on holiday to Biarritz and on a cruise, leaving Ernest in England. Edward's equerry, Sir John Aird, wrote in his diary that the prince had 'lost all confidence in himself and follows W around like a dog.'[27] When they returned, Edward composed and performed a bag-pipe melody in Wallis's honour. The first public reference to the fact that Edward and Wallis had been seen together, in the American magazine *Time*, was a sign of what was to come. In November King George tried to prevent Wallis joining a birthday party at Buckingham Palace and when she came anyway, avoided being introduced to her. In February 1935 the pair were skiing in Austria, with, once again, Ernest noticeably absent. Edward set aside two rooms for Wallis at Fort Belvedere, conveniently adjacent to his.

Edward and Wallis may or may not have had a physical relationship before their marriage in 1937 — and Edward insisted to his father that she was not his mistress — but the fact that speculation was rife was enough to threaten to taint the royal family's respectability.[28] 'He has not a single friend who is a gentleman,' George complained. 'He does not see any decent society.'[29] Whether the titillating rumours circulating about Mrs Simpson in the early 1930s — confined at this point to upper-class and establishment circles — were true or not was irrelevant. Social repu-tations are made or broken on the basis of gossip rather than verifiable fact. The author and politician Harold Nicolson, who knew the couple well, wrote in his diary, 'I have an uneasy feeling that Mrs Simpson, for all her good intentions, is getting him out of touch with the type of person with whom he ought to frequent.'[30]

What, the gossip asked, was the source of her obvious hold on him? The American journalist John Gunther, a friend of Edward's, had a simple explanation: 'She treated him like a man and a human being, not as an Heir Apparent and a puppet.'[31] But there were also sniggered sto-ries: of 'erotic techniques' Wallis had learned in Chinese brothels in the 1920s, when her first husband was stationed in Shanghai; that Edward was a homosexual in thrall to a masculine woman; or that — because of her obvious delight in taunting and sometimes openly humiliating him in company — the relationship was darkly sado-masochistic.

Edward's long-running lover Freda Dudley Ward once said she had never seen any sign that he was homosexual. 'I would have known. I think he may have been a masochist.'[32] One biographer commented, 'Sometimes she mocked or scolded him so cruelly that he burst into tears. The prince seemed to revel in his humiliation.'[33] Edward's mother, Queen Mary – as cold-blooded in her own way as Wallis – thought she was simply a witch who had cast a spell over her son. This she hoped the passage of time would break.

Dominatrix or witch, Mrs Simpson was not playing entirely straight with Edward. From the spring of 1935, the Metropolitan Police Special Branch had begun taking a close interest in the relationship between Edward and the Simpsons. A police report said of Wallis, 'She is reputed to be very attractive and to spend lavishly on dress and entertainment.' Her husband, Ernest, was described as the 'bounder' type. 'He makes no secret of his wife's association with P.O.W. [Prince of Wales] and seems to enjoy some reflected glory because of this and to make what capital he can out of it.' He was, the report went on, expecting 'high honours' when Edward came to the throne, and to be made at least a 'baron'.

In July 1935 Superintendent Albert Canning passed the latest, juiciest piece of intelligence to the commissioner, Lord Trenchard. Mrs Simpson, Canning said, had a lover, Guy Trundle, a 37-year-old Ford engineer and salesman, married in 1932 but a notorious adventurer. 'He meets Mrs Simpson openly at informal social gatherings as a personal friend, but secret meetings are made by appointment when intimate relations take place.' Trundle – the son of a 'clerk in holy orders' according to Special Branch – was reported to be out in society boasting that Wallis had even introduced him to Edward. Superintendent Canning said Mrs Simpson feared Ernest Simpson might be having her watched 'and in consequence she is very careful for the double purpose of keeping both P.O.W. and her husband in ignorance of her surreptitious love affairs.'[34]

Special Branch reports on their observation of the Simpsons and their contacts were circulated to the government ministers and officials that were considered to 'need to know'. The authorities gave the impression of being determined to gather as much information as possible about the relationship. It was as if a dossier were being compiled for future use, if required. On one occasion Special Branch officers followed Edward and Wallis as they visited an antique shop in Pelham Street, South Kensington. The officers reported back:

The conversation showed that they were on very affectionate terms and addressed each other as 'Darling'. A number of purchases were made and orders given for the goods to be sent to York House and marked 'Fort Belvedere'. The opinion of the dealer expressed after his distinguished client had left was that the lady seems to have P.O.W. completely under her thumb.

Canning had further news for the commissioner on 17 October 1935. 'The association of P.W. [Prince of Wales] with Mrs Simpson continues.' He said they had been on holiday together recently on the Continent. 'P.W. is said to have taken great pains to prevent Mrs Simpson appearing in any Press pictures.' He attached the 23 September edition of *Time* magazine showing how detailed and extensive the publicity was in the United States about the relationship between the two.[35] The British press proprietors could be relied on to stay buttoned up, to self-censor and make no reference to what was taking place.

At the end of his patience with his son, his temper fiery at the best of times, George called in Admiral Lionel Halsey, the head of Edward's household. Halsey recorded the king was anxious that the way in which Edward was conducting both his public and his private lives would 'wreck the monarchy and the Empire'. He and the queen, George said, had tried to follow a straight and proper course over a quarter of a century for the sake of the country but now 'he was on the point of being let down by his eldest son'.[36] He had begun to fear for the British Crown's stability if Edward came to the throne, telling Archbishop of Canterbury Cosmo Lang, 'What use is it, when I know my son is going to let it down?'[37] The king said to Queen Mary in the presence of her lady-in-waiting, 'I pray to God my eldest son will never marry and have children, and that nothing will come between Bertie and Lilibet [George's pet name for his granddaughter Elizabeth] and the throne.'[38]

The issue at stake was that in a relatively immature British democracy – women of 21 were unable to vote until 1929, many ordinary working men only as recently as 1918, later than some comparable countries – and with an economy in constant turmoil since the end of the First World War, forced into austerity by the 1931 financial crisis, the

monarchy provided a focus for national cohesion and a reference point
for the wider Empire. The Windsors and the political establishment had
seen from the fate of their royal cousins in Russia and Germany in 1917
and 1918 the chaos that could erupt when a monarchy squandered the
confidence of its subjects.

The Crown's survival did not only mean the preservation of a particular family's way of life but of the entire hierarchical and deferential
structure on which the British state and Empire were constructed.
As Thomas Jones – deputy Cabinet secretary to four prime ministers
– put it in 1936, 'We invest our rulers with qualities which they do not
possess, and we connive at the illusion – those of us who know better
– because monarchy is an illusion which works.'[39] But it was an illusion
all the same and workable only up to a point. One serious tremor – a
revelation that all was not what it seemed – and everything could come
tumbling down, the game might be over, not only for the Windsors but
for the 2 per cent of the adult population who owned 64 per cent of
the country's wealth.

As Edward came closer to the throne, he appeared to some to represent that awful possibility. His father George had no confidence in him,
telling the prime minister, Stanley Baldwin, 'After I'm dead the boy will
ruin himself in twelve months.'[40] Recovering from illness in 1928, he
had been even more emphatic, saying to the Duke of York (who subsequently become George VI), 'You'll see, your brother will never become
King.'[41] And to Edward himself he was once heard bellowing angrily
across the room in Buckingham Palace, 'You dress like a cad. You act like
a cad. You are a cad. Get out!'[42] George avoided mentioning his son's
'Mayfair Cockney' accent, popular among the prince's set, until, as Duke
of Windsor, he took up his wife's American twang.

Baldwin – who was to be central to the events that culminated in
Edward's abdication – made what in retrospect was a darkly brood-
ing speech to the Conservative Primrose League in the Albert Hall in
May 1935. 'The position of the Crown and of the King in this country
is not merely a matter of sentiment, important as that is. It is a matter of
the most profound political interest and importance.' It represented, he
said, a constitutional link 'which once broken can never be repaired'.[43]

It was almost as if Baldwin were issuing a coded warning to Edward that he could not continue as he was.

According to the close, but by now disillusioned, observer, Alan 'Tommy' Lascelles – Edward's private secretary until his despairing resignation in 1929 – Baldwin had arrived at his own conclusions about the heir to the throne's suitability for kingship as far back as 1927. On a tour of Canada Lascelles sat with Baldwin in a private room in Government House, Ottawa, and outlined his worry that Edward's 'unbridled pursuit of wine and women, and whatever selfish whim occupied him at the moment' threatened to make him 'no fit wearer of the British Crown'.

> I expected to get my head bitten off, but Baldwin heard me to the end, and, after a pause, said he agreed with every word I had said. I went on, 'You know, sometimes when I sit in York House waiting to get the result of some point-to-point in which he is riding, I can't help thinking that the best thing that could happen to him, and to the country, would be for him to break his neck.'

'God forgive me,' said Stanley Baldwin, 'I have often thought the same.'[44]

The British public knew nothing of this, encouraged as they were by a tame press to imagine that the political and royal establishment marched happily in step with Edward and that all was well.

5

It was not only Edward's loose personal life, his lax attitude to his constitutional role, and the type of people he chose to surround himself with, that were a matter of concern. There were growing suspicions about his political sympathies. The enduring myth was that he was a radical. If he were, that would more likely have been a radicalism of the right rather than the left. While he was prepared to give the Nazi salute in Germany, it is difficult to imagine him giving a clenched-fist salute if he had visited the Soviet Union. The playwright Noël Coward, Edward's close friend, noted in his diary three decades later, 'Secret papers have disclosed his pro-Nazi perfidy which, of course, I was perfectly aware of at the time. Poor dear, what a monumental ass he has always been!'[45]

For MI5 and Special Branch, the Soviet Union and the tiny Communist Party of Great Britain had been the main threat to national security through the 1920s. But with Mussolini's consolidation of his Fascist regime in Italy and – even more emphatically – with the coming to power in Germany of Hitler's National Socialists in 1933, interest turned gradually to the activities of the far right in Britain and its links with both these authoritarian states. Until then domestic fascist movements such as British Fascisti had been viewed as relatively harmless, eccentric but motivated by the sense of patriotism MI5 shared. This attitude was now changing. In 1934 MI5's head, Vernon Kell, presented the Home Office with his first report on 'The Fascist Movement in the United Kingdom'.

Edward's erratic combination of casualness and high-handedness disturbed the authorities, in his role as, first, heir and then as monarch in a parliamentary democracy. In July 1933 – six months after Nazis had come to power in Germany – the journalist and former diplomat Robert Bruce Lockhart noted in his diary that Edward admitted to his cousin Prince Louis Ferdinand, grandson of the former German Kaiser, that he was 'quite pro-Hitler'. Edward went on to say that it was 'no business of ours to interfere in Germany's internal affairs either re Jews or re anything else.'[46] This indifference towards virulent anti-Semitism in Germany was not, it has to be said, uncommon in British ruling circles at the time.

However, one-time Austrian ambassador to Britain and a friend of Edward's father George V, Count Albert von Mensdorff-Pouilly-Dietrichstein, was surprised at how far the prince went in his admiration for the Nazis. He quoted Edward as saying, 'Of course it is the only thing to do, we will have to come to it, as we are in great danger from the Communists here, too.'[47] An embarrassing seventeen seconds of footage kept hidden until 2015 shows Edward frivolously encouraging the future Queen Elizabeth (then 7 years old), her mother and sister, to practise the 'Heil Hitler' salute in the gardens at Balmoral, the Scottish royal castle, around this time. He would enthusiastically give this salute in Germany in 1937.[48]

It would be wrong to imagine Edward was working from anything as coherent as a worked-out political ideology. He operated with the ragbag of racial prejudices and sense of entitlement and self-preservation common to the privileged strata of the time. All the more so for having seen how the Bolsheviks had so easily ended the comfortably parasitic lives of his Romanov cousins and the enforced departure of monarchy throughout much of Europe. As recently as 1931 Spain's Alfonso XIII had been the latest of a string of crowned heads to be toppled from their thrones, in his case by an alliance of socialists and liberal republicans. But Edward's tendency was plain. In 1933 he told Prince Louis Ferdinand, a member of Germany's deposed Hohenzollerns, that dictatorships seemed very popular at present and that England might be needing one before much longer.

As well as Edward's often-expressed affection and admiration for Germany, MI5 were alert to his social and political connections with Oswald Mosley, the former Labour minister turned fascist. In 1931 Mosley set up the New Party, based primarily on his proto-Keynesian remedies for mass unemployment. When his party was humiliated at the October 1931 general election, Mosley turned to the authoritarian solutions he argued were working in Mussolini's corporate state. He formed the British Union of Fascists (BUF), the 'Blackshirts', in 1932. By 1934 MI5 had firm evidence that Mussolini was subsidising Mosley's movement to the tune of at least £60,000 a year. Even earlier there had been rumours, triggered by Mosley himself, that Edward was helping finance the New Party paper, *Action*. The story that Edward was now passing money to the Blackshirts – along with other wealthy donors – refused to lie down.

An interesting twist to this was that MI5 itself had aided Mussolini's rise in Italian politics during the First World War, paying him a subsidy of £100 a week in 1917 to oppose peace propaganda and to encourage a war-weary Italy to continue fighting on the Allied side. The payment was authorised by Sir Samuel Hoare, at the time an MP and MI5 station head in Rome. Mussolini used the payments to keep his newspaper,

Il Popolo d'Italia, functioning and to recruit a force of army veterans to attack peace protestors demonstrating in Milan. Hoare became British Foreign Secretary in June 1935.

In May 1934, meanwhile, among those in Edward's circle attending a Blackshirt dinner at the Savoy Hotel was his equerry and long-time crony, 'Fruity' Metcalfe – a friend of William Joyce, the most sinister of Mosley's political circle and the future 'Lord Haw-Haw' – proudly decked out in fascist uniform, as a picture in the up-market gossip magazine the *Tatler* showed. MI5 were already taking an interest in the pro-Nazi January Club, established by Mosley to cultivate high-society connections. Metcalfe was also a member of this. To complete the neat incestuous circle, Metcalfe's wife, Baba (known as 'Baba Blackshirt'), was Mosley's former sister-in-law and mistress, and currently having an affair with the Italian ambassador in London, Dino Grandi.

At the end of May 1934 Home Secretary Sir John Gilmour told Edward he was feeling increasingly anxious about the rise of the Blackshirts, perhaps in an effort to warn him that the prince's apparent sympathy with them had been observed. Another of Edward's equerries, Sir John Aird, recorded that in a conversation with the prince later that same evening, 'We agreed that, without knowing much about them, we both thought it quite a good movement except for Mosley.'[49]

Within a few months Edward's view of Mosley changed after the two held a long and friendly discussion about the BUF programme. Special Branch reported to the Metropolitan Police commissioner, Lord Trenchard, on 25 March 1935 that they had met at Lady Emerald Cunard's house in Grosvenor Square. 'Prince of Wales questioned Mosley regarding strength and policy of British Union of Fascists. These were explained at length by O.M.'[50] Mosley's explanations met with Edward's approval. Fascism – unlike communism – presented no threat to the survival of the monarchy, as Mussolini was showing in Italy in his relationship with Victor Emmanuel III. To underline the point, Mosley wrote early in 1936 that in a future fascist state there would be 'Absolute loyalty to the Crown. We shall in every way maintain its dignity.'[51]

The 'Leader', though, found no place in Edward's subsequent memoirs, which otherwise went into some detail about many aspects of

1930s politics. Times had changed and, despite Edward's close post-war friendship with Mosley in their comfortable Parisian exile, there were names it was tactful not to mention. Mosley was equally considerate in his own 1968 autobiography, *My Life*, saying not a word about Edward's political sympathies.

In 1935 Edward walked headlong into a trap set by the Nazis, naively some thought, but probably fully conscious of what he was doing. The regime realised that fellow feeling between men on both sides, former enemies who had endured the horror of the trenches, was a useful lever for securing sympathy for Germany's ambitions. Early in the year Joachim von Ribbentrop, Hitler's foreign affairs 'expert', soon to become German ambassador in London, suggested that the British Legion, the association of World War veterans, might want to send a delegation to Berlin to meet members of the German equivalent, the *Frontkämpferbund*. The Foreign Secretary, Anthony Eden, warned the Legion of the danger that they could used by the Nazis for propaganda purposes.

Edward, as the British Legion's patron, addressed members gathered at the movement's annual conference on 11 June and referred warmly to the forthcoming visit. 'I feel,' he said, 'that there could be no more suitable body or organisation of men to stretch forth the hand of friendship to the Germans than we ex-servicemen, who fought them and have now forgotten all about it and the Great War.'[52] In themselves the words were innocent, carrying no political significance. But Edward was speaking barely months after Hitler had defied the terms of the Versailles Treaty imposed on Germany in 1919 by reintroducing conscription to the armed forces, which the treaty had banned. German intentions in the longer term were clear to anyone willing to see them. Kell of MI5 noted in his diary on the day of Hitler's announcement, 'Straws in the wind'. His wife recalled that Kell 'had no doubts as to the eventual results of what both Mussolini and Hitler were planning.'[53]

The American-born writer and Tory politician Henry 'Chips' Channon, acquainted with many in Edward's circle and always well informed both politically and socially, recorded in his diary, 'Much gossip about the Prince of Wales' alleged Nazi leanings ... He has just made an extraordinary speech to the British Legion advocating friendship with

Germany; it is only a gesture, but a gesture that may be taken seriously in Germany and elsewhere.'[54] There was no doubt that Hitler did regard the speech as a heartening sign that Edward could be counted on as a reliable friend to Nazi Germany.[55]

George, always aware that the monarchy's survival as a pillar of Britain's unwritten constitution required painstaking practice of political neutrality, summoned Edward to Buckingham Palace. Here he warned his son against making controversial pronouncements that could be mistakenly interpreted as representing government policy. He should always adhere to the Foreign Office line in whatever he said. Preferably he should say nothing. Edward, still sulking according to one observer at a Court ball that evening, told the German ambassador, Leopold von Hoesch, that he was 'not retracting and was convinced he had said the right thing'. Hoesch reported this in a telegram to the German Foreign Office in Berlin.[56] No doubt MI5's informant in the German Embassy also took note of the message.

On another occasion Hoesch recounted Edward echoing Hitler's sentiments precisely in a long conversation. The prince, he said, had criticised the British Foreign Office for being 'too one-sided' in negotiations with Germany. 'He fully understood that Germany wished to face the other nations squarely, her head held high, relying on her strength and conscious that Germany's word counted as much in the world as that of other nations,' Hoesch reported to Berlin. 'I told the Prince in reply that what he had just said corresponded, as it were, word for word with the opinion of our Führer and Chancellor, such as I had heard it from his own lips.'[57]

Edward learned nothing from the British Legion experience, and at his father's funeral at Windsor on 28 January 1936 once more displayed his inability to resist meddling. Hitler despatched Carl 'Charlie' Eduard, Duke of Saxe-Coburg und Gotha, as his official representative at the ceremony. The duke was one of Queen Victoria's spread of great-grandsons, educated at Eton, a favourite cousin of Edward's. He was also a long-standing Nazi Party member and president of the right-wing Anglo-German Fellowship (to which 'Fruity' Metcalfe and other members of Edward's set belonged). Would it be useful, he asked Edward, if

Hitler were to meet the prime minister, Stanley Baldwin, to reinforce Anglo–German understanding? Edward – obviously intent on developing his own unofficial foreign policy – responded angrily, 'Who is King here? Baldwin or I? I myself wish to talk to Hitler, and will do so here or in Germany. Tell him that please.' What Edward said was blatantly unconstitutional. Hitler, the duke realised, would find the tone positively encouraging and sent a note of the conversation directly to Berlin marked 'Strictly Confidential. Only for the Fuhrer and Party Member v[on] Ribbentrop'.[58]

Similarly, over the Italian invasion of Ethiopia (then called Abyssinia) in October 1935, Edward had made no effort to hide his support for Italy, which he shared with Mosley's Fascists (they were conducting a 'Mind Britain's Business' campaign), and his opposition to League of Nations sanctions against the aggressor, limited and ineffectual though they were. He left the Italian ambassador in London, the staunchly fascist Count Dino Grandi – a frequent guest at Fort Belvedere – in no doubt about his sympathy with Mussolini's ambitions, calling British support for the League of Nations 'grotesque and criminal'.[59] Edward would have been distressed to hear Mussolini's far from flattering opinion of him. 'He's well known for his addiction to alcohol,' the dictator confided to his mistress Clara Petaccia. 'His other vice hardly matters, almost all Englishmen are like that.'[60]

Edward's interference was not only unconstitutional but crassly indifferent to the threat Italy's imperial project posed to British interests in Africa and the Mediterranean. He attempted in his memoirs to explain his motivation, stressing what he claimed was his anxiety that Britain should avoid antagonising Mussolini for fear of pushing him into a closer relationship with Hitler. The explanation given by Diana Mosley, wife of the fascist Oswald, is probably nearer to the truth, given Edward's enduring sense of white racial superiority. 'He probably thought Abyssinia would be better administered by Italians rather than Haile Selassie.'[61]

Edward's attitude to Italy and the Italians had undergone a striking change since the arrival of fascism on the scene. In July 1918, based at British military headquarters at Udine in Italy, he had sent photographs to Freda Dudley Ward in England. 'Aren't they an ugly crowd? & isn't that a terrible man with the big black beard!! But I'm sorry to say it's a pretty typical crowd of "dagoes"!!!!'[62]

When Ethiopia's ruler, Haile Selassie, arrived in London in June 1936 to begin five years of exile following Italy's defeat and occupation of his country, Foreign Secretary Eden asked Edward to grant him an official audience, which he said would be a popular gesture. Selassie had been named 'Man of the Year' by *Time* magazine in the United States. 'Popular with whom?' the king replied. 'Certainly not with the Italians.' He refused to do as Eden had requested, handing over the task to his brother, the Duke of Gloucester. Eden was seen by the Italians and by Edward as provocatively antagonistic to the Mussolini regime. Edward, with the air of a man smugly recalling a triumph, writes in his memoirs, 'Mr Eden, though disappointed, did not insist.'[63]

Edward had described himself as a 'misfit' in 1927. Two years later the prince told his private secretary, 'Tommy' Lascelles, who – after a painful hour-long explanation of why he could no longer tolerate his master's behaviour – had just handed in his resignation, 'I suppose the fact of the matter is that I'm quite the wrong person to be Prince of Wales.' Lascelles warned him that if he continued as he was he would lose the throne.[64]

The unease in governing circles, as George's health deteriorated and the day drew near, was that Edward was the wrong person to succeed his father as king. A few years before, the *Time* magazine had run an article telling how Edward teased his sister-in-law by calling her 'Queen Elizabeth'. The writer wondered 'how much truth there is in the story that he once said he would renounce his rights upon the death of George V – which would make her nickname come true.'[65] Even an astrologer had been prepared to chance his arm with an unambiguous forecast. In his *World Predictions* in 1931 the then widely known and often consulted clairvoyant Cheiro (an Irishman, William Warner, who also liked to call himself Count Louis Hamon) wrote:

The Prince of Wales ... was born under peculiar astrological circumstances which make his character a difficult one to understand ... It is well within the range of possibility that he will fall victim to a devastating love affair. If he does, I predict that the Prince will give up everything, even the chance of being crowned, rather than lose the object of his affection.[66]

6

On 25 September 1935 an MI5 officer noted that the Metropolitan Police Special Branch had passed across a copy of a report about McMahon and 'F. Mathews'. It is probable this involved the sometimes bizarre activities of McMahon and his friend 'Colonel' Matthews during Mrs Van der Elst's Putney election campaign (MI5 already had a file on Matthews – PF 261/9). But, as with much else referred to in the publicly available files, the document itself was removed and destroyed during the official weeding process.[67] A further Special Branch report in October on information McMahon had given the police on gun-running into the Irish Free State, presumably to build up the weaponry available to the Irish Republican Army, was also taken out.[68]

As the Bannigan family – McMahon's birth name – originated in Tyrone, a Northern Ireland county adjoining the now independent south, and relatives remained in the area, there was every reason to believe McMahon would have knowledge of Republican cross-border activities, even if only at the level of rumour. The IRA, already illegal in Northern Ireland, was about to be banned again in the south but would soon plan a renewal of attacks on the British mainland. Although what McMahon had to say had been of sufficient interest for Special Branch to share, MI5 head Vernon Kell told the Home Office permanent secretary that neither body found anything to act on as a result of his information.[69]

The next and far more active phase in McMahon's relationship with MI5 came on 12 October 1935, with a letter he had written to the Home Secretary, Sir John Simon, about work he was carrying out as an agent for the Italian military attaché. The letter made its way from the Home Office to the security service via the Foreign Office in what seems a typically dilatory fashion. Once again, the actual document was destroyed in weeding. But Kell thought its contents significant enough to discuss with John Ottaway, the officer heading MI5's enquiries and investigations section B4, before instructing him to call McMahon in for interview. Kell also ordered a Home Office Warrant to be raised, authorising the mail of both the Italian military attaché and an individual named Ponati, 'or any other cover name', to be intercepted.[70]

Ottaway was no novice, but he may not have had the subtleness of mind to deal with a man as complex as McMahon, to sift the truth hidden in untruth. Now in his sixties – he was born in 1870 – Ottaway had been an MI5 officer since 1920, joining on his retirement from a twenty-nine-year career with the City of London Police, the last eleven years as detective superintendent. Like many successful officers, he was an active Freemason. While with the City force he had led the hunt for Latvian anarchists who shot three police officers in Houndsditch, culminating in the famous Siege of Sidney Street in January 1911. When the killers were tracked down to a Whitechapel house Ottaway urged negotiating with their leader. He was overruled by army officers, who preferred a dramatic final shoot-out, and by the Home Secretary, Winston Churchill, who ordered the deployment of the Scots Guards, with an accompanying troop of artillery.

Two years later Ottaway headed the pursuit of suffragette bombers wreaking panic across London, though he never succeeded in apprehending the woman or women who planted a ticking 'mustard tin' device under the bishop's throne in the chancel of St Paul's Cathedral. In August 1915 he masterminded a raid on the Fleet Street offices of the anti-war Independent Labour Party newspaper, the *Labour Leader*, using Defence of the Realm Act powers to seize stocks of pamphlets and leaflets advocating a European peace conference to end the fighting.

In the 1920s, with the Soviet Union and the Communists now identified as the main threat to national security, Ottaway and his MI5 team trailed London party members who they believed maintained contact with Soviet intelligence through ARCOS, the All-Russian Co-operative Society, Russia's trading arm in Britain. Though a raid on ARCOS's Moorgate headquarters in March 1927 yielded nothing of real significance, and certainly not the stolen military documents expected, the British government ordered the body's closure, at the same time severing diplomatic relations with the Soviet Union.

The following year Ottaway was masquerading as a member of the 'Anti-Communist Union' in an operation to smoke out suspected Communist penetration of the Metropolitan Police Special Branch. Two Special Branch officers were dismissed after an internal disciplinary hearing in 1929 for 'supplying information to unauthorised persons'. They never faced criminal charges, partly for fear of the security can of worms a court appearance would open to public gaze. One result, however, was that in 1931 MI5 took sole rather than joint responsibility for investigating and tackling Communist subversion in the United Kingdom.

In the 1934 trial of a civil servant charged under the Official Secrets Act with divulging restricted information from Woolwich Arsenal, Ottaway, despite having been an MI5 officer for well over a decade, was described in the press when giving 'corrobative evidence' as an 'ex-superintendent of police acting under the directions of the War Office', with no reference in court to his actual role. It was true that he remained in practice the detective he had always been and hardly fitted the profile of the typical MI5 recruit. MI5's official historian found it revealing that the 'recreations listed by Ottaway on joining indicated that he came from lower down the social scale than most other officers: cricket and tennis rather than hunting and field sports.'[71]

Ottaway had been recruited to MI5 precisely because of his proficiency in the dull but essential work of surveillance, observing and collecting rather than assessing and judging evidence – police work rather than intelligence work. A 'watcher', he headed a three-man observation section B4, part of B Division, which had overall responsibility for investigations and enquiries under Brigadier Oswald 'Jasper' Harker, late of the Indian police. Ottaway's past career certainly added up to a familiarity with the shadowy frontier between crime and politics, the confusing blend of fact and fiction, truth and lies. But would this equip him to deal with a man as slippery and erratic as McMahon?

When McMahon met Ottaway for the first time on 17 October 1935, what he had to say about Italian intelligence operations in London was detailed and, given the worsening state of relations between the two countries, of some importance. MI5 had known since at least the spring of 1934 that the Italian dictator Mussolini was financing the British Union of Fascists, saving Mosley – as he claimed only half-jokingly – from having to sell his late wife's jewellery to maintain the organisation's existence. This, and the increasingly frequent and violent street clashes between Fascists and Communists, had persuaded Kell in 1934 of the need to compile his report on the activities of the BUF. The notorious June 1934 Olympia rally, with Mosley's crude anti-Semitic ranting and an unrelenting display of BUF brutality against hecklers, intensified uneasiness about domestic fascism.

The party, in Kell's view, represented a potential threat to national security. A further concern was the Prince of Wales's sympathy with fascism, his personal links with Mosley and – as time went by – Edward's growing dependence on Wallis Simpson, with her closeness to German and Italian diplomats. There was also the question of what Italian fascists living in Britain, of which MI5 had identified 870 by 1935, were involving themselves in, particularly in relation to the BUF. The Italian Embassy under Mussolini's close associate Dino Grandi was also known to have links with Mosley's movement throughout the early 1930s. Finally, Italian aggression in the shape of the invasion of Ethiopia in October 1935 was leading to diplomatic confrontation with the Mussolini regime.

Meeting an MI5 officer for the first time, McMahon confirmed what he had written to the Home Secretary in his letter, with significant additional information on the nature of his contacts, as Ottaway told Kell the following day.[72] McMahon said he had met an Italian official called Avella on 7 October in New Oxford Street, accompanied by an Italian Fascist called, he thought, Camatori. McMahon was carrying a letter from the Persian Consulate and specifications relating to armaments. As it emerged that the Italians were concerned about the supply of weapons to Ethiopia, it has to be assumed that McMahon had previously told the embassy he could provide intelligence on this. How, where and when he came by this information was not immediately clear.

Avella and Camatori took McMahon to the Italian Consulate in Portland Place and from there to the Italian Embassy. Here he was presented to Colonel Umberto Mondadori, the military attaché, who made copies of the documents McMahon had brought with him. McMahon told Mondadori he would be able to provide further intelligence on similar matters. Mondadori handed over a £5 note and a slip of paper on which he wrote the name and address of 'Mrs Ponti', with whom McMahon was told he should communicate in future, using the name 'Scott'.

McMahon told Ottaway that he had been to see the military attaché several times since 7 October, passing over papers provided to him by Colonel Matthews. Who were Matthews' contacts? Was he using McMahon or were they working together to extract money from the Italians? None of this was explained. Mondadori had paid McMahon a total of £27 for the intelligence. He offered a further £50 for three specific pieces of information he told McMahon he urgently needed: the activities of Solomon Hall and his brother, and in particular whether they were shipping aircraft abroad; whether the Soley Armament Company was selling weapons to the Ethiopian government; and what armaments, if any, Vickers Ltd were involved in supplying.

Mondadori was asking the right questions, though whether McMahon or the mysterious Colonel Matthews, using McMahon as a channel, were in a position to supply the answers the Italians required was another matter. The Soley Armament Company was a London-based business authorised to sell surplus British War Office weapons and equipment overseas. On 12 October 1935 the Board of Trade gave permission for the sale of 100,000 surplus Lee-Springfield rifles and 50 million cartridges to the Ethiopian army. But the licence was hurriedly withdrawn when the Foreign Office expressed fears that the shipment could antagonise the Italian government. A few weeks later, on 21 December, the Board of Trade gave Solely Armament permission to despatch sixty Hotchkiss machine guns to Ethiopia, provided all British identification marks were removed.[73] Vickers, meanwhile, had exported 2 million cartridges and a small consignment of light tanks to Ethiopia for use by Haile Selassie's forces against the Italian invasion forces.

The Halls were a Polish-Jewish family with close connections to the Ethiopian royal family dating back over many years. The brothers the Italians were interested in were David and Salomon (not Solomon). David, at this time counsellor of state to Emperor Haile Selassie, was visiting Germany in 1935 on a mission to buy arms, a fact the Italians seemed already to know.

Ottaway said McMahon had shown him other papers originating with Colonel Matthews, which the MI5 officer copied and returned. Matthews was clearly a person of interest and Ottaway included his private address in the report – 23 Haycroft Road, London, SW3. Matthews was referred to again in passing in McMahon's MI5 file, though MI5 already had a file on the colonel himself (PF 261/9), with cross-references to McMahon. When McMahon was later in prison, the authorities intercepted a letter from him to Matthews and passed a copy to MI5. The Prison Commission then intercepted a reply from Matthews in which he asked his friend not to refer to him as 'Colonel' on envelopes when writing.[74]

Having read Ottaway's report on his 18 October contact with McMahon, Kell spoke to Lieutenant Colonel Arnold of MI3c, a section of military intelligence at the War Office. They agreed the writing on the slip of paper McMahon had passed to Ottaway was definitely that of the Italian military attaché Mondadori. Kell noted on McMahon's file that Mrs Ponti was known to be the latter's private secretary and that she 'speaks English exceptionally well'.[75] Four days later Kell recorded that the Secretary of State had signed a Home Office Warrant authorising interception and examination of post addressed to both Mondadori and Ponti.[76]

Mondadori would also be playing another game, as MI5 became aware, using 'Colonel Pedro Lopez', a British subject of Polish origin (who was actually an actor, Henry Lawrence Bernstein), with a string of other aliases and links with intelligence services. Lopez had worked up a doctored-letter scam on behalf of the Italians to implicate the British government in alleged sales of 3 million dumdum rifle bullets – outlawed for military use by the Hague Convention of 1899 – to the Ethiopian army. *The Times* reported, 'The character of Lopez and the fact of his association with the Italian Military Attaché being known, the Foreign Office at this point gave the Italian Embassy a friendly warning.'[77] McMahon later claimed to the *Daily Express* he had provided the information that had enabled Colonel Lopez's exposure – this was never proved but was certainly not impossible given the range of his shadowy associates.

McMahon had established himself as a reliable informant to MI5 between October 1935 and April 1936, as Kell told the Home Office permanent under secretary, Sir Russell Scott, in a July 1936 memorandum. 'Some of the information was undoubtedly accurate, and as a result we were definitely able to ascertain that one Mrs Ponte [*sic*], a secretary employed by the Italian military attaché, was being used for certain intelligence work.'[78] But what was revealing was the way in which Kell tried to plant the sense that McMahon had suddenly and inexplicably ceased to be reliable after April 1936. Kell was writing five days after the 16 July attack on Edward and appeared to be attempting to create a smokescreen for MI5 to hide behind. He clearly had good reason to do this.

Ottaway had further contacts with McMahon on 30 November and 12 December 1935. The officer's reports on these meetings were removed from McMahon's file and destroyed before it was made public.[79] In a later written statement to Kell, Ottaway brought up the fact that McMahon had shown him a revolver he carried, probably in December 1935:

About two months after our first meeting, he produced a pistol and said it had been given him by the representatives of the foreign power referred to above for protection. I pointed out to him that it would be necessary for him to obtain a licence from the police to carry it.[80]

The legislation on gun ownership, the Firearms Act 1920, was not tightly enforced by the police and claiming the need for a pistol for 'self defence' would be seen as an acceptable reason for seeking a permit. But McMahon was precisely the kind of individual likely to be refused a licence by police: in the words of the Act 'a person of intemperate habits or unsound mind, or … for any reason unfitted to be entrusted with firearms'. The penalty for unlawful possession of a weapon and ammunition was a fine of up to fifty pounds and/or imprisonment for up to three months, with or without hard labour.

The most remarkable aspect was Ottaway's absolute lack of concern or even curiosity when McMahon produced the weapon. He simply told McMahon he needed a permit to carry a gun. As a police officer of many years' experience, he might have been expected at least to alert his former colleagues so they could question McMahon about the weapon and, if necessary, charge him with illegal possession. Presumably Ottaway feared that would risk MI5 losing what he saw as a worthwhile informant. As to how he came to have a revolver in his possession, McMahon told a series of stories. To Ottaway he said the 'foreign power' (Italy) had provided it for his protection. To the Italians he implied he was given the weapon by a British government department. Later, at Bow Street Police Court, he would say in response to his lawyer's question simply that he had 'obtained' the gun and that he never left home without it.

At this point – the end of 1935 – McMahon had made no mention of an assassination plot of any kind to MI5, but the significance of his possession of the weapon is obvious. Without a firearm McMahon posed no real threat. With one, he represented a serious hazard, as his run-ins with Mrs Van der Elst and then the steward at her Earlsfield election meeting in September had shown: he had threatened to shoot both of them. Bravado, obviously, but once a loaded gun comes into play the consequences will always be unpredictable.

7

What did McMahon's dealings with foreign embassies, the Italian and – it subsequently transpired – the German, involve? What was he giving them? What were they giving him? For McMahon the object was purely financial and there seemed at this point to be no political motive. He was later to tell a *Daily Express* reporter, 'For months before my arrest I was receiving payments from certain foreign sources for reporting on the activities of political refugees. It was detestable work. But I had to get money somehow.'[81] He said nothing about how and where he gathered this information or the nature of his contact with the people he informed on.

McMahon was clearly a man who put himself about, ingratiated himself into others' confidence, only to betray them. This was very much the character of the journalist he wanted and tried to be, but in this context the basest kind of gutter journalist. Was he using his cover as a 'journalist', with the single edition of his *Human Gazette* as a credential, to ferret out material he could then sell on to various embassies and agencies? Apart from his own statement to the *Daily Express*, there is no direct evidence, but this must have been the case: a smart voice, stylish clothes and a plausible manner – together with an accomplice in the shape of the elusive 'Colonel' Matthews – would be all it took.

On one occasion, conscious of the danger he was running in playing one intelligence agency off against another, McMahon told his MI5 handler Ottaway that he wanted to sever his connection with the Italian Embassy. Ottaway reported to his superior officer, Harker, that he had calmed McMahon. 'I assured him that everything would be well provided he told me all they wanted and before replying let me know what his replies were to be.' He persuaded McMahon to continue but, Ottaway added, 'I am perfectly certain he did not tell me nearly all that passed between them.'[82]

McMahon would also have had a contact in the German Embassy to whom he was passing intelligence on German political refugees. What he did not know, and what Ottaway would not have told him (and may have been unaware himself), was that MI5 had at least one informant of its own inside the Carlton House Terrace building. The highest ranked was Wolfgang von Putlitz, an anti-Nazi diplomat in his mid-thirties, head of the consular department since June 1934. Putlitz was recruited by Jona von Ustinov (father of the actor and writer Peter Ustinov), a press officer at the embassy who was dismissed in 1935 after refusing to provide proof that he was not of Jewish descent. He said he would, provided Joseph Goebbels, the Reich propaganda minister, was prepared to do so. Ustinov had already begun working for MI5 earlier in 1935.[83]

While McMahon was providing the embassy with what must have
been small-time gossip about the activities of Jewish and left-wing
refugees in London, Putlitz was supplying MI5 via Ustinov at their
fortnightly meetings with high-grade intelligence on German rearma-
ment, foreign policy and German Nazis operating in Britain. 'I would
unburden myself of all the dirty schemes and secrets which I encoun-
tered as part of my normal daily routine at the Embassy,' he later wrote.[84]
Putlitz continued passing valuable information of this kind until he was
posted to the Netherlands in May 1938, though his frequent warnings
that appeasing Hitler only served to encourage him had little impact on
British government policy.

What added to the murky atmosphere hovering around McMahon's
connection with MI5 was that the security service itself had as much
interest as the German Embassy in keeping tabs on that country's refugees, particularly those who had been compelled to flee because of their
Communist political affiliations or sympathies. MI5, German intelligence and McMahon may indeed have been keeping tabs on the same
people. There was certainly an element of mutual aid between MI5 and
the Gestapo in the early phases of the Nazi regime.

Once the Nazis had been installed in power, Guy Liddell, late of
Special Branch and now MI5's deputy director of counter-espionage
visited Berlin in March 1933 for discussions with the German secret
police, Abteilung 1A, soon to take on a new identity as the Gestapo.
Liddell's report on his return, 'The Liquidation of Communism and
Left-wing Socialism in Germany', followed his close examination of
files made available to him at Abteilung 1A headquarters, and demonstrated a shared anti-leftist sympathy between the two agencies.[85] This
would change when the direct threat Nazi Germany represented to
British interests could no longer be ignored.

The entanglements of McMahon, MI5 and the German Embassy give
the impression of fish swimming in the same sea, with shifting motives
of deceit, cynicism and even patriotism. One aspect of this is that
Ottaway was adamant that McMahon 'never disclosed that he was working for the Germans'.[86] But McMahon had clearly been passing MI5
information about, and was seen as connected to, particular Germans, as

cross-references in his file showed: Wuhl RL 8(2783), Heinz PF 19542, Smazi PF 44568, Fitzrandolph PF 42931, Winter PF 43099.[87] It is not unreasonable to suppose that in order to secure this information for MI5, McMahon needed to give the Germans something in return.

But what of the German political refugees McMahon was informing on? Where did he make contact with them? A letter received at Scotland Yard in July 1936 gave a clue. The informant told police that McMahon was an associate of a Dr Starkie who lived at a house in NW1. This was true. Starkie had been in McMahon's company during Mrs Van der Elst's Putney election campaign. 'Starkie's house,' the letter went on, 'is frequented by foreigners periodically without passports.'[88] Political refugees? Did some become aware of the double game McMahon was playing with them and try, in their turn, to use him? Passing disinformation to the German Embassy through McMahon would be seen as an effective political exercise, wrong-footing the Nazi regime as far as possible about resistance activities in refugee circles and in Germany itself. And could their use of McMahon go further, drawing him into a plot, real or contrived?[89]

There was one moment of comic irony in this world of international spooks when, on 12 December 1935, MI5 director Kell attended a lunch given annually by the Army Council at the Carlton Hotel for foreign military attachés – friendly and unfriendly – based at the London embassies. Among the other guests with whom Kell ate, drank and chatted was Colonel Umberto Mondadori of Italy, whose post he had only recently ordered to be intercepted, opened and read. Another guest was the German attaché, Major General Geyr von Schweppenburg.[90] The three would have accepted the rules of a game in which everyone might be snooping on everyone else, with varying degrees of competence and success.

8

McMahon had a further meeting with his handler Ottaway on 7 January 1936. There was a reference during their conversation to a German called Heinz, on whom MI5 already had a file (PF 19542). Once again, the report on what passed between the two men has been removed from McMahon's file and destroyed. Kell noted on 7 February, 'Mr Ottaway is still in touch with McMahon but there appears to have been a considerable lack of info. No doubt McMahon will notify Mr Ottaway as soon as he gets anything worth reporting.'[91] McMahon had not, in Kell's judgement and on the basis of his past record, yet lost his value as an informant.

McMahon himself, meanwhile, was showing signs of reverting to a tendency to unpredictable and irrational behaviour, again involving a weapon. A woman who had been acquainted with him around Notting Hill since 1933, Dorothea Maritch, told police that in February 1936 McMahon turned up at an estate agent's premises off Shaftesbury Avenue where she was working as a temporary typist. It was 6 p.m. and she was about to close the office for the day. McMahon told her he was hard up and asked her to lend him money. Maritch had past experience of his habit of being quick to borrow but slow to repay and she refused.

McMahon then produced a small automatic pistol, which he offered to sell her for two pounds. Maritch told the police officer who later interviewed her, 'I remember it was black and noticed that it was like one my husband had during the war which held eight cartridges.' McMahon said he had 'several refills' of ammunition at home. She asked him to leave. 'He implored me to give him a shilling for a drink but I refused as I had been let down so badly by him.'[92]

Money was a constant problem, with the McMahons often depending on Rose's earnings as a shop assistant to survive. Although over two years had passed since his release from prison, McMahon had not abandoned hope of compensation for what he saw as his mistreatment by the legal system. On 12 February he sent a petition to the newly installed King Edward VIII. 'Since a child I have never had a chance,' he wrote, 'and when a ray of happiness was beginning to illumine my life, it was extinguished through the harsh action of your Majesty's officers.' He ran through the story of police corruption in Notting Hill, his trial and appeal, repeating the pleas he had addressed to Edward's father in August 1934 and referring obliquely to his dealings with MI5:

In my agony of mind I appeal in the hallowed memory of your Majesty's father. If the Home Office cannot grant me some recompense for my unjust imprisonment, they can perhaps at least give me some work, even at 5s. a day. I have proved recently that my desire has been to help law and order. I have been the means of imparting valuable information, not for reward, but to prove that, although I have suffered much, I still remain a loyal subject of your Majesty. I have no unemployment benefit as I was an employer, and my poor wife is slaving to keep the home together. I am in debt.[93]

In further contacts with MI5 on 21 February, 30 March and 8 April McMahon gave Ottaway information on an individual called Jack Koski but the reports on what exactly he said have been removed from McMahon's file. But the most dramatic meeting between handler and informant took place on 17 April 1936. A note on McMahon's MI5 file says simply, '17 April 1936 B. note re recent activities of McMahon'.[94] 'B' is Oswald 'Jasper' Harker, Kell's second-in-command and head of B Division, in which Ottaway operated. The relevant attachment to the file, item 31A, which would contain his comments, has been destroyed.

Had Sir Russell Scott, Permanent Under-Secretary to the Home Office, not subsequently asked Kell to provide details of MI5's dealings with McMahon, there would be no evidence as to what took place at the 17 April meeting. Kell wrote in response to Scott's request:

On the 17th April 1936 McMahon approached Mr Ottaway, and informed him that he was in possession of information regarding a Communist plot to assassinate the Monarch, and that he was proposing to see Mr Baldwin's Private Secretary at 10 Downing Street with a view to placing the facts before the Prime Minister. This information was immediately given to Mr Norman Kendal, to whom I explained that this man had from time to time been giving us information. Mr Kendal asked at the time whether we had any objection to McMahon being seen by a police officer, and on my telling him we thought it would be advisable for a police officer to see McMahon, Mr Kendal made the necessary arrangements.[95]

Kendal, a former barrister and wartime army officer, was the Metropolitan Police assistant commissioner, with responsibility since 1931 for the Criminal Investigation Department and the activities of Special Branch. (It was to Kendal that McMahon had written with his second complaint about police corruption in February 1933, the letter that finally prompted action.)

Ottaway also wrote a statement setting out his own version of the 17 April meeting. He said that McMahon telephoned on 15 April, saying he urgently needed to see him:

> Consequently I saw him when he said that he was associated with certain persons who were planning to assassinate the King and that he would be prepared to tell the whole story providing the authorities would first guarantee him £1,000. He assured me that nothing was likely to happen for two or three months. I asked him if he was involved and he said he was, but only to the extent of supplying firearms. I pointed out to him the seriousness of the matter and requested him to give me full details, but he refused to do so unless the guarantee was forthcoming.

Ottaway asked McMahon why his associates wanted to kill the king 'and he said he knew nothing except that the assassin would be acclaimed a hero among a certain class of person'. Interestingly, Ottaway made no reference in his memorandum to Kell to McMahon implicating Communists in the plot, but he would in a later report.[96]

According to Ottaway, when he protested that asking for £1,000 was an unreasonable demand to make, McMahon said he would write a full statement and let MI5 have it the next day.[97] McMahon's recollection of the conversation differed from Ottaway's. He was insistent that he had never asked for £1,000. 'No sir, I said when I gave the information, would they look after my wife, would they give me some guarantee when I parted with the information that my wife would be looked after,

and they said "Yes".'[98] McMahon recalled that Ottaway had also promised him immunity from arrest in return for his co-operation, adding
that Ottaway said his superiors in MI5 could never put this in writing:
'Surely old chap you accept my word.'[99]

McMahon did not produce the promised statement and instead he
was interviewed by Inspector Cooper of Special Branch, an unhappy
experience for McMahon if his subsequent attitude to the officer was
anything to go by. A copy of Cooper's report, long according to Kell,
was attached to McMahon's file on 20 April 1936 but, as with so
many others, the document was destroyed in the weeding process. But
the effect of the report was dramatic. Harker noted on McMahon's
file the next day that Ottaway should read what the Special Branch
officer had to say at once, adding, 'In the circumstances I think we
had better drop this man.'[100] What were these 'circumstances'? It is
impossible to know without sight of the Special Branch report. What
had McMahon said, or what had Cooper recounted him as saying,
that had this sudden impact? Were MI5 taking the opportunity to
distance themselves from their informant, officially at least? If so, for
what reason?

On 6 May Harker repeated his instruction to 'drop' McMahon
more forcefully:

> In view of this informant's very dubious character, I do not consider
> in the absence of some other evidence that we should waste any time
> checking up on his yarns. Pl[ease] see that where extracts have been
> made in other files that a note is put to this effect.

Alongside this note was a handwritten list of MI5 file numbers and
names of individuals connected with information McMahon had given
in the past. Most names appear to be German.[101]

Kell's explanation to the Home Office permanent under secretary a
few months later differed slightly from Harker's, though no doubt the
two had discussed the action to be taken. Kell said that after reading
the Special Branch report 'and in view of McMahon's previous record
I instructed Mr Ottaway gradually to break off his association with

McMahon, as I felt that, while we had had some use out of him, he was too unreliable to be of real assistance'.[102] Harker's peremptory 'drop' had become Kell's break off 'gradually'. In his own statement Ottaway mentioned neither.

Despite Harker's instruction, MI5 maintained their interest in McMahon and his activities and on 22 April a newspaper cutting with a report on the case of McMahon v. Elst was attached to his file. Why the attentiveness to his involvement with Mrs Van der Elst? As the attachment was destroyed it has to be assumed that the story concerned McMahon's attempt at Marylebone County Court to force Mrs Van der Elst to pay for the cars he had procured for her 1935 election campaign. In June McMahon was still proving his use to MI5 when he passed information on an Italian agent named A. Mortara. An officer advised Kell on file:

As McMahon has produced this fresh information and we have not recently seen letters on intelligence matters going to Mrs Ponti, it seems worth while imposing a check on Mortara's correspondence, both at the Consulate and at his private address. Herewith H.O.W. [Home Office Warrant] for signature if approved, please.[103]

McMahon, meanwhile, was hoping to publish a second edition of his paper, the *Human Gazette*, in the summer and had persuaded a Mr Gordon, the owner of Windsor House at 46 Victoria Street, not only to provide financial backing but also to allow him to use an empty office free of charge. Readers of the paper had sent in articles, though McMahon was, not surprisingly, unable to pay them for their contributions.

On 1 July McMahon's hopes collapsed when he received a letter from Gordon saying he had found a paying tenant for the office from 15 July. McMahon would have to leave. When McMahon asked the reason for his sudden change of mind, Gordon replied, 'The police have been here.'[104] This could have only one interpretation for an agitated McMahon: the authorities were continuing to persecute him for having revealed corruption at Notting Hill police station and for proving he was right by his successful appeal against conviction for libel.

On 14 July, a Tuesday, Harker wrote in McMahon's MI5 file: 'B. note re information from McMahon re plot to assassinate the King (39A) and S.11 report on circumstances (39B)'. Both the note and the report were destroyed in weeding. Harker's 14 July observation is the first reference on the file to a plot to assassinate Edward, even though McMahon had told Ottaway in April the act was to take place in 'two or three months'.[105] The events that led up to Harker writing this note have to be pieced together from a later statement by Ottaway. What had happened at the latest contact was this:

> On the evening of the 13th July in consequence of a telephone communication from McMahon, I saw him at Victory House, Victoria Street, when he showed signs of nervousness and intimated that he would not be alive after Thursday 16th. I asked him what he meant, and he said that arrangements had been made that he and a companion should assassinate the King on Thursday during the presentation of the Colours. I again pointed out to him the seriousness of the matter and endeavoured to dissuade him from any such action, and pressed him to give me all details. He refused to do that, and said that nothing could prevent his carrying out his part of the plan, but that he had made the necessary arrangements regarding his private affairs in the event of his death.

McMahon told Ottaway the original plan was for Edward to be assassinated at Trooping the Colour (which had taken place on 23 June that year), but the attempt had been abandoned on the day for reasons McMahon did not at that point explain. Ottaway said McMahon told him, 'If you want to make a name for yourself, I would like you to meet me at 8 a.m. on the 16th and follow me.' Ottaway replied he was unable to do this as it was entirely a police matter. After discussion, McMahon agreed to give full details to the police. Ottaway noted, 'I told him that I would arrange for an officer to call on him the next day and he said he would be at his office.'[106]

Ottaway briefed Kell on his conversation with McMahon the following day, 14 July, and at 11 a.m. both men went over to Scotland Yard for a meeting with Assistant Commissioner Kendal, who by now fully understood the background to McMahon's involvement with MI5. Kell and Kendal had a long-standing working relationship dating back to the 1920s. There is no record on McMahon's file of what the three discussed in Kendal's office nor, indeed, any reference at all to a meeting having taken place. A document entitled 'Brief precis of case' attached to the file on 17 July, which may have included details of the discussion, has been destroyed.

McMahon, meanwhile, was in an anxious state, drifting aimlessly. Over the past few months he had managed to make a scant income selling odd snippets to newspapers in his guise as a 'freelance journalist', together with whatever the Italian and German embassies had been paying him for the material he was passing them on political refugees. The single edition of the *Human Gazette* he had managed to publish had dragged him deeper into debt. Only his wife's wages as a shop assistant kept their home afloat. Working from the rent-free Victoria Street office, McMahon's routine had been to drop in at the Two Brewers in Buckingham Gate at lunchtime just after midday. He had become well acquainted with a barmaid there, Mary Blencowe.

On Wednesday 15 July, two days after his revelation to Ottaway and the day he was due to lose his office, McMahon made his way to the Two Brewers. He ordered meat and two veg and a glass of mild. Lunch finished, according to the barmaid Mary Blencowe, McMahon stood to leave and then said, 'I am going away, and you will never see me again.' The barmaid replied she was sorry to hear that as he had been a good customer. McMahon's final words were, by her account, dramatic. 'Something dreadful has happened. I would like to tell you, but I can't. You will see it all in the papers.'[107] McMahon would later deny having said this.

That evening, 15 July at about 8.30 p.m., McMahon composed a letter to the Home Secretary, Sir John Simon, at his office in Windsor House, handwritten on two sides of yellow paper. He later said he felt the situation impelled him to write when Gordon told him the visit by police officers had persuaded him to deny McMahon further use of the office. The letter set out McMahon's anguish and frustration as he condemned the 'organised persecution by your hirelings' – the police – his unjust imprisonment in 1933 for trying to 'stop a systematic blackmail campaign carried on by certain of your subordinates', the way in which his family home and the opportunity to work had been 'wrested from me'. He pleaded for justice, which he said was every British subject's right:

> As previous appeals to the King have been unsuccessful, I now demand full satisfaction, within 14 hours, of a cessation of such un-British conduct by your servants: also a retraction of the vile persecution levelled against me; and, further, that you cease to continue publishing and prevent such persecution. In the event of your failing to do so I will exercise my own prerogative and obtain the necessary satisfaction which I, in my tortured mind, consider adequate. This is no silly boast. I demand justice irrespective of the consequences. G. A. McMahon.[108]

It was Wednesday 15 July and the clock was ticking.

III

'The Dastardly Attempt'

1

The Silver Jubilee celebrations on 6 May 1935 honouring George V's twenty-five years on the throne were an outstanding triumph for the Crown as an institution and for the king personally, the 'father of the Empire'. An invented 'tradition', the day was declared a public holiday and marked with a service at St Paul's Cathedral, a royal progress through London, and a flourish of pageants, fetes and street parties across the country. Towards evening the king and queen waved to the cheering crowds below from the Buckingham Palace balcony, repeating the performance next day by popular demand.

A reserved man, wary of showing or acknowledging emotion, George was touched by these displays of the regard and affection many of his subjects had for him. 'But I cannot understand it. I am quite an ordinary fellow,' he said. 'Yes, sir, that's just it,' the Archbishop of Canterbury replied. A more cynical view was taken by the journalist Claud Cockburn who portrayed the day as an admission by a shaky national government of the need to 'play the royal card for all it might be worth'.[1]

Edward as Prince of Wales had a vital part, often reluctantly, in boosting the monarchy's popularity in Britain and the Empire. But the last months of George's life were overshadowed by a concern for the throne's stability when his son succeeded, as he must. For such an undemonstrative man, George was outspoken in expressing his fears to a range of individuals: the head of Edward's household, Admiral Halsey; the Archbishop of Canterbury; the Countess of Airlie; and to the prime minister, Stanley Baldwin. 'After I'm dead the boy will ruin himself in twelve months,' he told Baldwin.[2] On 19 January 1936, as George lay dying, Henry 'Chips' Channon, the Tory MP and writer close to Edward's clique, noted in his diary, 'My heart goes out to the Prince of Wales tonight, as he will mind so terribly being King. His loneliness, his seclusion, his isolation will be almost more than his highly-strung and unimaginative nature can bear.'[3]

George V died on 20 January 1936, in the depths of a bitter winter, eased from life five minutes before midnight by the royal doctor's injection of a cocaine and morphine cocktail, timed to ensure the story broke in *The Times* next morning rather than in the raffish evening press. Both Queen Mary and the Prince of Wales had told the doctor, Lord Dawson, that if death was inevitable they did not want the king's life needlessly prolonged.

George and his advisers had learned from the fate of his royal cousins Nicholas in Russia and Wilhelm in Germany that the monarchy's survival depended on appearing to be of some use to society, to serve a function beyond simply reigning. Whatever his own misgivings, Edward as Prince of Wales had a public charm that perfectly fitted the new age of celebrity. His popularity was used to serve a political purpose, buttressing the ties of Empire through his glittering tours in the 1920s, expressing sympathy for the unemployed and the poor in his journeys round the kingdom. His charitable projects and sympathetic speeches were used to soften the edges of a persistent class crisis that the Depression of the 1930s threatened to sharpen.

Edward was able to give the impression that – although he had no solution to offer to the many dire problems the country faced – he was at least able to commiserate with the victims. But for established politicians his unpredictable comments on, for example, unemployment and slum housing, could be taken as implied criticism of government, threatening to raise hopes that would prove difficult to meet. However, much as Edward claimed to be a 'rebel', he did not criticise the economic and political system as such, nor had he any radical proposals for change. He was open about this when setting out his overall attitude in his memoirs, where he wrote of his 'distinctly conservative outlook'. He went on, 'I believed, among other things, in private enterprise, a strong navy, the long week-end, a balanced budget, the gold standard, and close relations with the United States.'[4] In short, his worldview was – apart from his fondness for America – uncomplicatedly ordinary for a man of his class and time.

One historian paints a vivid picture of the person who came to the throne in January 1936:

> He exuded a warm charm to most people he met, though he could get bored and fidgety, and enjoyed a glitzy, hedonistic lifestyle of travelling, partying, West End nightclubs, weekending, yachting, swimming, hunting and playing golf, spending money extravagantly, being at forty-one a middle-aged 'bright young thing' in the mould of the previous decade.[5]

There was much in this description the public – shielded by press and broadcasting from the truth about the ageing playboy – would find attractive, a monarch who suggested the future rather than the past. But there were elements that worried those who saw their task as keeping the show of state on the road. A *Times* article setting out to extol the late king's virtues could be read as a veiled warning about – and perhaps to – Edward, the establishment thinking out loud. George was, the piece declared, 'remarkably painstaking, orderly and thorough ... Temperate, even abstemious, he was an early riser ... He was very methodical. He would go laboriously through the day's work ... He read every State paper, and discussed each subject with the expert ...' The *Times* leader writer, whether he knew it or not – and as an establishment voice he probably did (and the newspaper's editor, Geoffrey Dawson, who was close to Prime Minister Baldwin, certainly did) – was describing a figure precisely the reverse of King Edward VIII. And, as if to underline the awkwardness of Edward's bachelor state – the first unmarried king since George III in 1760

– and to hint at his as-yet publicly unknown relationship with a married woman, George was commended in the piece as 'never so happy as in his own family circle, and he will be remembered as a model of husband and father'.[6]

Edward presented himself as a king for the new age by flying from Sandringham to London on 22 January for the Accession Council in St James's Palace, the first British monarch to take to the air. Here he was formally proclaimed 'our only lawful and rightful Liege Lord Edward the Eighth'. The shadowy figure of Wallis watched the proclamation ceremony from a palace window, caught by a photographer. Shortly after the formalities were finished she said to Edward, 'This has made me realise how different your life is going to be.' He pressed her arm. 'But nothing can ever change my feelings toward you.'[7]

The prime minister, Stanley Baldwin, also had strong feelings about the couple. On the day of George's death he called Duff Cooper, Secretary for War and one of Edward's social circle, to Downing Street. Baldwin surprised Cooper by saying he wanted to talk about the new king's relationship with Mrs Simpson. 'He thinks that if it becomes generally known the country won't stand it,' Cooper recorded in his diary. '"If she were what I call a respectable whore," he [Baldwin] said, he wouldn't mind, by which he meant somebody whom the Prince occasionally saw in secret but didn't spend his whole time with.' Cooper was unsure what Baldwin expected him to do but guessed he was meant to find a way of encouraging Mrs Simpson to 'clear out'.[8] The irony in all this was Cooper's own reputation among those in the know as a keen womaniser, protected, like Edward, by an understanding press. Perhaps Baldwin had in mind a variation on the principle of setting a thief to catch a thief.

On 23 January Edward marched with his brothers behind a gun carriage bearing their father's coffin from King's Cross station to Westminster Hall, where the casket was to lie in state. The heavily bejewelled Imperial State Crown rested on the flag-draped coffin. As the procession entered New Chapel Yard the carriage lurched and the crown shifted. The Maltese cross, mounted on top, fell into the roadway. Edward saw this out of the corner of his eye and, as a Grenadier Guards sergeant major scooped the cross from the road and slipped it into his pocket, he was heard to say, 'Christ! What will happen next?'[9] Edward later recalled, 'It seemed a strange thing to happen; and, though I am not superstitious, I wondered whether it was a bad omen.'[10]

Neville Chamberlain, Chancellor of the Exchequer in Baldwin's government, had written to his sisters after the accession ceremony on 22 January, 'I do hope he pulls up his socks and behaves himself now he has such heavy responsibilities, for unless he does so he will soon pull down the throne.'[11] Chamberlain had earlier drafted a memorandum, which Baldwin suppressed, urging Edward to 'settle down', to wear drabber clothes, to avoid expressing opinions on social issues, and to attend to his boxes.[12] But Baldwin obviously shared Chamberlain's worries and had for some time, telling the Labour leader Clement Attlee he doubted that Edward would 'stay the course'.[13]

The question of the 'red boxes' confirmed Edward's unwillingness, his inability, to accept the routines underpinning a constitutional monarch's role. He understood in theory the importance of dealing with the official papers delivered each day for his attention. He said of his father, 'The picture of him "doing his boxes", to use his own phrase, had long represented for me the relentless grind of the King's daily routine.'[14] It was a task Edward found difficult and unpleasant. Lloyd George, a mature confidant since Edward's installation as Prince of Wales in 1911, once warned him that if he aspired to the role of constitutional monarch he would first need to be a constitutional Prince of Wales. This was a lesson that passed Edward by.

The boxes, delivered by courier, contained state papers for the king to read and where necessary sign: Foreign and Colonial Office telegrams and despatches; appointments to government posts, military commissions, the Church of England and embassies abroad to be approved; together with the most confidential of Cabinet documents and minutes. Much of what had to be done was routine, certainly not intellectually demanding, but Edward admitted he had neither the taste nor facility for what he called this 'interminable amount of desk work'.[15] But dealing with them lay at the heart of the monarch's role in the governance of Britain.

Edward began enthusiastically enough, signing what was required, marking documents to indicate he had read them, occasionally discussing with officials items he found particularly interesting. But then his self-indulgent nature re-asserted itself, a slide began, his staff having to cover up for his lack of attentiveness. He complained to Wallis Simpson about 'those d---d red boxes full of mostly bunk to read', and as time passed barely skimmed the papers.[16]

More and more frequently he kept the red boxes at Fort Belvedere for days on end, sometimes returning documents with ominous cocktail-glass stains. Ominous because cocktails were the symbol of decadence in the 1930s. Highly secret Cabinet minutes and memoranda lay strewn across sofas and tables, files on view to any guest he happened to have invited for the weekend, including, one story said, secret plans for a battleship. Edward was once seen sharing a box's contents with Wallis as if they were of no more significance than a morning newspaper, praising her comments to his friends 'with ecstatic admiration'.[17]

A strange paragraph appeared in the *Daily Express* in July, with no apparent context, headed 'Cabinet Secrets Are Safe'. Sir John Simon, the Home Secretary, was quoted as having said at a meeting in Woodford, Essex, 'Cabinet secrets are entirely safe, because the only people who know anything about them are very responsible Cabinet Ministers, who, of course, are under the most solemn obligations to keep the secret until it is made public.'[18] It was as if there had been something on the tip of Simon's tongue that he could not quite bring himself to spell out. Clive Wigram, a shrewd and dedicated palace official now acting as Edward's private secretary had been accustomed to George's methodical work routine. Wigram was aghast as complaints mounted about Edward's attitude, his irregular hours, his brusque and insensitive treatment of palace officials, and his lax handling of state business.

One royal biographer describes the often-discussed contrast between Edward's bachelor life in the days before he came to the throne, a hangover from the 1920s, and that of his married brother Albert, Duke of York:

While the Yorks lived in domestic bliss, the Prince of Wales was a man about town. He took up flying, he summered on the Riviera rather

than on Deeside, he spent many long evenings entertaining his friends
in chic London nightclubs.[19]

Not, it was clear, what the political and royal establishment wanted in
a monarch. When Baldwin had first heard of the depth of Edward's
attachment to Wallis Simpson and the possible impact on the monarchy's future, he is quoted as saying, 'The Yorks will do it very well.'[20]
The ground was being prepared.

In February 1936 Wigram attended a meeting at the prime minister's room in the House of Commons to discuss the drift already taking
place under Edward. Present were the country's most influential admin-
istrators – Warren Fisher (head of the civil service), Maurice Hankey
(Cabinet secretary and clerk of the Privy Council) and Robert Vansittart
(Foreign Office permanent secretary). That these three civil servants
constituted the Secret Service Committee, which had responsibility for
overseeing the intelligence services, MI5 and MI6, underlined the meeting's significance.

Wigram recorded their conversation in a memorandum. It was
common knowledge among senior civil servants that Edward was showing state papers to Mrs Simpson and discussing their contents with her.
Vansittart said the French and Swiss Embassies in London had reported
back to their governments on her influence over the king. The Foreign
Secretary, Anthony Eden, Vansittart said, believed she was 'in the pocket'
of the German ambassador, Leopold von Hoesch.[21] Baldwin's closest
political confidant, former Tory party chairman Lord Davidson, had
echoed this, writing to the prime minister in a memorandum, 'Mrs S is
very close to Hoesch and has, if she likes to read them access to all Secret
and Cabinet papers!!!!!'[22]

After the meeting Wigram raised Whitehall's uneasiness about the
security of confidential documents with Edward. The king brushed
him off, saying he was always careful and that he read the papers in
his car en route from London to Fort Belvedere. Wigram noted, 'As
HM leaves about 3 a.m. in his car, I did not feel there was much light
to read!' Wigram told Edward that he would be leaving his service
when the period of official mourning ended, informing Baldwin he

had come to the conclusion that Edward's attitude and behaviour left him with no alternative.

Wigram had also taken his concerns to the Lord Chancellor, Lord Hailsham, the country's chief law officer. What Wigram had to say to Hailsham was explosive:

> I did not think the King was normal, and this view was shared by my colleagues at Buckingham Palace. He might any day develop into a George III, and it was imperative to pass the Regency Bill as soon as possible, so that if necessary he could be certified.[23]

Alec Hardinge, Edward's assistant private secretary and soon to succeed Wigram, complained of the new king's irregular hours, combined with an irresponsible attitude to work that made the serious conduct of affairs difficult, if not impossible. Godfrey Thomas, who had spent many years as the Prince of Wales's private secretary, expressed his view a few days after Edward came to the throne that he was 'not fitted to be King and his reign will end in disaster'.[24]

As if all these failings were not enough, there was Edward's relationship with Wallis Simpson. The upper classes had long accepted with pragmatic hypocrisy that a male monarch would marry a wife for dynastic breeding purposes and keep a mistress, or mistresses, for pleasure. But this arrangement only worked if it was undertaken discreetly and the truth kept from the royal subjects. Was Edward prepared to follow this tradition, to play the game with discretion?

Whatever his faults, Edward was no hypocrite when it came to his attitude to religion or following his emotions. He refused, for example, to keep up a pretence of being a diligent Anglican, almost entirely abandoning ritualistic weekly churchgoing. Baldwin once complained he had never before 'met anyone so completely lacking in any sense of what is *beyond*'.[25] Wallis, writing to her aunt Bessie Merryman in February 1936, said, 'It's a very lonely job – and it's a tragedy that he can't bring himself to marry without loving.'[26]

At the same time Ernest Simpson had become less inclined to simply play his part in the three-cornered game with Wallis and Edward.

He told the king he had decided Wallis might have to choose between them. He asked the king what his intentions were. Edward replied, 'Do you really think that I would be crowned without Wallis at my side?'[27] 'Chips' Channon described how Edward and Wallis's relationship was seen by their peers:

> It appears that the King is Mrs Simpson's absolute slave, and will go nowhere she is not invited, and she, clever woman, with her high pitched voice, chic clothes, moles and sense of humour is behaving well.[28]

'Behaving well' on the surface. The police knew otherwise. Wallis, unusually for Edward's past run of lovers, had been the subject of Special Branch interest for the past twelve months, once the seriousness of the relationship had become plain. Police observation of the Simpsons had revealed Wallis's simultaneous affair with the London motor salesman, Trundle. Her social contacts and her right-wing political sympathies had led the Foreign Secretary to suspect she was passing information to the German Embassy. Mistrust of this kind, combined with Edward's carelessness with state documents, added up to one thing – the king posed a growing threat to national security.

Edward, according to his memoirs, had already decided he must and would marry Wallis. A family Christmas at Sandringham in 1935 had been, he wrote, a torment. His father was thin and weak, a man in bad health. 'I felt detached and lonely. My brothers were secure in their private lives whereas I was caught up in an inner conflict and would have no peace of mind until I resolved it.'[29] Edward was increasingly in the company of a small circle of friends acceptable to Wallis at Fort Belvedere, where he spent much of his time. Even his long-standing crony 'Fruity' Metcalfe was excluded for a while by Wallis as a bad influence. 'Mrs Simpson's invitations came to rank as commands,' a journalist wrote in *The New Yorker* magazine. 'Her position in London is without precedent in history for an American.'[30]

Despite Edward's commitment to Wallis – unknown to most of the public, common knowledge in ruling circles and along Fleet Street

– newspapers continued to tout the myth of Edward as the lonely but eligible bachelor. In March 1936 the American United Press agency compiled a list of what it claimed were the top seven candidates for his hand: 'The Princesses Eugenie, Irene, and Catherine of Greece; the Grand Duchess Kira of Russia; Princess Juliana of The Netherlands; Princess Alexandrine-Louise of Denmark and Princess Friederika of Brunswick-Luneburg.'[31] Hitler saw the possibilities and had, reportedly, been angling since 1934 for Friederika's family to arrange her marriage to Edward, twenty-two years her senior.

Hitler's interest partly arose from his failure to understand the actual political role and authority of a British monarch. The resolutely Nazi Duke of Saxe-Coburg und Gotha (the name the Windsors had dropped in 1917), was Hitler's emissary at George's Windsor Castle funeral in January 1936 and had reported back to Berlin:

> The King is resolved to concentrate the business of government on himself. For England, not too easy. The general political situation, especially the situation of England herself, will perhaps give him a chance. His sincere resolve to bring Germany and England together would be made more difficult if it were made public too early.

The duke added in his despatch that Edward suggested he made regular visits to London for confidential talks of this kind, that is discussions carried on behind the backs of British government ministers.[32] Once again, there can be little doubt MI5's informant in the German Embassy had word of this and passed it on. Baldwin, the prime minister, subsequently told Edward one left-wing Clydeside MP had said to him, 'I see we are going to have a Fascist King, are we?'[33]

The implications of Edward's succession had struck not only Wallis, with her declaration of how different his life would be, but also the political establishment, elements of which were lining up to demonstrate their anxiety that the wrong man had come to the throne. In April the Earl of Crawford, an influential former Conservative chief whip, expressed his fear of what the British public's reaction would be when the truth about the king's life was exposed, as was inevitable:

I feel certain that a crisis must occur and without much delay as our newspapers will not long forego their claim to discuss what is already the subject matter of articles in France and America, probably in Australia too. And then what is the little man going to do – how can he face that storm?[34]

It was a short step from believing the wrong man was king to concluding it might be legitimate to remove him in whatever way presented itself. Much had been invested in Edward as the figurehead for a new age, in his popularity as Prince of Wales, and in the hope that he could mature into the role of monarch once he had succeeded. But if he failed to give a return on the outlay, an alternative existed. As Edward had told Kitchener in 1914 when he pleaded to be allowed to join his regiment on the Western Front, there was a brother waiting in line.

The 27 May 1936 Court Circular – the official record of royal public engagements – reported the presence of Mr and Mrs Simpson as Edward's guests at dinner at Buckingham Palace, with the prime minister and Mrs Baldwin, the Mountbattens, the American aviator Charles Lindbergh and his wife, among others. On 9 July Wallis's name appeared on the Court Circular without that of her husband. *The Times* was later to comment that this opened the door for the American press to give 'prominence to the gossip which had been circulating in London'.[35]

In Britain itself, only the Communist *Daily Worker* openly joked about Edward and Wallis, and even that was done mildly. The party leader, Harry Pollitt, addressing a National Peace Congress in Leeds on 28 June, said, 'If gas masks are to be given out we should demand the same kind of gas masks for our wives as will be given to the Duchess of Kent and Mrs Simpson.' Most of the audience appeared to get the point.[36] The former prime minister, Ramsay MacDonald, complained that Mrs Simpson's appearance alone in the Court Circular was bound to have a bad effect.

'The people do not mind fornication, but they loathe adultery.'[37] The deluge was approaching.

2

McMahon's movements and actions between the evening of Wednesday 15 July and the morning of Thursday 16 July are, not unexpectedly, as muddled and difficult to follow as many of the events in his life. As far as the man himself is concerned, they shift depending what aspect of his story he is telling. Much, though not all, of what McMahon was thinking and doing over those two days has to be reconstructed from exchanges during his appearances at Bow Street Police Court and the Old Bailey.

On 14 July John Ottaway and MI5 director Vernon Kell had briefed Assistant Commissioner Norman Kendal at Scotland Yard on McMahon's latest revelations about the plot to assassinate the king on 16 July. McMahon had told Ottaway he was prepared to give the police more details. Inspector Cooper of Special Branch was sent to interrogate McMahon. Cooper had previously questioned him about the conspiracy in April. Cooper's subsequent report had prompted Harker, Kell's deputy at MI5, to recommend dropping McMahon as an informant. This time McMahon, who did not feel comfortable with Cooper, told him he would say nothing without the guarantee of a safeguard, as he feared for his life.

On Wednesday 15 July, Inspector Clarke of Special Branch was despatched to interview McMahon, who seemed to have an easier relationship with this officer and was prepared to be more open with him. Clarke arrived at McMahon's soon-to-be-vacated office in Victoria Street about 12.45 p.m. and, according to a later Home Office account of the meeting, McMahon told the inspector that the plot was 'a st affair'. He mentioned an individual named George Thompson as one of the conspirators. McMahon said that weapons had been supplied by a 'late consul named Heinz'. (McMahon had previously mentioned him to Ottaway in January and MI5 already had a file on a person of that name – PF 19542.)

McMahon promised Clarke he would go to Scotland Yard later in the afternoon to dictate a full statement, but failed to turn up. When the two met again that evening around 11 p.m. McMahon said men called Bill and Tom were also involved in the plot, but he had become unsure now whether the attempt would be made.[38] Nevertheless, he told the inspector he had been instructed to meet others involved in the conspiracy at the Express Dairy, a cafeteria and shop on Edgware Road, the next day, 16 July. The Home Office report said this was to be a little after 10 a.m. but McMahon later testified his instructions had been to get there between 8 a.m. and 9 a.m. Clarke pointed out an officer who would accompany McMahon, presumably at a distance. McMahon believed this was an assurance that he would be followed by police throughout the morning on 16 July.[39] This, he thought, would protect him and enable the arrest of the plotters.

In the evening McMahon wrote his undated letter to the Home Secretary, Sir John Simon. That is not disputed. But he gave two explanations as to why. The first – which he would give at Bow Street Court on 31 July – was his anger at being deprived of his Victoria Street office through, he believed, continuing police harassment. The sequence of question and answer ran:

'Were you trying to frighten him?' – 'Not exactly. I thought he would pay more attention.'
'You said you would exercise your own prerogative if he failed to give you satisfaction. What was your prerogative?' – 'I was thinking of making some demonstration somewhere.'
'Did you intend in that letter to threaten to endanger anyone's life or to alarm anyone?' – 'Certainly not.'[40]

But at the Old Bailey, responding to his lawyer, McMahon's explanation was entirely different: he had been forced into writing the letter by the conspirators organising the plot to kill the king. He was under their direct surveillance and compelled to act on their instructions. 'How did you come to write your letter to Sir John Simon?' – 'It was dictated to me by two of the men.'[41] Their intention was to make it appear that McMahon's action against Edward was motivated by his grievance against the police and the Home Office.

All that can be said with any certainty is that McMahon did write a letter to the Home Secretary, that he posted it – as a postmark showed – in the area where he lived, Paddington W2, and that a postman delivered the envelope to Simon's house early in the morning of 16 July. What did McMahon do after posting the letter? Once again the stories conflict. McMahon gave the impression at Bow Street Court that he spent the evening of 15 July at home and did not leave until about 7.45 a.m. the next morning, 16 July. (His landlady told a newspaper reporter she thought he left at 7.15 a.m., rather than his usual 8.45 a.m.) But he told an acquaintance, Goldwin Faulkner, whom he visited that morning, 'Oh, I've been out nearly all night. I have been around at a club and I've had some drinks.'[42]

McMahon claimed he spoke to one of the conspirators early on the morning of 16 July. Was this at the club he had mentioned to Faulkner? It is not clear. According to McMahon the unnamed man told him the meeting place had been changed from the Express Dairy to the corner of Kingsway and Holborn, half a mile or so away. From that time on, McMahon was convinced he was never out of the sight of one or more of the plotters, making it impossible for him to let the police know of the new rendezvous. At 9.45 a.m. McMahon telephoned Sir John Simon at his Chelsea home from a kiosk in Kingsway. He later said the conspirators had forced him to make the call, three of them standing outside a telephone box in Kingsway listening while he spoke. He was asked at the Old Bailey:

'Why did they want you to do that?' – 'It was only afterwards that I found out the reason for encouraging me to telephone. It was to show I had some other grievance.'
'You mean so that if you were captured no suspicion would be thrown on anyone but yourself?' – 'Yes.'

Stephen Bach, Simon's personal private secretary, took the call. McMahon asked if the Home Secretary had made a decision about the request he had made in his letter. Bach knew nothing about the letter and, as far as he was concerned, McMahon was unable to explain what he wanted. Bach concluded, he later told police, that 'the man was mentally affected'. When Bach suggested calling the Home Office, McMahon 'replied with words to the effect that he must have justice or he would take the law into his own hands.' Shortly after the call, Simon and Bach left for the Home Office, where Bach found McMahon's letter in a bundle of post he had been carrying from Simon's house.[43]

The only apparently independent witness to McMahon's movements on the morning of 16 July was Goldwin Faulkner, an insurance agent. He first met McMahon – who knew him as 'Captain' Faulkner – in March or April 1936 at an estate agent's offices in Bloomsbury. Faulkner was there to arrange letting a room. McMahon was with two or three people, talking. McMahon mentioned his paper, the *Human Gazette*, to Faulkner and said he was planning a second edition. Faulkner had coincidentally bought a copy of the first edition from McMahon in Piccadilly the previous year. The two met again at the same office a few days later and McMahon brought up a vague business plan he had been considering. On another occasion McMahon helped Faulkner with a property dispute and Faulkner gave him four or five shillings for his assistance.

According to Faulkner, they had no further contact until McMahon knocked at the door of his Shaftesbury Avenue flat on 16 July. Faulkner was preparing his 5-year-old son's breakfast and invited McMahon in. He told McMahon he planned to take the boy to Hyde Park later that morning to see the king present new colours to the Guards. McMahon replied, according to Faulkner, 'Well, I'm going along there too. Do you mind if I come along?' He showed Faulkner's son a picture postcard he had in his pocket of Edward VIII wearing ceremonial robes.

The three left Faulkner's flat together, walking up Charing Cross Road, taking a bus from Oxford Street to Marble Arch, then strolling into Hyde Park, Faulkner holding one of his son's hands and McMahon the other. After they had passed the stands erected for prominent guests,

Faulkner arranged to hire chairs to stand on for a better view when the ceremony began. McMahon said he would not need one. 'I'm going away, don't worry about me, I'll see you again.' Faulkner recalled that was about 10.30 a.m. 'I noticed nothing unusual about him.'[44]

One surprising aspect of Faulkner's statement to the police was his failure to mention how McMahon had turned up at his office in February 1936, drunk, and trying to borrow money from his typist, Dorothea Maritch, and then when this had failed, he had offered to sell her a gun. McMahon's possession of a pistol and ammunition was surely memorable. Possibly Maritch did not tell Faulkner about the incident, though this seems unlikely. As to Faulkner being a captain, the rank McMahon believed he had held, a 'Goldwin Lloyd Faulkner' was commissioned into the Royal Flying Corps as a probationary second lieutenant on 20 November 1915 but resigned his commission on 3 December 1916.[45]

According to McMahon, he had not arrived at Faulkner's house on 16 July by chance. He later said he had an appointment to see Faulkner that morning, but he neither described nor was he asked the purpose.[46] When had they first arranged the meeting? What were they to discuss? Faulkner told the police they had met three or four times in the past. To judge from the notes of the police interview, the officers had a remarkable lack of curiosity about his relationship with McMahon. Did Faulkner have a connection with MI5 of which McMahon was unaware? Was he part of the conspiracy? It seems more than a coincidence that Faulkner should have planned to attend Edward's presentation of the colours in Hyde Park on the day that McMahon was going armed to Constitution Hill.

'Captain' Faulkner, like 'Colonel' Matthews (who supplied some of the information McMahon passed to the Italian Embassy and on whom MI5 had maintained a file for some time), was one of those elusive figures in McMahon's life, unexplained and inexplicable, but a definite presence. Were Faulkner and Matthews connected? Did Faulkner know more than he let on about McMahon and his intentions on 16 July? Were Faulkner and Matthews both MI5 informants, together or separately, and exploiting McMahon as a patsy, a 'useful idiot'?

McMahon left Faulkner and his son in the park waiting for the presentation of colours to the Guards to begin and made his way back to
Hyde Park Corner. Feeling depressed about the position he was in – 'I
remembered that I barely had the price of a meal' – he went into a
pub and then thought of returning home. Instead he walked across to
Constitution Hill. Standing on the pavement, people happy and contented around him, he considered suicide, shooting himself with the
revolver he was carrying in his left-hand trouser pocket.

Taking the folded *Daily Telegraph* he was carrying in his pocket,
McMahon wrote a message to his wife. 'May, I love you.' But then he
thought of the effect his death would have on her. 'Why kill myself? I
will make a last gesture.' He stepped back from the crowd, deciding he
would throw the newspaper at the king as he passed, be arrested, and
draw Edward's attention to the wrongs he believed he had suffered.[47]
That would be McMahon's story at Bow Street Court. When he reached
the Old Bailey, it would change significantly. Prosecuting counsel, the
Attorney General Sir Donald Somervell, asked him about the money he
had been offered to shoot the king, £150:

> 'You led the people whom you say had been offering you this sum to
> believe that you would make such an attempt: Is that right?' – 'Yes.'
> 'Your intention in Hyde Park was to do an act which they would
> regard as an attempt on his life?' – 'Yes, sir.'

McMahon felt certain he was being watched by the conspirators. He was
also afraid the police were not following him, as he had expected. As far
as he was concerned, if he faltered the other plotters would punish him
and one of them would make sure the king was assassinated.[48] The pistol
was in his pocket, four bullets in the chambers, the fifth left empty to prevent – as he thought – the gun discharging accidentally. In his jacket he
carried two more bullets. McMahon had never fired a weapon in his life.

3

On the morning of 16 July 1936 the king was buttoned into the uniform of colonel-in-chief of the Grenadier Guards, setting off to ride
from Buckingham Palace to the parade ground in Hyde Park, accompanied by his brother the Duke of York. Both wore the fancy dress in
which male royalty masquerade as warriors. The function of this recently
invented tradition was to insinuate into the public mind the belief that
this elevated position had been achieved through force of arms rather
than accident of birth. In Edward's case the pretence was all the more
poignant as at five feet seven inches he was conspicuously shorter than
the minimum height required of the guardsmen he nominally com-
manded as colonel-in-chief. As he himself described the contrast in
height, 'I was a pygmy among giants.'[49]

The occasion was the handing of new colours to six battalions of the
three senior Guards regiments, the Grenadiers, Coldstream and Scots. The
day was sunny and warm, the sky flecked with clouds. As 6,000 troops
paraded, forming three sides of a square, Edward dismounted, taking up
position on a low platform before them. His mother, Queen Mary, had
arrived earlier by car and was sitting in a pavilion behind Edward, with
other members of the royal family, including the Duchess of York and
her daughters, the princesses Elizabeth and Margaret. Wallis Simpson was
there, watching from an adjoining stand. Crowds of spectators had been
assembling since early morning, among them McMahon's acquaintance
Faulkner and his son.

The Chaplain General to the Forces blessed the richly embroidered
flags. Edward briefly addressed the troops, reading a speech that Winston
Churchill had put a finishing touch to. The king praised the traditions
of the Guards, their loyalty and courage in battle. He recalled both the
horrors and the comradeship of the war:

> With all my heart I hope, and indeed I pray, that never again will our
> age and generation be called upon to face such stern and terrible days.
> Humanity cries out for peace and the assurance of peace, and you will

find in peace opportunities of duty and service as noble as any that bygone battlefields can show.[50]

The ceremony completed, at a quarter past midday Edward began the ride back to Buckingham Palace, massed bands leading the way, ranks of Guardsmen following with rifles, fixed bayonets gleaming in the sun, colours flapping in a light breeze. Major General Bertram Sergison-Brooke – General Officer Commanding London District, nicknamed 'Boy' – rode on Edward's right and the Duke of York, the king's brother, to his left, both a little way behind. The procession passed through the Wellington Arch, turning into the tree-lined Constitution Hill, with cheering and waving men, women and children on both sides of the road. Then – close to the spot where the 18-year-old Edward Oxford had fired two pistol shots at Queen Victoria on 10 June 1840 – there was a sudden commotion, a flurry of action.

4

What took place is confusing even now.[51] Witnesses standing nearby on the pavement – including police on duty lining the route – were unsure what exactly they had seen and told conflicting stories. One onlooker, Mrs Alice Lawrence, was sure she had observed McMahon in conversation with a smartly dressed man with a moustache and a noticeably tall hat shortly before the incident.[52] Was that one of the conspirators McMahon feared were watching him to ensure he carried out his task, or had it been Faulkner a little earlier? Mrs Lawrence was never called to testify at McMahon's trial.

The uncertainty continued as the prosecution subsequently presented evidence in court. As McMahon's solicitor, Alfred Kerstein, would point out, 'No two witnesses are telling the same story.' This was only to be expected given the speed with which the incident occurred. McMahon compounded the uncertainty by giving different versions of what he did and why. However, one thing was clear: he had been allowed to walk the streets of London carrying a loaded revolver and to stand, armed, on the pavement as the king approached.

Having decided to make a gesture rather than kill himself, McMahon returned to take a place in the three- or four-deep crowd on the Green Park side of Constitution Hill, standing in the second or third row. His appearance on 16 July contrasted sharply with that of the poised and elegantly uniformed king, symbolising the social distance between them, a chasm impossible to bridge. McMahon, wearing a shabby and badly fitting brown three-piece suit with belt and braces, cheap but highly polished shoes and spectacles, his thin hair balding, was agitated, muddled and determined, but uncertain on what. One witness recalled him taking an envelope from his inside pocket, repeatedly studying a picture of Edward in his coronation robes. This was the postcard McMahon had shown Faulkner's son earlier that morning.

As the procession passed through Wellington Arch, McMahon called to a mounted policeman in the roadway, 'Take your damned horse out of the way, I want to see the procession.' The officer asked, 'Is that an order or a request?' McMahon replied, 'A request' and the policeman turned away. A woman said that, as the king came nearer, McMahon pressed forward, spreading his arms to push her aside from the kerb, almost knocking her over. Edward was now ten or twelve feet away and McMahon reached into his pocket to take out the revolver, holding it under cover of the copy of the *Daily Telegraph* he was carrying.

Press versions of the incident showed how varied the recollections were immediately after the dramatic event. The London *Evening News* that day said, 'MAN AIMS A REVOLVER AT THE KING "It Was Loaded in Four Chambers": Yard Statement'. The next day's *Daily Mirror* was in no doubt what had occurred, the paper's front page blazing: 'ATTEMPT ON THE KING'S LIFE … HERE IS THE MAN WITH THE LOADED PISTOL … AND THE 'SPECIAL' WHO SAVED THE KING'. The story below continued, 'The King was saved by a middle-aged Hackney Special Constable, who was only on duty for the day.' The part-time volunteer police officer was Anthony Dick from Essex, a travelling salesman for an Old Street firm of French polishers:

Dick was watching the procession when he saw a glint of metal in the sun. He turned to a man on the outskirts of the crowd and saw he was holding a revolver close to his body. With complete disregard of his own safety the special constable pounced on the man ... With a sweep of his arm he knocked the weapon out from the crowd to hit the hooves of the King's horse.[53]

Dick said he had acted instinctively:

Anyone in my place would have done the same. As soon as I saw a little woman in grey make as if to strike the man and cry out, 'It's a revolver!' I smashed out at him with my fist.[54]

The incident was clearly unexpected and had come as a shock to the officers lining the route. Their commanders made no effort to advise them that an armed attack might be imminent, despite McMahon's repeated warning to MI5 and Special Branch.

A *Times* reporter at the scene had seen McMahon force himself to the front of the crowd. The journalist's impression was that McMahon had 'raised a hand holding a revolver and appeared about to fire at the King'. The gunman's view suddenly obscured by a mounted policeman's movement, he 'thereupon threw his revolver across the hindquarters of the constable's horse straight at the King'.[55] The *Yorkshire Post* London correspondent differed slightly in his report of what had occurred. 'Several statements of witnesses declare that the hand of the man who was arrested was seized by both a woman and a police officer, and that the revolver was "jerked" into the air.' Another woman on the pavement screamed, 'An insult to the King, a revolver'. Her husband lunged forward, shouted, 'You swine' and punched McMahon's face.[56]

One witness to the attack was a 78-year-old Marylebone woman, Mrs Mary Ann Clarges, who had been in Windsor in 1882 when a gunman stepped from the crowd and fired a pistol at Queen Victoria. She had now come to Green Park to see Victoria's great-grandson, Edward. As the king drew near, Mrs Clarges heard a cry, 'Oh, look! Stop him, stop him'. She later said:

I turned and saw a revolver waved in the air only a few paces away. I screamed, and then a hand appeared as though from nowhere and thrust up the one holding the revolver. I saw a struggling mass where the hand holding the revolver had been and people were crying: 'Hold him, hold him.' I saw the police pull the man away, and then I fainted.[57]

Special Constable Dick had – it at first appeared – fended McMahon's hand away, grasping him by the jacket collar and pinioning his right arm. As McMahon cried, 'Don't choke me', three or four people who had seen what was happening surged in, shouting and punching. A woman screamed, 'Let me get at him', while another cried out for McMahon to be lynched on the spot. The *Daily Express* described 'an infuriated mob' kicking and scratching in a scrum in which McMahon's spectacles were torn from his face and trampled underfoot.[58]

Two further police officers rushed in, forcing McMahon's attackers aside, seizing him by the arms and shoulders, dragging him to the edge of the roadway, partly for his own protection. In the confusion a constable took the man who had first punched McMahon into custody, leading him towards Hyde Park police station. The revolver, which had struck the king's horse on the near-side hind leg, lay on the ground as Edward paused, looked down, and then rode slowly on. A policeman walked his horse across, dismounted, picked up the weapon, checked to see whether it was loaded, and placed it in the pocket of his riding breeches.

Edward's memory remained sharp over a decade later. He recalled in his memoirs a sudden commotion breaking out on his left, a bright metallic object flying through the air, skidding under his horse. He thought at first it was a bomb:

For one icy moment I braced myself for a blast that never came. There was a convulsive stir in the crowd as several policemen threw themselves upon the man. General Sergison-Brooke, himself a man without fear, threw an anxious look in my direction. Turning to him, I said, '"Boy", I don't know what that thing was; but, if it had gone off, it would have made a nasty mess of us.' The General gave a smile of relief, and we rode on as if nothing had happened.[59]

When Edward at last heard that McMahon had been armed with a revolver and not a bomb, he wrote briefly to Sergison-Brooke, 'We have to thank the Almighty for two things. Firstly, that it did not rain, and secondly that the man in the brown suit's gun did not go off!!'[60] *A King's Story* makes it plain that Edward had not been warned by MI5 or Special Branch that they had known for at least the preceding forty-eight hours of the threat he would face that day.

There is a significant piece of evidence to show how seriously both Edward and Wallis took the incident. In 1935 they had commissioned Cartier the jeweller to make a diamond-set bracelet to which over the subsequent years they attached pendant gold crosses, nine in all, each marking a special moment in the couple's lives together. One was the day of their marriage in 1937. Another was inscribed: 'God Save The King For Wallis 16-VII-36', the date on which both believed Edward had escaped an assassination attempt.[61]

McMahon was taken to Hyde Park police station in a state of panic, perhaps fear. He could not fail to realise the enormity of what he had been involved in on Constitution Hill and, given his experience of the forces of law and order, the danger he might face. A beating from the police would not be out of the question, as he would have learned from his Notting Hill acquaintances and his fellow inmates in Wandsworth Prison a few years earlier. As the police and their prisoner crossed the park McMahon heard Special Constable Dick say, 'These bloody foreigners coming over here to shoot our king,' McMahon told Police Constable Thomas Griffiths defensively, 'I could easily have shot him, but I only threw it.'

The police searched McMahon at the station, finding two further rounds of pistol ammunition in his left-hand jacket pocket and the picture postcard of the king. A little later, the copy of the *Daily Telegraph* on which McMahon had written 'May, I love you' was added to the collection. Griffiths asked McMahon his name and address. 'I shan't tell you until I have had a drink of water, as I am ill.' An officer brought him water. McMahon said, 'My name and address is on the correspondence.' At that moment John Remes, the man who had punched McMahon, was escorted into the room, still suspected of being an accomplice. McMahon had to be restrained as he threw the glass at him.

Griffiths then asked McMahon for his age and occupation. 'I shan't tell you any more until I have seen my solicitor.' In the charge room he said, 'I wish I had done the job properly.' At this point Griffiths cautioned him, taking McMahon to a cell to await the arrival of a detective from Scotland Yard. McMahon said, 'I wrote to the Home Secretary last night and telephoned him again this morning.' He repeated that he could have shot the king. 'It would have been better if I had shot myself.'[62] His collar and tie were removed to prevent any attempt at suicide.

Detective Chief Inspector John Sands was placed in charge of investigating the incident and arrived at Hyde Park police station at about 12.45 p.m., accompanied by Detective Inspector Sydney Kidd. He was first shown the revolver McMahon had carried, with bullets still remaining in four of the five chambers. Sands went to McMahon's cell a few minutes later to tell the prisoner he would be transported to Canon Row police station for questioning. McMahon would have been familiar with that particular police station as it was there that he had been charged with criminal libel in 1933. Sands told McMahon he was investigating an allegation that he was in possession of a firearm with intent to endanger life. McMahon said nothing.

As the police car set off from Hyde Park to Canon Row, McMahon was about to say something to Sands, who cautioned him again, warning him that anything he said might be used in evidence. McMahon repeated what he had earlier told Griffiths. 'It is all the fault of Sir John Simon. I wrote to him last night, and phoned him this morning.' Sands reported McMahon as saying under questioning, 'I did not want to hurt him in any way. I only did it as a protest.' Had he actually said this? McMahon's story would later be different. At 4.15 p.m. Sands charged McMahon under Section 7 of the 1920 Firearms Act with unlawful possession of a Chicago Arms Company revolver 'with intent to endanger life and property'. McMahon asked for a solicitor.[63]

Sands was a detective with long experience, a member of what the popular press dubbed the 'Big Five', senior officers of Scotland Yard's Criminal Investigation Department. The son of a Norfolk police inspector, he held the record at the Yard for successful murder investigations. He was frequently called on by provincial police forces to help solve serious crimes. As recently as March 1936 he had been in Hull investigating the apparently motiveless murder of a 70-year-old shopkeeper known as the 'Fairy Godfather'. Sands would be promoted to detective superintendent in August, going on in September to be appointed head of the elite Flying Squad.

The king, meanwhile, still not knowing what the object landing close to him had been, thinking it may have been a bomb, rode on through the cheering crowds to Buckingham Palace. It is difficult not to admire Edward's imperturbability in the face of attack, about which he had been given no warning. He showed no sign of the shock that could have been expected. Reaching the palace, Edward halted at the main gate, waved up to greet his mother, Queen Mary, who was standing on the balcony, then wheeled his horse about to take the salute from the six Guards battalions as they marched back to Wellington Barracks.

This final part of the ceremony over, Edward rode into the palace courtyard. It was here that his equerry, Sir John Aird, told him the missile was a revolver and that it had been loaded. Aird had been riding close by in the procession and had at first thought of dismounting to see what the object might be, but the trousers of his Guards uniform were so tight he was afraid he would be unable to climb back on his horse. Changing from his military uniform into plus fours, a shirt and golf shoes, Edward went to the Coombe Hill course near Kingston upon Thames to spend the rest of the afternoon playing golf. A club member said the king had rarely looked so well. 'We saw the King play a marvellous shot from the seventeenth tee. He appeared to be in the best of health, and enjoying his game tremendously.'[64]

Edward was given the official review of the afternoon incident from the Home Secretary, Sir John Simon, when he returned to St James's Palace that evening. The report added nothing to what newspapers were already saying and left much out. Simon said that the perpetrator was an

Irishman using the assumed name McMahon and that he had acted in pursuit of a grievance against the government:

> While standing in the crowd near Wellington Arch, before the Royal Procession reached the spot, he asked a mounted policeman to move so that he could obtain a better view. A special constable saw him draw a revolver as the King approached and was able by his prompt action to knock the weapon out of McMahon's hand. The revolver was picked up by another mounted policeman and was found to be loaded in four of its chambers.[65]

'Afterwards,' Edward later wrote, 'I used to refer to the incident jokingly as "The Dastardly Attempt", the phrase used by one of my older courtiers in indignantly describing it.'[66]

That evening, Thursday 16 July, Special Constable Dick was called to Scotland Yard to be congratulated on his presence of mind and swift action by the Metropolitan Police assistant commissioners Norman Kendal and Sir Percy Laurie. The latter had been in command of police on duty at Hyde Park that day. Kendal knew the actual (and hidden) background to the attack, that McMahon had revealed a plot to assassinate Edward as early as April 1936. Kendal had discussed McMahon's latest revelation about a conspiracy with MI5's head, Vernon Kell, and McMahon's contact John Ottaway, on 14 July, just two days previously. Had Laurie also been aware? The intention appeared to be that this prior knowledge should remain under wraps.

5

Late in the afternoon of 16 July, McMahon was taken to Bow Street by Detective Chief Inspector Sands for his first court appearance. The most colourful and dramatic report appeared in the *Daily Express*, probably the work of the paper's reporter Lindon Laing, who was to build up a close relationship with the McMahons and their solicitor, Alfred Kerstein, during the course of the case. Laing was a 30-year-old

Durham miner's son who went on to become the *Express* news editor. The police suspected Kerstein of heightening the drama of McMahon's court appearances to give Laing a good story. The *Express* would be paying McMahon's wife for her co-operation while he was serving his prison sentence.

Crowds were gathering in Bow Street when McMahon arrived with Sands in a police car shortly before 4.30 p.m., officers clearing the way through market stalls in the area to gain entry to the courtyard. As the car drove in several people shouted abuse at McMahon. In the courtyard itself groups of off-duty police officers were waiting for a glimpse of the prisoner, who was hurried into the building by Sands.

When the door to the small first-floor courtroom opened there was a rush of spectators, mostly men. Among those hurrying for a seat was Assistant Commissioner Kendal, who knew from MI5 and his Special Branch officers all there was to know about an assassination plot. The Chief Metropolitan Magistrate, Sir Rollo Graham-Campbell, took his seat on the bench, and McMahon was brought in through a door marked 'Prisoners Only'. He limped into the dock, his face bruised, cheap brown suit crumpled, thinning hair swept back. He had no collar and tie and his shirt was torn open, exposing his chest. The *Daily Express* reported:

> He stared quickly about him as he took the four steps that carried him to the dock, and then thumped nervously with clenched fists on the rail before him. He fidgeted from one foot to another, clasped and unclasped his nicotine-stained fingers. Beads of perspiration stood out on the bald part of his head.[67]

The clerk read out the charge against McMahon of unlawfully possessing a revolver. Sands then gave evidence on the arrest, outlining briefly what McMahon had told police officers in the course of the afternoon. Sands produced a shiny revolver from his jacket pocket in evidence, wrapped in a white handkerchief, laying it dramatically on the witness box ledge. He asked the magistrate to remand McMahon in custody for eight days while his investigation continued. The magistrate asked if there were any questions. McMahon's solicitor, Alfred Kerstein, rose and looked towards Sands. 'You say that the revolver was loaded in four chambers. I take it the gun has not been fired at all?' – 'No. There is no evidence that the gun has been fired for some considerable time.'

The magistrate concluded the twenty-minute hearing, ordering a remand in custody until Friday 24 July, with a request for a medical report. As two officers led McMahon from the dock, Kerstein stood again:

> I think it is also right that I should take the earliest opportunity – in view of certain sensational statements which have appeared in the evening press – of saying most emphatically that there was no attempt at assassination or attempt to fire the weapon. I must say that at this stage, because of certain reports which may prejudice my client at his trial.[68]

Half an hour later McMahon left the court accompanied by Sands and Kidd for the drive in a saloon car south of the Thames to Brixton Prison, trailed by another police car and seen off by a large crowd, booing and jeering. Officers lining both sides of the road struggled to hold the mob back. On the way McMahon checked with Inspector Kidd when his next court appearance was due. Kidd told him 24 July. 'I shall be dead before then,' McMahon said. 'I intended to shoot myself in front of the King, but I lost my head.'[69]

6

In the public mind, there was no doubt that Edward had narrowly escaped assassination. One newspaper described the reaction of passengers when a London tram stopped on Gray's Inn Road and they saw a newspaper placard with early headlines. 'A second later they were pouring into the road to buy papers and, throwing rigid convention to the winds, turning joyfully on total strangers and shaking them by the hand … Safe … safe … it didn't go off … the police got him …. what a mercy …' Filming was abandoned at Ealing Studios as a producer called out,

'Ladies and gentlemen, you will be as distressed as I am to hear of an attempted assassination of the King.'[70]

In London theatres, it was reported, audiences and actors joined together in singing 'God Save the King' at the close of performances. In cinemas the appearance of Edward on a newsreel of the day's events was greeted with cheers. There were bursts of applause when the commentator mentioned the elusive 'Woman in Grey' who reputedly prevented McMahon from firing his revolver and showed the king riding calmly back to Buckingham Palace after facing the armed attack. The newsreel, shown in over 260 cinemas throughout Britain, was captioned 'Attempt on the King's Life', though it displayed only Edward reviewing the Guards, riding to the palace and McMahon's arrest. The newsreel title led to the film's distributors facing proceedings for contempt of court, along with the *Daily Express* and the London *Evening News* for words used in their reports.

It was not only the British public that believed the king had had a fortunate escape from death at McMahon's hands. Foreign politicians were given the same impression from the reports they received. From Berlin the German Chancellor, Hitler, sent a telegram to Edward: 'I have just received the news of the deplorable attempted attack on your Majesty. I beg to tender to your Majesty my heartiest congratulations on your escape from this danger.' Mussolini telephoned Italy's embassy in London immediately on being told of the attack, referred to 'the attempt against the life of His Majesty the King', and instructed the chargé d'affaires to 'convey his heartfelt felicitations at the escape of the King from danger'. Pope Pius XI expressed his 'satisfaction and gladness at the safety of the King'.

The French Chamber of Deputies sent a telegram associating itself with 'the joy of the British people at seeing its beloved and respected Sovereign escape the menace of an attempt on him'. Every major American newspaper made the attack the main story, the *New York Herald Tribune* declaring, 'King Edward is so popular a figure in this country that the mere thought of the incident has yielded a sense of personal shock.' The most lyrical congratulation to Edward on his escape appeared in the Greek newspaper *Athinaika Nea*:

The pistol fell from the trembling hand before it could be raised, and this could not have been otherwise. In the midst of the fervent adoration of a mighty nation for its King a hand raised against him could not but be fatally paralysed.[71]

The prime minister, Stanley Baldwin, had despatched an immediate message to the king when reports of the attack reached Downing Street. He told the Cabinet he had written on their behalf 'in order to express in appropriate terms their thankfulness at His Majesty's escape, together with an expression of the loyalty and devotion of His Majesty's servants'.[72]

The impact of events on McMahon's family was overwhelming, as police and reporters descended on their Glasgow tenement flat (the 'house' McMahon would claim he had bought them), exposing the family to unwelcome and distressing public scrutiny. McMahon's father, Patrick Bannigan, in his eighties and almost completely blind from an accident at work some years before, spoke with tears in his eyes to journalists. 'To think that one of my family would come to this. It is now ten years since I have heard from Jerry. What has happened to him in the interval I do not know.' Bannigan was anxious to keep the news from his wife, Eileen, also in her eighties and confined to bed for the past three months. He said he feared the shock would kill her. He believed his son's drinking was the cause of his behaviour. 'I only pray the court authorities have him medically examined before dealing with him.' A childhood friend still living in Glasgow wondered whether McMahon's mental balance had proved too delicate for the pace of life in London.[73]

Out of touch with his parents for so many years since leaving Scotland, McMahon finally wrote from Brixton Prison. He warned his father to be wary of reporters, saying the least comment was likely to end up as a 1,000-word story once a newspaper went to work on it. 'I have noticed that the various papers have published certain statements which you are alleged to have made. If you have not already received any payment for such please demand it now, as the Press have been splashing money about.'[74]

7

As the news of the attack on Edward came in at Scotland Yard, senior Metropolitan Police officers would realise that not only had an outrage of potentially epic proportions taken place but – if the truth emerged of McMahon's contact with the authorities – that they and MI5 would face accusations of negligence for having done nothing to prevent it happening. On 18 July, two days after the incident, the *Daily Express* printed a prominent front-page article in bold type, obviously planted by the Metropolitan Police as a pre-emptive defence against criticism. Referring to McMahon's letter to the Home Secretary, the report said:

> The nature of the man's letter to Sir John Simon was such that it was handed to Scotland Yard on Wednesday morning. Officers assigned to watch him traced his movements that night. When observation was placed on his flat the following day, it was found Bannigan had gone off in the early hours of the morning.[75]

This was plainly nonsense, dishonest nonsense at that. McMahon had not written the letter until Wednesday *night*, 15 July, and it did not arrive at Simon's house until Thursday morning, 16 July, the day of the attack. How, then, could the letter have been in police hands on Wednesday *morning*, before McMahon had even sat down to write it? Was this a small mistake or something else? Either the *Express* reporter was confused about the days – and this was unlikely – or the police were. The other possibility – and given what followed, the most likely one – was that the police were simply lying, intending the public to be fooled into believing the forces of order had taken every step to prevent an attack. The final paragraph of the police statement underlined this. They were quoted as saying there would be no more 'incidents' of this kind:

> There will be fresh, far-reaching check-up of persons holding arms certificates; Scotland Yard's black list of undesirables and trouble-makers, compiled in co-operation with Empire and foreign police authorities, will be under constant, intensive scrutiny.[76]

This was as good as an admission that the police had previously done none of these things, despite the warning that an attempt would be made on the king's life, and that they had failed in their duty to shield Edward from harm. Someone had blundered and a desperate game of back-covering was now in progress. The obvious points to make are that McMahon did not have an arms certificate (that was why he was charged with illegal possession of a weapon) and that the police (and MI5) had every opportunity to keep McMahon under 'constant, intensive scrutiny', but had failed to do so.

Sir Philip Game had been Metropolitan Police commissioner since November 1935. If any heads were to roll, his should by rights have been the first. There were two immediate reasons for the authorities to downplay McMahon's attack, its significance minimised. First, to save face, Game's in particular. Second, to avoid the need to reveal that MI5 and Special Branch had known since 17 April 1936 that an assassination was being planned and that they had been told on 14 July the date and place of the attack.

The Home Secretary made a statement to the House of Commons on the evening of the attempt. 'The whole House will be profoundly thankful,' he declared, 'that the risk to which his Majesty was exposed was so promptly averted.'[77] What the Members of Parliament listening were never told was that the risk, rather than being averted, could so easily have been prevented.

Chief Inspector Sands was called to Game's private office at Scotland Yard the same evening to discuss the course his enquiries into the attack should take. Sands then went on to meet the Home Secretary at the House of Commons. The *Daily Express* was the most informative in presenting the official police view of events, one designed to ensure essential elements of background information were left out. On the meeting between Game and Sands, the *Express* reported that the commissioner:

> ... has called for a report giving fullest details of George Andrew McMahon, alias Jerome Bannigan, his medical history, the exact information concerning him in possession of Scotland Yard prior to the threat to the life of the King. He will then be able to decide whether

there was sufficient justification for subjecting Bannigan to any additional observation than that usually given to persons known to be
nursing some grievance against the State.[78]

Sands did as he was instructed, presenting a twelve-page report on 20 July,
four days after the attack. It was a study in the avoidance of embarrassing facts. Sands wrote that he had restricted his enquiries to the events
of 16 July. The effect was to ensure there was no need for any awkward
references to McMahon's dealings with MI5 or the Metropolitan Police
Special Branch in April and July 1936.

Sands referred to George Andrew McMahon being the alias of Jerome
Bannigan, 'an Irishman', noting his conviction and imprisonment for
fraud in Scotland in 1927, his conviction in London in 1933 for defamatory and malicious libel, followed by a successful appeal. 'Since this date
the prisoner has harboured a grievance that he is entitled to substantial
damages and he has voiced his complaint in many directions. The present outrage is the culmination.'[79] The official line had been determined:
a lone attacker with a grudge.

Sands reported that the story began with McMahon's letter to the
Home Secretary, which arrived at Sir John Simon's house on the morning of 16 July. (This, of course, contradicted what Scotland Yard had told
the *Daily Express*.) McMahon, the chief inspector reported, 'speaks of
organised persecution for some years, demands full satisfaction within
fourteen hours, failing which he will exercise his own prerogative
and obtain the necessary satisfaction which he, in his tortured mind,
considers adequate'. Sands then undermined his argument about the
significance of the letter by saying it contained 'no mention of a suggested attack upon His Majesty'.

The chief inspector quoted evidence from selected witnesses
including, among others, the barmaid Mary Blencowe, whom
McMahon told that she would never see him again after 16 July;
John Remes, who tried to assault McMahon, and his wife Queenie;
Margaret Biden, who saw McMahon raise his right hand and produce something 'made of metal and gleaming'; Lily Yeoman, roughly
pushed aside by McMahon as the king approached; and Special

Constable Anthony Dick, who was said to have knocked the revolver from McMahon's hand.

Sands summed up the evidence:

> The facts as disclosed herein and our enquiries in all directions fail to prove conclusively that at any time did McMahon present the revolver at His Majesty or attempt to pull the trigger. There can be no doubt he was seen to take the weapon from his pocket, and whatever his project, he was prevented from carrying it into effect by those around him. No person heard a click of the trigger. We must stand by the evidence that either the revolver was knocked from McMahon's hand or thrown by him and the weight of evidence is in favour of the latter.[80]

Sands makes no reference to the crucial events preceding McMahon's letter to Simon that directly relate to the attack. There is nothing about McMahon's claim to the MI5 officer Ottaway on 17 April of a conspiracy to assassinate the king in the next two or three months; nothing about Special Branch interviews with McMahon; nothing about McMahon's warning to Ottaway on 14 July that an attempt would take place 'during the presentation of the Colours'; and no mention of the failure by the police to intervene before rather than during the incident. The picture Sands sought to paint was that the attack on the king was a sudden and unexpected event on 16 July that no person in authority could possibly have foreseen.

8

There was no shortage of witnesses to the events on Constitution Hill. The problem was that the stories they had to tell were confused and contradictory, even among those closest to the action. Scotland Yard issued an appeal through the press for anyone 'in the immediate vicinity of the man arrested, and who witnessed the occurrence' to come forward. Scores did by telephone and an officer was detailed to plough through the messages. Many claiming to have vital information called personally at Scotland Yard, officers then having to laboriously take down statements that amounted, on examination, to nothing.

Even more people wrote, and the letters, often anonymous, were held for analysis at Canon Row police station. The appeal, not unexpectedly, garnered little of actual value, but served as an irresistible magnet to the deluded, the attention seeking and the downright malicious.[81] The letters revealed a thriving underground psychology of fear, paranoia and fantasy not unlike that of McMahon himself.

'A Loyal English Subject' declared in a letter dated 17 July that he felt duty-bound to inform the police that he knew of 'a young band of Communists who hold secret meetings in a room at Leyton, Essex'. Their leader, he said, was called Edmund Jones. 'The young man is always talking of doing away with the Royal Family.' He thought the authorities should keep an eye on them. A man from Newbury, Berkshire, reported that on 12 July, four days before the incident, he had a crossed line on his telephone and heard a snatch of conversation 'between two ladies which was – if they don't get Edward this time they will at the Coronation'.

'A Friend of the People' placed the conspiracy's centre in London's cosmopolitan Soho district:

> The plot was made in a Certain Club & Restaurant in Frith St. That's as much as I dare say. Should I be seen approaching a police officer or police station my life would not be worth a penny. I can assure you that they intend to try again but by different means. Although I joined this Sect not knowing its actual portent I am against murder in every respect … Watch from Ports of Folkestone and Dover. Three members will be arriving next week.

McMahon's Irish origin provoked a predictable response. A writer said it was a well-known fact that IRA gunmen habitually left the top chamber of a revolver unloaded, as McMahon was reported to have done. 'There may be a connection.' An anonymous letter arriving at Scotland Yard on 20 July suggested keeping 'a sharp look out on Marylebone Irish Catholics. McMahon has not done that all by himself. That's all been

planned. There's a gang of them.' At the other extreme, a writer calling himself 'the Rev Dr Stanley McKelvie' thought it was significant
McMahon lived in Westbourne Terrace:

> I happen to know that in the same Terrace are bitter atheists. Now I
> am a broad minded fella, having travelled a lot: but I also know that
> atheism and anarchy go hand in hand. So it is quite possible that in
> this locality is a hot-bed of subversionists. I know nothing to bear this
> out: and have no more information. But it is worth keeping an eye in
> this direction.

A letter-writer called Richard Anson claimed McMahon had often been
seen attending not only Communist but also Irish Republican meetings
in Hyde Park. Anson wondered if the revolver McMahon carried might
be linked with the shot fired recently at the fascist leader Mosley's car. 'In
conclusion for your information McMahon is a writer of Communist
literature.' A police superintendent noted on the file, 'The writer of this
letter for several years has communicated information to Special Branch
which has been found to be valueless.'

Special Branch found a letter posted directly to the king at
Buckingham Palace, rather than to Scotland Yard, more promising.
Charles Skinner of Battersea wrote:

> On seeing that the 'criminal' was the notorious 'Jerry McMahon' I
> was relieved because apart from the undoubted danger to someone by
> careless handling of a loaded revolver, I am convinced from personal
> knowledge of McMahon that he has not the courage and never had
> any intention other than seeking notoriety and free drinks for himself.

Skinner had served eight years in the Metropolitan Police Special
Branch until his resignation in 1920 and seemed a useful prospect. Two
officers from the unit were despatched to interview him. They were
disappointed to find on questioning Skinner that he had not been in
contact with McMahon since 1933 and possessed no up-to-date information that would prove of any use to the investigation.

Mrs Florence Hollyer of Portsmouth offered a dream, a premonition of Edward's violent death she had had in February 1936, six months before the attack. She said she had recorded this in her 'Dream Diary' and had written to the Metropolitan Police commissioner alerting him to what she was sure was an imminent – if unspecified – danger to the monarch. Mrs Hollyer promised she would remain in touch with Scotland Yard. 'When I again receive any warning dreams on matters touching our Royalty, will you be pleased to "sift" the matter. Imagination or Inspiration as well as brains and intellect, is needed in the Force more especially in these troublous days. I am sure you will agree.'

Another enthusiastic informant, Gertrude Byrd of Bristol, had no doubt Germany would be found to have been behind the incident. 'This was a movement of German Agents,' she wrote. 'His Majesty's life is in great danger almost any minute. Germany will spring upon us any moment.' She claimed she had tried in the past to warn the prime minister, Stanley Baldwin, that the king was in peril and that he should not travel in an aeroplane. A Macclesfield man thought publicity itself represented a danger. 'May I appeal to you to keep the report of the proceeding of the attack upon His Majesty the King from the press; the reason for my appeal being that it will only have a tendency to bring dangerous foreigners into this country for the Coronation.'

Among these letters, absurd, deluded or vindictive as many were, one recommendation emerged, so patently sensible that the authorities immediately took steps to adopt it. Police lining the route of a royal procession normally stood with their backs to the crowd. It would be more useful, and observation would be more effective, three correspondents suggested, if police faced the crowd during these events. McMahon's movements, one said, would have been seen earlier. 'This simple suggestion may appear unorthodox and against etiquette,' a London man wrote, 'but that it contains any intentional slight against His Majesty is entirely absent from my thoughts.'

9

The day after the incident on Constitution Hill the *Daily Express* gossip column 'These Names Make News' ran a small piece on the camera-man who had taken the dramatic photographs of McMahon's arrest. The column was written by Tom Driberg, a complex character who during the course of his life spied on the Communist Party for MI5, acted as a double agent for the KGB, and eventually became a left-wing Labour MP, resuming work for MI5 keeping an eye on fellow Labour members. He was, as well as being a devoted Anglican, a recklessly enthusiastic homosexual at a time when such acts were against the law. Written in the newspaper's breathless style, Driberg's story ran:

> Man who took exclusive *Daily Express* pictures of arrest of man concerned in Hyde Park incident yesterday was taught photography, as a small boy, by an aunt of King George V.
> His father was employed on the royal estate at Windsor.
> He is grey-haired, rosy Ernest Brooks, formerly War Office official cameraman, who accompanied the then Prince of Wales on Empire tours.[82]

The article sent Scotland Yard on a wild goose chase that even Driberg's colourful imagination could not have foreseen. An even more intriguing fact Driberg missed in his story was that Brooks had indeed been closely connected with the Windsor family but had fallen out of favour in 1925, stripped of his British Empire Medal and Order of the British Empire. Travelling by steamer from South America as the Prince of Wales's official photographer, Brooks captured Edward sporting a woman's kimono and wig as he played the part of a flapper in an on-board amateur farce. The picture was splashed across the pages of British and American newspapers, to George V's annoyance and Edward's embarrassment.

Brooks had previously been in trouble five years earlier for a photograph he took of Edward capering apparently naked in a pool with his cousin and close friend Lord Louis Mountbatten. As a result of his latest misdemeanour in 1925, Brooks's official career was abruptly terminated and, to underline royal disapproval, his name was erased from the register of honours. Brooks continued to make a living as a photographer, but by 1936 was down on his luck, scrabbling about for odds and ends of work. A story took legs that Brooks had set up the threat to Edward with McMahon to give him a dramatic photo-opportunity and a sizable pay packet. The police would spend a few days frittering away time and manpower investigating this.

A man who refused to give his name took a cutting of the *Daily Express* story to Scotland Yard, telling a detective it seemed remarkable that Brooks should have been in exactly the right place at the right time to use his camera at the very moment McMahon was arrested. He wondered if the police realised Brooks was 'a disgruntled person in that some time ago he was deprived of his Royal Warrant'. He further wondered whether Brooks and McMahon were acquainted in any way. The head of the Criminal Investigation Department noted on the report, 'Chief Inspector Sands should just keep this in mind whilst he is making his enquiries.'[83]

Scotland Yard detectives proceeded to waste three days interviewing an illustrator for the *Daily Sketch* (who said he had first heard a version of the story in the Sun public house in Long Acre), and the paper's chief crime correspondent, William Ashenden. The latter – having initially been to Scotland Yard simply to ask if there were any substance to the tale – found himself under interrogation. There had, he said his editor had told him, been a conspiracy between Brooks the photographer, McMahon, a Romanian journalist called Michaelis, and Netley Lucas, a small-time confidence trickster well known among Fleet Street reporters. Ashenden said in his statement:

> The plot consisted of using the services of McMahon for £500 to throw the revolver at the King and having Ernest Brooks standing by with a camera to take photographs of the incidents which would naturally follow. The best pictures were sold by Brooks to the *Evening Standard* for 100 guineas and to other London newspapers for 30 guineas.

Michaelis, Ashenden went on, took advantage of his prior knowledge by calling *The Star* immediately, giving them a clear and detailed story, which enabled the newspaper to beat its rivals. During the weekend following the 16 July incident, Ashenden said, Michaelis was heard boasting to other journalists in the London Press Club in Wine Office Court, off Fleet Street, what he knew about the real background to the case. Ashenden added that he had not personally checked any of this and was simply repeating what his editor had told him. What he had done, however, was to ask McMahon's solicitor, Alfred Kerstein, whether his client could shed light on any such plot. McMahon told Kerstein the entire tale was absurd.[84]

Chief Inspector Sands reported on 22 July:

> I was reliably informed last night that this fantastic story was concocted and told as a joke among a number of journalists in a public house, for the express purpose of it being overheard by a reporter of the 'Daily Sketch', [Ashenden] who is not generally liked by others and who was apparently disappointed in the lack of 'copy' he obtained. The story was added to and distorted before it reached this office. It has caused much work for nothing.[85]

Embarrassed for having apparently fallen for the story, the senior officer who first set the hare running noted, after reading the chief inspector's report, 'The question is, shall we officially caution Ashenden, or shall we ask the Director [of Public Prosecutions] to consider Ashenden's conduct under public mischief.' Neither action appears to have been taken. What was truly astounding was that the police had devoted more time and manpower chasing this absurd yarn than they had spent on investigating McMahon's claim of a plot to kill the king.

Among others questioned by the police in the wake of the attack was the mysterious 'Colonel' Matthews, something he complained about to McMahon. 'You have in the past so lied to me I don't know what to believe,' Matthews wrote to his friend. 'I've had endless worry over your affair; I know nothing about it but have had detectives bothering me.'[86] Another name floating to the surface in the days following the incident attracted even greater police interest – the well-known anti-hanging campaigner Mrs Violet Van der Elst.

The *Daily Express* on 17 July, the day after the attack, reported a 'friend' of McMahon's pointing out an association between McMahon and Mrs Van der Elst, implying, though not saying, that she might be connected with the attack in some way. When another newspaper made a similar point, Mrs Van der Elst vigorously denied even knowing McMahon, though given the extensive coverage of the Marylebone County Court case in April over hire cars – the story was even covered by *The Times* – she could hardly have expected this to stand up for long. But why had she felt the need to lie?

A café owner signing himself 'Britisher' had a complex tale to tell Scotland Yard involving Mrs Van der Elst. McMahon, 'Britisher' claimed, was an associate of a Dr Starkie of 27 Oakley Square, NW1. (This much was true. Starkie was the struck-off doctor who had been in McMahon's company during Mrs Van der Elst's November 1935 election campaign.) 'Starkie's house is frequented by foreigners periodically without passports.' Starkie would claim he was collaborating with McMahon on writing a book, but this was a lie. 'This man is head of a dope organisation' and the group were also involved in the white slave trade and forged passports. The writer said he knew this was true because they frequented his café. 'Britisher' regretted he could not divulge his name or address. To do so would endanger his life. 'Strangely enough each one of these men have applied to Mrs Van der Elst for money or presenting some schemes to her.'[87]

The letter interested the police as 'Britisher' was not the only person suggesting Mrs Van der Elst was implicated. Sands, leading the overall investigation, reported to the head of CID: 'In the early stage of the enquiries, it was known that the prisoner had been associated with the notorious Mrs Violet Van der Elst and rumour was rife that she was "behind" him in the outrage on His Majesty.' Sands attached copies of statements and newspaper cuttings to his memorandum.[88]

An earlier accuser had been J.M. Williams, the Conservative Party election agent for Wandsworth and Putney. On 17 July – the day after the incident – Williams called at the Home Office in Whitehall and asked to speak to a junior minister, Geoffrey Lloyd, for whom he had acted as political agent in the past. An official made a note of what Williams had to say, promising to pass it to Lloyd. Williams had worked for Mrs Van der Elst in her unsuccessful attempt at the Putney seat and he outlined the dispute over hire cars that had ended up in the county court. What he then had to say was – if true – explosive. Williams accused McMahon of trying to blackmail Mrs Van der Elst. The note continued:

> Mr Williams is convinced in his own mind that in the incident of yesterday McMahon acted only as a catspaw for Mrs Van der Elst – who, he thinks, would stop at nothing in her attempts to attract attention to her campaign against capital punishment and probably insisted on McMahon 'doing something' in return for the money which he was demanding from her. Mr Williams had a good deal to do with Mrs Van der Elst and says that he knows her to be anti-Royalist, having heard her speak disparagingly of the Royal Family on more than one occasion.[89]

The Home Office civil servant added in his note that Williams was not prepared to take this information directly to Scotland Yard as he was convinced senior Metropolitan Police officers had placed themselves under 'obligation' to Mrs Van der Elst by making use of her house at Wittingdean, near Brighton, for weekends and holidays. Williams said McMahon's involvement with Mrs Van der Elst was well known to officers at Notting Hill police station, including Sergeant Tracey. The sergeant, of course, was one of the officers McMahon had accused of corruption in 1932, which had led to McMahon's trial for criminal libel the following year, his release on appeal and his grievance against the authorities.

Other individuals acquainted with Mrs Van der Elst (and, to a lesser extent, with McMahon) appeared to corroborate much of Williams's story, in particular her attitude to the monarchy. Lionel Howes of Kilburn, also a Conservative Party political agent, told a detective sergeant on 17 July that on a number of occasions Mrs Van der Elst 'has spoken very disrespectively [*sic*] of the whole Royal Family and in particular in violent terms of the present King. She has told me that McMahon holds the same views as herself.'[90]

Reginald Clifton of West Kensington, who had acted as Mrs Van der Elst's assistant agent in Putney, told police that during the winding up of one election meeting at the Star and Garter ballroom in Richmond, 'Mrs Van der Elst pulled the pianist away from the piano as she was playing the National Anthem and shouted "I do not believe in the King". McMahon was in the ballroom at the time.' Clifton claimed that when he was at her house in Addison Road on 3 April 1936, 'She said to me words to the effect that she intended to publish in her book called "Humanity" matters bearing on the private life of the King.'[91]

Mrs Van der Elst's statement to the police – given, she complained, when she was suffering with a temperature of 102 degrees – appeared to put an entirely different light on her relationship with McMahon, for whom she obviously felt pity and contempt edged with disgust: 'This man has been to me a terrible menace.' Sands plainly believed her, or – for whatever reason – saw it as the safer course to take. He rejected as entirely unreliable gossip the allegations coming from Clifton, Howes and Williams, which, he reported to the head of CID, had 'not been substantiated in the least degree'.[92] Why three apparently respectable individuals should be making similar claims about Mrs Van der Elst Sands did not say.

Mrs Van der Elst had her own opinion of how seriously McMahon should be taken: 'I believe this man was only humbugging. I do not believe he ever meant to kill the King.' But in this same interview she described an unstable and reckless man, 'a menace' who told her he would shoot her because: 'You are too well known, and also I feel I would like to.'[93]

10

There was a baffling development when the Italian Embassy involved itself in the case. On 24 July Assistant Commissioner Kendal, who had been kept informed in detail from the outset by Vernon Kell about McMahon's revelations, sent a confidential report across to Harker at MI5 headquarters. The dossier contained allegations concerning McMahon that the chargé d'affaires at the Italian Embassy had made to the British Foreign Office.[94] What the Italian official had to say added to the mystery surrounding McMahon's story about a plot to kill the king, and perhaps was intended to.

According to the chargé d'affaires, McMahon visited the Italian Embassy in Mayfair on 1 May 1936 and told the consul general, Andrea Rainaldi, that he had reliable information about a plot to assassinate the duce, Benito Mussolini. This would perhaps have come as no surprise – between 1922 and 1936 there had been seventeen recorded attempts on Mussolini's life; eight of those charged had been executed and thirty-seven imprisoned. McMahon was told to go to the Italian Consulate the next day. He did and was interviewed by an Italian police officer. McMahon passed over the names and addresses of what he claimed were fourteen conspirators, thirteen in Milan and one in Antwerp. He refused to reveal the source of his information but asked for money to defray his expenses.

When the authorities in Italy checked the Milan names they discovered six were dead and had been for some time. The other seven were respectable tradesmen about whom there was no suspicion. The individual in Antwerp was also considered to be entirely innocent. The chargé d'affaires told the Foreign Office that coincidentally a man had come forward in Yugoslavia with a similar story to McMahon's. He added that during his visit McMahon had partially revealed a revolver, ten inches long and made of bright metal. (Press reports had already described the pistol McMahon had with him on 16 July as 'shiny'.) McMahon told the Italians he was working for 'a British government department' and had official permission to carry the weapon for his protection.

The report raised questions about Italian motives and about the nature of McMahon's game. What did the Italian Embassy hope to achieve by coming up with this account now rather than in May when McMahon had – so they now said – first brought them the story of a plot against

Mussolini? Given worsening relations between Britain and Italy since the invasion and occupation of Abyssinia, it could hardly have been through any wish to help the Metropolitan Police with their enquiries. Were they perhaps hoping to put the British authorities off the scent by portraying McMahon as an incorrigible fantasist? But why, when they presumably would not have known at this stage that McMahon had told MI5 there was a plot against Edward?

What scent were they hoping to put the British police off? Did the Italian Embassy know MI5 were aware of McMahon's dealings with the military attaché, Colonel Umberto Mondadori? Had there been a double game in which McMahon kept MI5 informed about his contact with Mondadori and the attaché about his contact with MI5? If not, were the Italians concerned that McMahon, now in police hands, would blurt out that he had been working for Mondadori? Did they fear the police would then suspect a connection between McMahon's involvement with them and the attack on Edward? Were they attempting, clumsily, to divert British attention with the message, 'Don't believe a word McMahon says'?

What did this second conspiracy story say about McMahon? Did any plot exist at all? Were they fantasies McMahon had concocted in an attempt to boost his value to MI5 and to Italian intelligence? Or did he genuinely believe in the existence of both conspiracies? Had one or more of his dubious contacts fed him tales as a prank, knowing he would not be able to resist passing them on? Were political refugees who suspected McMahon was giving the Italian Embassy information about their activities setting him up? Had they given him a story about a spurious assassination plot to discredit him in the eyes of Italian intelligence? Was the mysterious 'Colonel' Matthews, who weaved his way through McMahon's life during the mid-1930s, and on whom MI5 kept a file, involved in any way?

11

It was no surprise that the highly competitive popular press would go over the top in reporting the 16 July incident, one of the biggest stories so far of the decade. The over-enthusiasm of two newspapers led to their prosecution for contempt of court. On 22 July the Attorney General, Sir Donald Somervell, acting for the Director of Public Prosecutions, took proceedings in the High Court against the proprietors and editors of the *Daily Express* and the London *Evening News* over stories they had published on 17 July, the day after the attack on Edward. The effect, Somervell told judges sitting on the King's Bench, was to gravely prejudice McMahon's right to a fair trial.

Somervell pointed to a story in the *Evening News* headed 'Revolver Affair of no Political Significance', with sub-headings running down the page: 'Jerome Bannigan', 'The Story of the Man Now Known as McMahon', 'McMahon Felt that He Had a Grudge', 'His Unsuccessful Claim for £4,000 Against Two Detectives', and 'Said to be Mentally Unstable'. The *Evening News* – prompted no doubt by Scotland Yard – had moved on from the original assassination story. Somervell raised particular objection to one paragraph: 'He has been known to people who have had business relationships with him as a man with a boorish temperament and a lack of mental balance. His behaviour at times brought him to the notice of the police, who regarded him as a "harmless lunatic nursing a grievance".' The final sentence, of course, could only have been based on information leaked by police officers, who were no doubt paid by reporters. The Attorney General also expressed concern about the *Daily Express* comment, 'Jerome Bannigan, otherwise George Andrew McMahon, club-footed Irish "reformer", man with a grievance against authority'. Somervell told the judges, 'Their Lordships would be aware of the possible adverse effect on people's minds if it were stated that an accused person was using an alias.'[95]

On 29 July the three judges hearing the case fined the editors and proprietors of the *Daily Express* and the *Evening News* £500 for contempt in what they had published, plus costs. The *Daily Express* editor, Arthur Christiansen, apologised but added that the events of 16 July had been of a 'rare nature'. He had published the criticised story with 'the sole object of relieving the disquietude which I felt existed in the minds of the public as to the possibility of a recurrence of an event of this nature'.

McMahon's legal team – solicitor Alfred Kerstein and barrister St John Hutchinson – had also joined the action, objecting to the newsreel shown in cinemas throughout Britain with an opening caption 'Attempt on the King's Life', together with the poster displayed outside cinemas headed 'Assassination Attempt'. Gaumont British Distributors were fined £50, plus costs.[96]

12

In February 1936 Edward had told Ernest Simpson, 'Do you think I would be crowned without Wallis at my side?' On 21 July, five days after the attack on the king, Simpson booked into the Hotel de Paris at Bray, close by the Thames at Windsor, ten miles from Fort Belvedere. The hotel had been popular among the 'bright young things' Edward epitomised when he was Prince of Wales. Simpson signed in as 'Ernest A. Simmons' and his female companion – Wallis's close friend, Mary Raffray – as 'Buttercup Kennedy'. Custom demanded that in cases of contrived adultery the couple should take breakfast in their room, ensuring that hotel staff could honestly swear to having seen the man in question sharing a bed with a woman who was not his wife.

Two days later Wallis Simpson wrote to her husband saying she had discovered that rather than being away on business, as he had told her, he had been staying at a hotel with another woman. 'This only confirms the suspicions I have had for a long time. I am therefore instructing my solicitors to take proceedings for divorce.'[97] She asked Edward to recommend a firm of solicitors and he put her in touch with his own, George Allen. 'Are you quite sure, Mrs Simpson, that you want a divorce?' Allen asked at their first meeting.[98] The 'dastardly attempt' having failed to come off, the next opportunity to remove Edward from the throne was beginning to take shape.

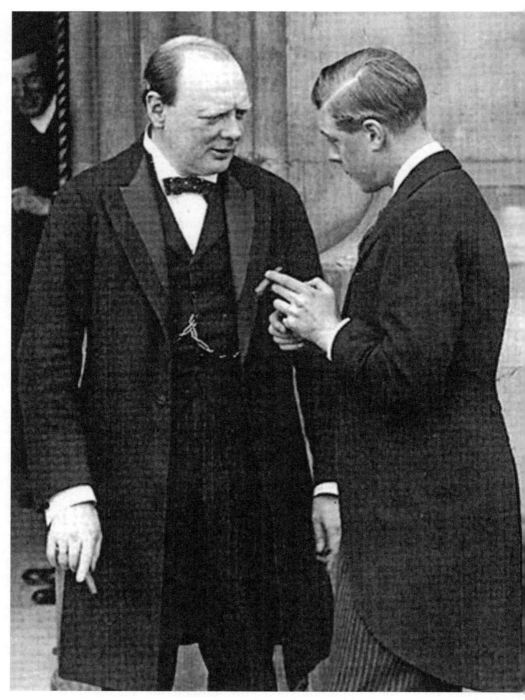

Edward VIII, as Prince of Wales, with Winston Churchill in 1921. Churchill was a leading supporter of Edward during the abdication crisis in 1936. (Unknown photographer/Wikimedia Commons)

Govan, Glasgow, where McMahon lived as Jerome Bannigan until he left Scotland in his twenties. (Unknown photographer/Wikimedia Commons)

Vernon Kell, director of MI5 from 1909 until his dismissal in 1940, wearing military uniform. (By kind permission of the Estate of Lady Kell)

THE HUMAN GAZETTE

BRITAIN'S PREMIER NEW NON-SECTARIAN & NON-POLITICAL JOURNAL

VOL. I. No. 1.   FEBRUARY, 1935.   Price 2d.

" A fellow feeling makes one wondrous kind."—David Garrick.

MANAGING EDITOR

SPECIAL FEATURES

- WANDSWORTH PRISON
- TOO OLD AT THIRTY
- BRIBERY IN BUSINESS
- UNMORAL GIRLS
- VACUUM CLEANER VAMPIRES
- BABIES AND BUNKUM
- THIS FREEDOM
- HYDE PARK VULTURES
- IS NUDISM IMMORAL?
- HOW TO LAND A JOB
- ARROWS FROM OUR BOWS
- WHY I SHALL NOT MARRY
- WANTED HE-MEN

SPORTS, CINEMA, AND HOUSEHOLD NOTES, Etc.

NEXT ISSUE FULL PARTICULARS OF SEVERAL **ORIGINAL COMPETITIONS**

The *Human Gazette*, No. 1, February 1935, the sole issue of the magazine McMahon was able to produce. (Unknown photographer/ *Daily Express*)

King Edward VIII as Admiral of the Fleet, 1936. (Grainger Historical Picture Archive/Alamy Stock Photo)

Prime Minister Stanley Baldwin, who had a low opinion of Edward as monarch and played a central part in his abdication. (Walter Stoneman/George Grantham Bain Collection/Library of Congress)

MI5 Director Vernon Kell in the late 1930s. (By kind permission of the Estate of Lady Kell)

Edward rides on to Buckingham Palace immediately after McMahon's attack, Major General Bertram Sergison-Brooke alongside him. (The Print Collector/Alamy Stock Photo)

McMahon being arrested following the attack; Special Constable Anthony Dick can be seen gripping his right wrist. (D & S Photography Archives/Alamy Stock Photo)

Front page of the London *Evening News* in the aftermath of the attack. (John Frost Newspapers/ Alamy Stock Photo)

John Sands, the detective chief inspector who investigated McMahon's attack. One of Scotland Yard's 'Big Five', he was promoted in 1936 to superintendent and then head of the Flying Squad. (Unknown photographer/*Daily Express*)

McMahon's wife Rose and solicitor Alfred Kerstein on their way to the Old Bailey for the trial on 14 September 1936. (Unknown photographer/*The Sphere*)

McMahon's wife greets him on his release from Wandsworth Prison on 12 August 1937. The couple was driven off in a *Daily Express* car to be interviewed. (Unknown photographer/*Daily Express*)

McMahon and wife Rose in 1938, the year after his release from prison. He attached this photograph to letters he sent to prominent public figures asking for money to support his 'fight for justice'. (Unknown photographer/The National Archives UK/Metropolitan Police Service)

Duke and Duchess of Windsor, the titles Edward and Wallis Simpson took after his abdication in December 1936. (Vincenzo Laviosa/Wikimedia Commons/Public Domain)

IV

McMahon's Trials

1

At the conclusion of McMahon's first court appearance at Bow Street a few hours after Edward had faced the armed attack on 16 July, the magistrate, Sir Rollo Graham-Campbell, remanded the defendant in custody for eight days. Chief Inspector Sands, the Scotland Yard detective leading the investigation, and Inspector Kidd took him by car to Brixton Prison. McMahon was confined to the medical wing where he was treated for the bruises and scratches sustained during the scuffle on Constitution Hill. Later he was put through a series of tests to enable medical staff to present a report on his physical condition and mental state.

The prison senior medical officer, Dr H.A. Grierson, suggested in his initial report that McMahon's present predicament arose from his grievance against the police and the failure to secure the compensation for wrongful imprisonment in 1933 to which he felt entitled. 'From my examination and enquiries I find no reason to consider his ideas as having arisen from any disease or defect of the mind. In fact, while under my care, he has been normal and rational in conduct and conversation and has not shown any indications of insanity.'[1] McMahon never lacked plausibility, at least on first encounter. After McMahon's next appearance at Bow Street Court Grierson decided he might need to reconsider his assessment.

Meanwhile, equipped with new spectacles to replace the pair lost during the scrap on Constitution Hill, McMahon began composing his version of the incident in a notebook. This does not seem to have survived. He was allowed only one visitor on Friday 17 July, his solicitor Alfred Kerstein, who interviewed McMahon for ninety minutes in a private room. Other prisoners were not told of the charge McMahon was facing, presumably for his safety.

McMahon's wife tried to visit him but was at first refused entry. She said she had no doubt the charge against her husband was ridiculous and that she would stand by him. The Home Office eventually gave her permission to see McMahon for an hour. The *Daily Express*, whose journalist Lindon Laing already seemed to have gained exclusive access to her, reported that during the visit McMahon 'sobbed, begging forgiveness for the distress he caused her'. Through his wife, McMahon appealed for a woman standing immediately behind him on Constitution Hill on the day of the incident to contact his solicitor. 'He declares she must have had a perfect view of all that happened, and states she was talking to another woman in German.'[2] Was McMahon muddying the water? Nothing came of the appeal.

Edward, meanwhile, spent the day after the attack discussing plans for his coronation, due on 12 May 1937, with the Duke of Norfolk, who, as Earl Marshal, had charge of the arrangements. The meeting was joined by Edward's brother Albert, Duke of York, a member of the organising committee. Throughout the country, factories and workshops were beginning production of commemorative mugs – 7 million in all were turned out – and plates, bunting, flags and banners, while towns and villages set about planning street parties and other celebrations. The British Colour Council, it was reported, 'have standardised the official colours for bunting, flags, &c, and in co-operation with the Paint and Varnish Federation will produce a range of colours which will beautify our buildings'.[3] However, in official circles Edward's obsession with Wallis Simpson was raising doubts over whether his coronation would be taking place at all.

Everything suggested that the authorities had agreed that, for public consumption, the 16 July incident should be treated as the act of a disturbed eccentric airing a grievance. But behind the scenes fears remained that a murderous conspiracy did actually exist, that McMahon was an active participant, and that the king was still in danger. On 24 July Secretary for War Duff Cooper summoned MI5's director, Vernon Kell, to the War Office. Cooper and his wife Diana were members of Edward's Fort Belvedere social circle and were due shortly to accompany the king and Mrs Simpson on holiday.

Cooper told Kell that McMahon's solicitor, Kerstein, had disclosed something worrying to the barrister who would appear for the defence, St John Hutchinson. McMahon had revealed that a further attempt on the king's life would be made abroad. Hutchinson told Cooper (a personal friend) that he had acknowledged that confidential discussions between client, solicitor and barrister were privileged, but he felt he had no choice but to share the story with him.[4] In fact, McMahon later said, he had asked Kerstein to inform 'the authorities' that another attempt on the king's life would be made in France.

As Edward was shortly to travel to France to unveil a Canadian war memorial at Vimy, and then proceed to a summer holiday at Cannes on the Côte d'Azur, the story was taken seriously. Kerstein also told Hutchinson that McMahon had admitted for the first time past contacts with officials at the German Embassy. After discussing the threat with Cooper, Kell crossed to Scotland Yard to talk to the commissioner, Sir Philip Game, and Assistant Commissioner Kendal. They agreed Kell would ask the governor of Brixton Prison, Captain Stevenson, to have 'a friendly chat' with McMahon and try to draw him out. Stevenson, when Kell put this to him, thought questions might come better from the prison medical officer, Dr Grierson, as he and McMahon had become 'very friendly'. But when they spoke, McMahon told the doctor he knew nothing about any such threat to Edward in France.

The common factor in all this was McMahon's solicitor, Kerstein, who police suspected was embellishing and sensationalising events to keep himself in the public eye. It did begin to look as if Kerstein and McMahon had entered into some kind of an agreement with the *Daily Express*, which was publishing the most colourful pieces about the prisoner and his wife. There was also a rumour that Kerstein was ultimately hoping to cash in on the drama by writing a book giving the 'inside story' of the whole affair, though if that were his intention none ever materialised.

The alarm was raised again when a postcard addressed to McMahon arrived at Brixton Prison on 25 July signed cryptically 'S.B.' Was this further evidence that the conspiracy still had life? So concerned were Dr Grierson and the prison governor, Stevenson, that they drove from South London to Kell at MI5 headquarters with the card. The three then made their way to the office of Metropolitan Police Commissioner Game to discuss the best course of action. Game suggested showing the card to McMahon and asking him if he could throw any light on the sender's identity.

In the course of the morning the postcard went from Brixton Prison, to MI5 headquarters, to Scotland Yard, and back to the prison. At the end of this circuitous journey McMahon, finally allowed to view the card, said he had no idea who the sender could be. Had everyone, including the heads of MI5 and the Metropolitan Police, had their time wasted by a simple prankster?

2

Kell's main concern now as head of MI5 was to keep from the public the fact that he and his officers had been aware since April 1936 of a plot to assassinate the king and that they had, on the face of it, done little or nothing to prevent an attack. Would McMahon go to Bow Street Court on 24 July and reveal from the dock his contacts with MI5 and their and Special Branch's failure to act effectively on his revelation? He had, after all, been left unhindered to confront the king with a loaded revolver. Sir Russell Scott, Permanent Under-Secretary to the Home Office, had wind of MI5's relationship with McMahon and was clearly concerned at the implications. He instructed Kell to compile a report on everything he and his officers knew about McMahon.

Kell's response on 21 July (with a copy sent to Commissioner Game at Scotland Yard) was a two-page typed memorandum setting out details of the organisation's involvement with McMahon from the interception of his letter to the *Daily Worker* in August 1933 to his revelation in October 1935 that he was working for the Italian military attaché. Kell admitted McMahon had at this point supplied MI5 with accurate information about Italian intelligence activity in London.[5]

Kell went on to describe to Scott how in April 1936 McMahon told his MI5 contact Ottaway about a 'Communist plot to assassinate the Monarch'. Kell forgot – though perhaps he deliberately failed – to mention that McMahon had showed Ottaway a revolver he carried and that the officer's advice had been that he needed a police permit. Kell said that after reading the report of a Special Branch interview with McMahon, he decided to sever contact with McMahon because he was 'too unreliable to be of real assistance'.

But on 13 July, Kell said, McMahon warned Ottaway an attack on Edward was imminent. He shifted responsibility for what happened next by saying that he had placed 'all the facts' before Assistant Commissioner Norman Kendal and 'explained the whole matter to him'.[6] While it was true that MI5's role was to gather intelligence and the police's role was to make arrests, it did appear Kell – having said he had informed Kendal – was hoping any blame for the events of 16 July could be placed on the police.

Kell's hope of keeping MI5's involvement secret was soon threatening to unravel. At 12.15 p.m. on 21 July Ottaway telephoned his immediate boss, 'Jasper' Harker, the head of B Division, to say McMahon's solicitor had asked for an interview. Harker immediately called Kell to discuss how best they should respond to Kerstein. Kell at that exact moment had Sir Russell Scott with him in his office and this call from Harker may have been what prompted Scott's instruction to Kell to write the report on what exactly MI5 had been doing with McMahon.

Kell's advice to Harker was to refer Kerstein's request to the Director of Public Prosecutions, Sir Edward Atkinson, who was responsible for mounting the case against McMahon. The DPP turned to the Attorney General, Sir Donald Somervell, who would present the prosecution in court. From these high-level consultations, a form of words emerged that everyone hoped would see Kerstein off:

Your request has been referred to D.P.P. who, under the instructions of the Attorney General, is responsible for the prosecution. The Director is of the opinion that no evidence which Mr Ottaway would give is in the least degree relevant to the charge which will be proceeded with at Bow Street on Friday. In consequence he cannot consent to the solicitor for the defence interviewing Mr Ottaway, but Mr Ottaway will appear to a sub poena.

Harker discussed the DPP statement with Kell and Ottaway, then telephoned Kerstein. In the conversation that followed Harker said he was Ottaway's superior officer, read the statement aloud, and told Kerstein future dealings should be with the DPP directly and not MI5.[7] McMahon's solicitor – who himself was the subject of an MI5 personal file, PF 63449 – refused to be brushed aside so easily. MI5's reluctance to talk suggested he might be on to something worth pursuing. That McMahon had twice brought up with Ottaway a plot to kill the king, first in April and again in July 1936, was far from irrelevant, despite MI5's efforts to keep these facts hidden. What else would emerge at an interview with Ottaway?

Kerstein wrote at once to the Director of Public Prosecutions saying he was 'very anxious' to interview Ottaway and asked him to reconsider his decision not to allow this. The DPP telephoned Harker at 11 a.m. on 22 July to give him the news that Kerstein was persisting. Kell and Harker then met the DPP at his office to go over the question again 'from various angles', as Harker described the discussion. Unable to reach a conclusion, the three agreed to seek the opinion of Somervell, the Attorney General.[8]

Kell, Harker and Director of Public Prosecutions Atkinson met Somervell in his office at the Law Courts in the Strand at 2.30 p.m. The senior Treasury counsel, Eustace Fulton, was also present. (Fulton and McMahon were acquainted. Fulton had been prosecuting counsel in 1933 when McMahon was convicted at the Old Bailey of libelling the Notting Hill police officers, the conviction against which he successfully appealed.) As a government minister, Somervell was sensitive to the political implications of what might appear obstructiveness on

MI5's part. He feared that any appearance that McMahon's defence was being hampered might be raised in the House of Commons. Somervell was probably thinking of the small group of radical Independent Labour Party MPs, possibly even the sole Communist elected in 1935, all of whom would welcome an opportunity to embarrass the government.

The five agreed that Ottaway would be allowed to speak to Kerstein, accompanied by another MI5 officer. Obviously, Somervell said, Ottaway would be obliged to refuse to answer some questions on security grounds. Atkinson telephoned Kerstein and arranged for the meeting to take place at the War Office the following day, 23 July, exactly one week after McMahon had pulled his revolver on Edward.[9]

Harker ordered Ottaway, McMahon's MI5 contact, to prepare a statement for Kerstein to read, 'saying exactly what he knew in connection with this particular matter'. Ottaway's two-page typed memorandum described the April and July conversations about the assassination plot. Ottaway was at pains to emphasise McMahon's demand for £1,000. A sentence at the end referring to their 13 July meeting appeared an afterthought intended to cover MI5 against criticism over Ottaway's apparent lack of concern about the gun McMahon had shown him at the end of 1935. 'McMahon told me at this interview', Ottaway wrote, 'that he had disposed of the pistol previously referred to and led me to think that he did not then possess one.'[10]

Given how persistent Kerstein had been in his determination to interview Ottaway, he seemed remarkably mild and compliant when the meeting finally took place at the War Office in Whitehall. Ottaway was accompanied by Harker and a shorthand writer. Harker reminded Kerstein that Ottaway's statement was being shown to him 'in absolute confidence'.[11] Kerstein replied that he had no intention of taking advantage of that confidence in any way, that his only concern was to do his duty to his client. Harker handed the typed pages to Kerstein to read. Harker noted that, having taken the statement in, Kerstein appeared depressed.

Kerstein then turned to question Ottaway briefly. Was the revolver loaded when McMahon produced it at their meeting? Ottaway replied that he could not say either way. The weapon could have been loaded or unloaded. Kerstein said he had no plans at the moment to call Ottaway to give evidence at Bow Street the following day. His decision would depend on the answers the police witnesses gave in evidence. But if he did call Ottaway it would be to answer the question: 'Was it not a fact that McMahon had openly stated that he was in possession of a revolver?' Harker's note of the meeting recorded that Kerstein raised two further points with him:

> Firstly – could I tell him whether McMahon's information on subjects in which I was interested had been of any use. I said I was afraid I could not do so. He then asked – could I tell him whether there was any truth in the statement McMahon had made regarding the alleged conspiracy. To this I replied that he must ask the police as I had not investigated this, as it was no concern of the Directorate of Military Intelligence.[12]

Harker had not lied, but he had been careful to avoid telling the truth. The conversation took a new turn when Kerstein said he did not want Harker to think he was proposing any kind of bargain, but it was possible McMahon had other information the authorities would find useful. Harker replied that he considered it safer to leave matters as they stood until court proceedings had concluded. Kerstein thanked the two MI5 officers for their help and was about to leave the office when Harker raised a last point – an understandable one, but strange in the circumstances. 'I asked him, purely as a matter of curiosity, explaining that if it caused him any embarrassment he need not answer me, whether he thought his client abnormal or insane. He replied: "Not normal, but not insane."'[13]

3

What was noticeable about McMahon's appearance at the Bow Street Court committal hearings on 24 and 31 July 1936 was how nobody – neither defence nor prosecution – raised his involvement with MI5 or the fact that he had twice warned of a plot to kill the king. This would hardly have happened spontaneously or out of forgetfulness. McMahon gave the obvious explanation in his letter to the probation officer, Colonel Bevis, in 1937: 'During the Police Court hearing my solicitor was entreated not to mention anything about the plot or War Office connections, being assured that a "silence" would be a help to our King's safety.'[14] There was more to it than this, as McMahon knew and as later events would show. The implication was that the solicitor, Kerstein, had been told (or perhaps even promised) McMahon could expect to be treated leniently if he kept to himself anything that might embarrass MI5 or the police.

Early in the morning on 24 July, more than 500 people were queueing in the street outside the court hoping to gain entry; at their head was an ex-serviceman, medals on his chest, and three clergymen. The Bow Street officials had announced that no more than thirty members of the public would be accommodated because of the demand for seats from the press. In addition to the original charge under Section 7 of the 1920 Firearms Act of illegally possessing a weapon with intent to endanger life and property, McMahon faced two further charges. These were under Section 2 of the 1842 Treason Act, introduced following the attempt on Queen Victoria's life on Constitution Hill: presenting near the king's person a revolver with intent to break the public peace, and with intent to alarm the king.

For the prosecution, Attorney General Sir Donald Somervell ran through the main events since McMahon had walked into the Two Brewers in Buckingham Gate on 15 July and spoke to the barmaid, Mary Blencowe, as if that were when the story began. He briefly described the incident on Constitution Hill, and concluded with McMahon's last appearance at Bow Street on 16 July. He then called witnesses to give evidence. Miss Blencowe confirmed that McMahon told her she would not see him again, disputing the suggestion from Kerstein, McMahon's solicitor, that he had been referring to the imminent loss of his office in Victoria. A journalist noted that McMahon stood in the dock:

...neatly dressed in a brown lounge suit, with a brown tie, and wearing glasses. He had a notebook in his hand, listened attentively to the evidence, but his agitation was so great and his hand trembled to such an extent that he seemed incapable of making notes.[15]

Kerstein's tactic appeared to be at this stage to attempt to undermine witnesses' evidence by querying their memory of events and then playing on contradictions between them. Questioning John Remes, the Brighton night porter who had punched McMahon, Kerstein showed a particular interest in the camera he dropped just after photographing the king. The reason for Kerstein's curiosity became apparent when he questioned Anthony Dick, the special constable who had knocked or grabbed McMahon's arm. Dick said he had seen 'a black object' in McMahon's hand and then observed it lying in the road by the king's horse. Was he quite sure it was not a camera, Kerstein asked, suggesting a possible confusion between Remes's camera and a revolver. Dick said he had no doubt.

> Kerstein: Did you notice in what direction the black object was pointing when you first saw it? – No, I couldn't say that.
> Kerstein: Did you notice in what manner the object fell through the air before it fell in the roadway? – It was like a ruler, or something like that.
> The Chief Clerk: Did it go high in the air? – Not too high. About a man's height.[16]

Other police witnesses were uncertain which of them had been the first to seize McMahon, whether the object that flew through the air was shiny or black, and whether it had been knocked from McMahon's hand or he had thrown it. Constable Thomas Griffiths said that on the way to Hyde Park after his arrest McMahon had said, 'I could easily have shot him but threw it instead. It would have been better if I had shot myself.' Kerstein asked, 'If I had shot myself in front of the King?' – 'That was all he said.' 'He did not say in front of the King?' – 'No.'

Questioning Chief Inspector Sands, the Scotland Yard detective leading the investigation into the incident, Kerstein read out McMahon's letter to the Home Secretary, Sir John Simon, in its entirety. Sands agreed

McMahon believed he had a legitimate grievance against the police dating back to his imprisonment in 1933 and that he had also written a number of letters to Buckingham Palace.

> Kerstein: In the course of your inquiries have you ascertained if the prisoner has ever threatened the King? – I have not.
> Kerstein: To be perfectly fair to the prisoner, the communications addressed by him to Buckingham Palace have not been threatening so far as you know? – So far as I know. I am speaking in the absence of them, but I do not think they contain threats.

Eustace Fulton, the senior Treasury counsel assisting Somervell, told the magistrate the prosecution had submitted sufficient evidence to justify committing McMahon for trial on all three charges. Kerstein disputed this, saying he had never before seen a collection of witnesses contradict one another so blatantly. No reasonable jury, he said, would convict on a single one of the charges. The accusation that McMahon was in possession of a weapon with intent to endanger of life was particularly weak, Kerstein claimed. The chance to fire a fatal shot had been there, but McMahon had not seized the opportunity.

> Magistrate: The word 'life' in the charge is very wide. It might be his own life or someone else's. There is evidence with regard to the statement made on oath that he intended to shoot himself in the presence of the King.
> Kerstein: In that case, if the prosecution had been properly presented, the proper charge would have been attempting to commit suicide.

Kerstein said the evidence the court had heard in no way indicated that McMahon intended to harm or assassinate the king. 'A revolver was seen to fall into the roadway where the King was passing. Within an hour or two some newspapers had placards that an attempt had been made to assassinate the King.' How, asked Kerstein, could McMahon expect a fair trial in these circumstances, when any twelve persons would inevitably, he was sure, already be biased against him? The magistrate disagreed.

He believed he had seen sufficient evidence to commit the defendant for trial on all charges. Kerstein consulted McMahon, who said he would want to give evidence and to call witnesses of his own. The magistrate remanded him in custody for a further seven days.

How Kerstein had decided he would run McMahon's defence seemed clear from this first day's hearing: minimise the gravity of the offence, raise doubts about witness evidence, and avoid any reference to McMahon's contact with MI5 and his revelation in April and July of a plot to kill Edward. This suited the prosecution, MI5 and senior Metropolitan Police officers, who were concerned the public should be led to believe that nothing of importance or significance had taken place. But did it suit McMahon? Would he, unpredictable at the best of times, be prepared to continue to play the game at his next appearance on 31 July? If he was, the major difficulty would still be to explain why he was carrying a loaded gun on Constitution Hill.

4

Now the Brixton medical officer, Dr Grierson, had become better acquainted with McMahon he was beginning to reconsider his previous opinion on his mental state. Grierson's initial report to the Bow Street magistrate had been that McMahon appeared normal and rational, with no 'indications of insanity'. In his 31 July report he said he now preferred to 'defer expressing a final opinion'. He understood McMahon would be committed for trial from Bow Street. McMahon would remain under observation in the prison hospital and Grierson would submit a report 'in due course'.[17]

On his second committal appearance at Bow Street on 31 July, McMahon limped into the dock and was allowed to sit through the hearing as he was questioned. Kerstein took him through the course of his life from the accident at the age of 12, which had left him permanently disabled, his move to London six or seven years previously, his discovery and exposure of corruption among Notting Hill police officers, the resulting loss of his job as a sports club secretary, his conviction and imprisonment for criminal libel, and his subsequent successful appeal. McMahon described how the police continued to harass and persecute him. He described the Home Office's failure to compensate him for wrongful imprisonment, his petitions to King George and King Edward. Kerstein read aloud a section of his petition to Edward on 12 February 1936:

> May I as one of the least of your subjects offer my condolence in your recent sad bereavement, and now that you have experienced such sorrows and heartache through the passing of your beloved father may I beg you to ease the suffering and sorrow I have been experiencing for many years by commanding the Home Office to recompense me for the irreparable suffering they have occasioned my wife and I. Since a child I have never had a chance.

Kerstein asked him, 'Have you ever sent any communication either to his late Majesty, or to the present King, or to the Home Office, or any other authority that was threatening in tone?' McMahon answered, 'No.'[18]

McMahon said that at the end of 1935 he had obtained a revolver and ammunition, but did not say, and was not asked, how or where. 'I was doing certain work and I was imparting information, referred to in my petition, to the authorities, and it necessitated my carrying a revolver for my own safety.' That was his one and only reference that day in court to his involvement with the police or MI5. He said he had never fired that revolver or any other firearm.

McMahon described his publication in 1935 of the magazine the *Human Gazette* and the difficulties he had faced in raising money to produce a second edition. He had then lost access to his office in Victoria. McMahon disputed what the barmaid at the Two Brewers had said in evidence. His version was that he told her there had been 'an unpleasant setback' and that he would not be in the area again for some time. He did not refer to 'something dreadful' having happened and neither did he say 'You will see it in all the papers'. His letter to the Home Secretary, Sir John Simon, had certainly not been intended as a threat, simply an attempt to secure his attention.

Turning to the events of 16 July on Constitution Hill, McMahon said
he felt he had lost all control of himself. He wrote a message to his wife
on his newspaper and contemplated suicide, but then decided instead
on making a last gesture. At this point in his evidence McMahon broke
down and sobbed, continuing in a broken voice, scarcely audible. He said
he had intended to throw the newspaper at the king in the hope Edward
would demand an explanation. 'I then remembered what I had written
on my paper, and then, almost before I could realise it, I remembered
about the gun … I put my hand in my pocket and took out the gun.'
Kerstein asked, 'Did you ever point it at anyone?' – 'Definitely not.'
He said he stooped and slithered the gun along the roadway where the
procession was about to pass. McMahon disputed that the revolver had
been knocked from his hand. 'It might have gone off if it had been.'

Kerstein: Did you intend your revolver to hit anyone, or anything?
– No.
Kerstein: Did you not think the revolver might be discharged as it fell
to the ground? – No, that is why I slithered it.
Kerstein: Did you intend to alarm his Majesty? – No, I certainly did
not. I was seeking his intervention. Why should I seek to alarm him?
Kerstein: Did you intend to cause a breach of the peace? – No, that is
why I selected the spot where very few people were about. I did not
want to alarm.

It was now the turn of the Attorney General, Sir Donald Somervell, to
cross-examine McMahon. He was interested in the letter McMahon had
written to the Home Secretary the evening before the 16 July incident.
He asked McMahon what he meant when he demanded 'satisfaction'
of his grievance within fourteen hours, written in capital letters and
underlined twice. 'Were you thinking of something that might happen
at the review of the Guards?' McMahon said he had intended go to
Simon's house, or to the Home Office, on the morning of 16 July. That
was what he meant when he wrote fourteen hours. 'I am suggesting',
Somervell said, 'that when you wrote this letter you were intending to
do some act – leaving out for the moment what it was – at the review

on the following day.' McMahon denied there had been any such intention in his mind.

Somervell asked why McMahon had taken a revolver with him if his objective were not to endanger life. 'In order to make a gesture to draw attention to oneself on an occasion of this kind it is quite unnecessary, is it not, to use a loaded revolver?' There were other articles he could have thrown. 'I wish now I had had some advice about it,' McMahon responded.

Somervell referred to McMahon's statement 'I could easily have shot him but threw it instead', asking, 'Does not that sentence show that at any rate the idea of shooting his Majesty had entered your head?' – 'No, sir.'

Re-examining his client, Kerstein wondered why he had not unloaded the revolver before throwing it. McMahon said there had been no time. 'If I had been seen to take out the revolver someone would have caught my hand and said that I intended to shoot someone.'

The Attorney General asked the magistrate to commit McMahon for trial on all three charges. Kerstein argued that his client had no case to answer as far as the allegation against him under the Firearms Act was concerned, intent to endanger life and property. He went on:

> It is only by his acts that you can judge what his intention was that morning, whatever might have been his intention on the previous day or at any other time, and in that connection you will remember that he says that he never intended to harm the King, or any one else – and there is no evidence that he did.

Kerstein accepted that a jury should consider both charges under the Treason Act, possessing a firearm with intent to break the public peace and to alarm the king.

The magistrate sent McMahon for trial at the next session of the Central Criminal Court, the Old Bailey, on all three charges. On his return to the hospital wing at Brixton Prison, McMahon wrote to a Hampstead priest of his acquaintance, 'In the interval since my arrest, the bitterness has been greatly leavened, and when the full facts are divulged at my trial all trace of anger will have disappeared.'[19] When McMahon next appeared in the dock, what he had to say would call into question everything that had gone before.

5

On the day the British press covered McMahon's committal for trial at the Old Bailey, 1 August, the *Daily Mirror* reported in detail preparations for the king's planned Mediterranean cruise on the steam yacht *Nahlin*. The holiday, Edward's biographer Frances Donaldson suggests, 'was the beginning of what would shortly be the end, the point at which every historian writing of the Abdication must inevitably start.'[20] The luxurious vessel − appointed with a swimming pool, gymnasium and dance floor − belonged to one of Britain's wealthiest women, the widowed Lady Annie Yule. Edward paid her £6,000 to rent the yacht for a four-week summer cruise.

Wallis Simpson wrote excitedly from Fort Belvedere to her Aunt Bessie on 1 August that she would be sailing with Edward on the yacht along the Dalmatian coast and 'possibly going to the Greek islands and a visit to the King there − also perhaps to Prince Paul in Yugoslavia − all depending entirely on the political situation in Europe which changes from day to day − no place seems very safe for kings'.[21] She made no mention of the fact that her husband would not be accompanying her on this holiday, nor that steps were being taken for them to divorce.

The previous day Edward had driven himself in a black Buick (followed by his chauffeur in a Rolls-Royce) down to Southampton, where the *Nahlin* was moored, to check his requirements were being met. All the books in the ship's library had been removed to make space for construction of a bedroom. A sofa, bed, wardrobe and other furnishings were being hoisted aboard. Stores conveyed in two naval lorries from Buckingham Palace included, the *Mirror* reported, 'baskets of linen and cutlery, several cases of champagne and red and white wines, lager, numerous cases of lemon and orange quash and lime juice.'[22] Transport from Fort Belvedere carried the king's personal luggage in trunks, together with rugs, cushions, a parcel of gramophone records, pneumatic exercise mattresses and thousands of golf balls for Edward to amuse himself driving into the sea.

Edward had originally planned to join the *Nahlin* at Venice but he was persuaded by the Foreign Secretary, Anthony Eden, that this was diplomatically unwise. Eden feared the king's appearance on Italian soil would undermine British disapproval of the regime's interference in the Spanish Civil War and the occupation of Ethiopia. Instead, the yacht sailed to the tiny Dalmatian port of Šibenik to await the arrival of Edward and his guests. These included an assistant private secretary, an equerry, War Secretary Duff Cooper and his wife Lady Diana, and two American friends of Wallis, Herman and Katherine Rogers. A still-peeved Duke of Windsor later recalled, 'In thus bending my plans to suit the exigencies of British foreign policy, I subjected myself to an indescribable night journey by train into Yugoslavia with a clanking and jolting such as I had never before experienced.'[23]

Edward – masquerading for the duration of the holiday as the 'Duke of Lancaster' – was greeted as he crossed the border from Austria by the regent, Prince Paul, and the British chargé d'affaires in Belgrade, John Balfour. As Wallis had said, assassination was in the air – King Alexander of Yugoslavia had been killed on a visit to France less than two years before. When Edward and Wallis were taken for a break in their journey to tea with Prince Paul and his wife Princess Olga, their car was driven at manic speed by a chauffeur warned to avoid a feared ambush by Communists or Croat nationalists – nobody was sure which. The couple then went on to Šibenik, where they boarded the *Nahlin*, decked out, according to Edward's equerry Sir John Aird, 'like a Calais whore-shop'. Balfour, meanwhile, had been embarrassed to be told by a Romanian diplomat that when his king travelled abroad he always left his mistress at home.

Whatever pleasure Edward, Wallis and their guests experienced during the cruise, the trip certainly gave a great deal of enjoyment to the American and European press, unshackled by British respect, and to the crowds who turned out to cheer the couple wherever the *Nahlin* dropped anchor. They clearly knew everything about the nature of

Edward's relationship with Wallis. The bulk of the British public, who were indirectly paying for the month-long holiday, remained in the dark about their king's affair with a still-married woman, shielded from the truth by an abjectly obedient press. Escorted by two Royal Navy destroyers, the *Nahlin* sailed down the Dalmatian coast, stopping off at Corfu, where Edward met the newly restored King George of Greece, through the Corinth Canal to Athens and on into the Aegean.

At every port that the yacht moored, photographers seized their opportunity to capture intimate images of Edward and Wallis, the king making so little effort to hide their relationship that Wallis pleaded with him to try to be more discreet. She later recalled, '"Discretion," he said, almost proudly, "is a quality which, though useful, I have never particularly admired."'[24] But as the ostensibly 'innocent' party in the impending divorce from Ernest it would not do for her to appear just as unfaithful. A contemporary commented, 'Everywhere Mrs Simpson was beside him … there was no denying that the King was supremely happy.'[25] But one member of the on-board party, Lady Diana Cooper, thought she saw a shadow over the affair, writing back to England, 'Wallis is wearing very, very badly. Her commonness and Becky Sharpishness irritate', and in her diary she noted how coldly Wallis treated Edward, giving the impression she was already bored with him.[26]

When the *Nahlin* reached Istanbul, Edward met the Turkish dictator, Kemal Ataturk. Wallis wrote on a picture postcard of the city to her Aunt Bessie, 'A lovely lazy holiday and interesting things to be seen.'[27] After spending an evening with the couple, Ataturk saw the danger, commenting that the intensity of Edward's attachment to Wallis would lose him his throne. True to form, Edward invited Ataturk to Britain on a state visit, without informing the British Foreign Office, his freelance diplomacy provoking official embarrassment and annoyance.

The cruise gave every impression of being Edward's declaration of war against the British political and royal establishment, a final assertion that he would live his life as he pleased. Did the couple sleep together on the yacht, Lady Diana Cooper was later asked by an inquisitive friend back in London. 'I haven't the least idea. How should I know? Though I'm perfectly sure they did.'[28] The holiday coming to its end, Edward crossed Yugoslavia by train without Wallis, stopping for a few days in Vienna, then flying to England from Zurich on 14 September – the day McMahon was driven across London from Brixton Prison for his trial at the Old Bailey. 'Now Tommy,' the king said to his private secretary on his return, 'back to striped trousers and coats again, back to school.'[29]

Wallis, meanwhile, travelled on to Paris, where she found letters from Aunt Bessie and from friends in the United States waiting at her hotel in the Rue de Rivoli. Whether it was her shock at the sight of cuttings from the American press as she later said in her memoirs ('Yankee at the Court of King Edward' and 'Mrs Simpson, Ever at Ruler's Side' were two of the headlines), whether she had – as Lady Diana Cooper believed – become bored with Edward, or she was simply playing hard to get, she telephoned the king on 16 September. She followed up their conversation with a letter. Wallis said she had decided to seek a reconciliation with her husband. They would be a couple again, she declared, and her relationship with Edward was over. 'I must really return to Ernest for a great many reasons … I know Ernest and have the deepest affection and respect for him. I feel I am better with him than with you – and so you must understand.' She believed Edward would be a finer monarch without her. 'I am sure you and I would only create disaster together.'[30]

Edward's response was distraught and self-dramatising, as Wallis would have come to expect from his previous behaviour. According to his private secretary, Alan Lascelles, after reading the letter Edward telephoned her and threatened to kill himself. If she did not go with him to Balmoral, the royal family's Scottish castle, as he had asked, he would cut his throat. He followed these threats up with a letter, 'You see I do love you so entirely and in every way Wallis. Madly tenderly adoringly and with admiration and such confidence.'[31] Wallis relented and promised to join him in Scotland for the remainder of the summer.

6

What McMahon's wife Rose (he often called her May) made of his part in the events of 16 July and the days following can only be guessed at.

When her husband was arrested she told the press she would stand by him, as was only to be expected. There was no doubting the strong bond of affection between them, despite the constant strangeness of his behaviour. McMahon's letters from prison to his wife invariably begin 'My dearest May' and end 'Yours lovingly, Jerry', always with a row of crosses signifying kisses. He expresses concern about her health, never fails to compliment her appearance and tells her how important her visits are to his well-being.

But there had clearly been tension in the past over McMahon's secretiveness and his unexplained activities. Not quite spelling out what he meant, he wrote guiltily:

> I really regret that I never availed myself of your valuable help, had I only done so, I may never have got into this awful mess, because I know you would have kept my secrets, but May I loved you far too much to let you know the awful Truth, hence those little differences, when you used to question me as to my doings and absences.[32]

Writing to his parents in Glasgow a few days after the Bow Street hearing, McMahon praised his wife: 'The poor girl is bearing up bravely and has been a tower of encouragement throughout all my difficulties, but for her I would really have given up all thought or care for my future.'[33]

Did he give any clue in his letters, which he could be sure were being read by the prison authorities, about what he had been thinking on 16 July, what had actually been taking place? He was adamant that shooting the king had never been his intention, though a man facing trial on serious charges would hardly say otherwise. On 12 August he wrote to the papal nuncio at St Peter's in Rome (not in London where he was based), protesting about the pope having sent a telegram congratulating Edward on his escape from assassination. 'No such <u>attempt of Assassination was ever made</u>, nor has <u>such a charge been made against me</u>.' He asked the nuncio to pass the letter to Pope Pius XI.[34]

McMahon hinted to one friend that he had more to reveal about the incident and its background than had so far come out. He told William Davie, the proprietor of a social club he frequented (and perhaps had been at the night before the incident), that when the truth was known his action 'will assume a totally different character'. He added, 'I would like when you next throw back a Scotch to please remember me and say a true Scotchman's prayer on my behalf.'[35] To Rose he wrote that his disclosures when he came up for trial at the Old Bailey – 'my trump card' – would be dramatic. 'I am going to accept Mr K's advice to divulge all, though personally I would rather not, as it in my estimation is going to have far-reaching consequences.' Referring obliquely to his contacts with MI5, he added, 'Still my supposed friends have not strictly kept to their promises.'[36]

He played up his new notoriety for all it was worth when he wrote on 19 August to the manager of Lockwood & Bradley, which described itself as 'London's Leading Tailors – Direct from the Mills to the Millions'. McMahon said that he had been a customer of the firm two years previously and wondered if they still had his measurements: he now wished to put in a repeat order. 'The order was Black Jacket, Vest and striped trousers and naturally being thoroughly satisfied I now desire a similar smart outfit, especially in view of my appearance at the Old Bailey.'[37]

McMahon tried to give his wife the impression he was looking forward with confidence to the Old Bailey trial. Once the truth was revealed, all would be well. He wrote on 24 August:

> It will only last a few days, so dearest I do not want you to be there, just carry on at your usual duties and everything will work out satisfactory. One consolation, if one can term it such, is that I cannot possibly get more than 20 years on all charges, but putting all jokes aside, when I play my trump card which is to divulge everything in court, I am confident that I shall be having tea with you just after my trial.[38]

In the meantime, there was a revelation of what the officer leading the investigation, Detective Superintendent Sands (newly promoted from chief inspector), actually knew about the background to the case, as opposed to what he had restricted himself to in his report. It was the story the authorities were still at pains to keep hidden. On 11 September Charles Owen, a detective inspector in A Division, wrote a memorandum describing a conversation he had had two days previously at the entrance to the Old Bailey with William Ashenden, the *Daily Sketch* crime reporter well known to the police. Owen said Ashenden knew he was working with Sands on the investigation and seemed eager to share something he had heard from Kerstein, McMahon's solicitor. Ashenden suggested that facts Kerstein intended to present in McMahon's defence 'would be of an astounding nature'. Owen told Sands that Ashenden had made four points:

(1) That police when searching McMahon's rooms after his arrest had overlooked a number of live cartridges and a list containing the names of numerous persons who had been concerned with McMahon in the outrage.

(2) That McMahon had been (or would be) paid the sum of £150 by German fascists for his part in the affair and had in fact been 'put up' to carry out the attempt by them.

(3) That he had been meeting his co-conspirators in flats and hotels in London, but had double-crossed them and had made use of the occasion to give effective notice to his own personal grievances.

(4) That he had been previously engaged on espionage work for the War Office.

The reporter had, Owen wrote in the memorandum, asked him whether the authorities were aware of these facts and whether they would take steps to have them suppressed at the trial. Owen said he had refused to continue the conversation with Ashenden. Sands and Owen subsequently discussed what Ashenden had said. Sands advised Owen to bring it to the attention of the Director of Public Prosecutions.

What is significant is what Sands wrote on Owen's memorandum when he passed it up the police hierarchy to the assistant chief constable. Sands noted that the methods the *Daily Sketch* reporter used had occasionally been dubious, 'but in this instance, from rumours I have heard from other directions, there is good reason to believe that Ashenden's story is substantially true'.[39] In his investigation of the 16 July incident Sands had, officially, restricted his enquiries to the day itself and the previous twenty-four hours. His report had purposely ignored every-thing that had happened before 15 July, when McMahon had written to the Home Secretary. His hands had been tied by his superiors. But his comment on the memorandum that Ashenden's story was 'sub-stantially true' showed he was well aware of the complete background, including McMahon's contacts with MI5, his possession of a pistol, and that he had warned MI5 and Special Branch there was a conspiracy to kill the king.

7

A few days before McMahon's trial was due to open at the Old Bailey, his solicitor, Alfred Kerstein, and his defence barrister, St John Hutchinson, visited him at Brixton Prison, where he was being held on remand. 'I understand', McMahon wrote to his wife after the meet-ing, 'that if I adopt a certain course the chief charges will be dropped.' Hutchinson advised him to give the matter careful thought before deciding on his course of action.[40] What this course was, he did not say, though it clearly involved saying as little as possible about the back-ground to the charges against him. But if he acted on the suggestion, he must have wondered, how could this be reconciled with his deter-mination to 'divulge all'?

A queue began forming outside the Old Bailey two hours before the opening on 14 September 1936 of what the *Daily Mirror* declared was guaranteed to be 'one of the most sensational court dramas ever heard by a British jury'.[41] Of the over 200 people waiting, only thirty-five were allowed into the courtroom. McMahon – the black coat and grey-striped trousers ordered from his tailors, Lockwood & Bradley, having arrived in time – stood smartly but nervously in the dock, refusing the offer of a seat. He faced one charge under the Firearms Act: unlaw-fully possessing a firearm and ammunition with intent to endanger life. There were two further charges under the Treason Act: presenting at or near the person of the king a revolver with intent to break the public peace; and unlawfully and wilfully producing near the king a revolver with intent to alarm the king. As each of the charges was put to him, McMahon replied 'Not guilty'.

The twelve-strong jury hearing the case in Court No. 1 was made up of nine men and three women. Mr Justice Greaves-Lord, Conservative Member of Parliament for Norwood from 1922 until his appointment as a High Court judge in 1935, presided over the trial. Sir Donald Somervell, Attorney General in the Conservative-dominated national government, led for the prosecution, accompanied by Eustace Fulton (prosecuting counsel in McMahon's 1933 criminal libel trial). St John Hutchinson and John Maude appeared in McMahon's defence.

Outlining the case against McMahon, Somervell told the court, 'So far as the evidence that will be called is concerned, the story starts on July 15.' But, as Somervell knew, the complete story began months before that in April 1936, when McMahon first warned his MI5 contact Ottaway of a plot to kill the king. More recently, on 14 July, McMahon told Ottaway that the attack was about to happen. Somervell was, and always had been, determined to restrict his arguments and the evidence he presented to 15 and 16 July to avoid any reference to McMahon's contacts with MI5 and Special Branch and to their prior knowledge of the attack on Edward.

The trial opened with evidence from the witnesses who had been at the Bow Street hearing on 31 July. Questioned by Fulton, who was assisting the Attorney General with the prosecution, Mary Blencowe, the barmaid at the Two Brewers, repeated that McMahon told her on 15 July, the day before the attack, 'I am going away. Something dreadful has happened. I would like to tell you, but I can't. You will see it in the papers.' Fulton asked, 'Did he say when?' – 'No.' John Remes, the night porter from Brighton, said that when his wife called out, 'An insult to the King, a revolver', he looked to his left and saw McMahon with his arm in the air. Remes said he shouted, 'You swine', and struck out. 'He had his glasses on, but I hit him all the same.'

Lily Yeoman from Leytonstone said that McMahon had pushed his way to the front of the crowd as the king approached. She saw something bright in his hand. The king stopped saluting and stared in the direction of McMahon, whose arm was raised. 'My eyes were rooted to the object from the moment it left his hand until it hit the ground,' Yeoman said. Questioned by the judge, she demonstrated the movement she had observed by raising her hand and bringing it back slightly over her shoulder. Hutchinson, McMahon's barrister, asked, 'There was nothing between McMahon and the King?' – 'No, nothing.' 'If he had wished to, he could quite easily have fired?' – 'That is correct.'

Samuel Green, a retired journalist from Sidcup, described 'the shadow of a hand in front of me, a backhand throw, and then at the horse's legs I saw a pistol.' He had seen McMahon take a picture postcard of the king from his pocket several times. After the police had taken McMahon away, Green picked up the newspaper McMahon had been holding, which had fallen to the ground in the struggle with police and examined it. 'Words written on the margin were: "May, I love you."'

Special Constable Anthony Dick had been hailed as the hero of the day immediately after the 16 July incident for knocking the revolver from McMahon's hand. Metropolitan Police Assistant Commissioner Kendal had summoned him to his Scotland Yard office for personal praise. But now Dick was less certain about what had actually happened. He told the court that as the king approached he saw McMahon's hand in the air. 'I just managed to knock his arm and then I got hold of him.' Somervell asked, 'Can you say whether or not when you knocked his arm the object left it?' – 'I cannot say.' 'Did you see anything thrown?' – 'Yes, in the air it looked like a black object.' So, it now appeared, the weapon may have been thrown rather than knocked from McMahon's grasp.

Hutchinson began cross-examination of Dick: 'After the event – I am not blaming you – the Press and your comrades made you the hero of the occasion?' – 'Unfortunately, yes.' Dick said he could not recall which of McMahon's hands he struck, 'Not with the excitement of the whole thing.' But he was equally certain he had struck McMahon's hand. Hutchinson put it to him that two witnesses who were close to the scene were certain McMahon's hand had not been hit. Dick maintained he was sure he had. Hutchinson asked, 'You do not suggest to me that the pistol was still in his hand when you knocked it?' – 'No.' Mr Justice Greaves-Lord intervened, as if to assist Dick in extricating himself from an awkward position. 'You saw the hand up, which you knocked, but in your opinion a dark object left the hand?' – 'Yes.' 'A pistol was not very far away when you knocked the hand?' – 'No, sir.'

Two officers who had joined Dick in arresting McMahon then gave evidence. Police Constable Ernest Mayne said he saw McMahon rush forward, apparently making for the king. Mayne dashed in, grabbing McMahon by both arms. As he did so he saw a shining object in the air. 'I watched it fall under the forelegs of the King's horse. I could then see distinctly that it was a revolver.' McMahon's counsel, Hutchinson, asked, 'It could not have got as far as it did by someone knocking it out of his hand?' – 'I don't think so.' 'If it had been knocked out of his hand it would, more or less, have fallen near his feet?' – 'Yes.' The third officer who had seized McMahon, Police Constable Thomas Griffiths, repeated what his prisoner had said soon after arrest: 'I could easily have shot him, but threw it instead.' He agreed to Hutchinson's suggestion that the revolver could not have been knocked out of McMahon's hand.

Hutchinson's line of defence was plain. He was working to erase from the jury's mind any idea they may have picked up from newspaper reports and cinema newsreels that McMahon had set out to Constitution Hill on 16 July to assassinate the king. By stressing that the revolver had been thrown by McMahon rather than knocked from his hand – and there seemed to be sufficient evidence from witnesses to justify that – he was reducing McMahon's action that day to a simple, desperate cry for attention. No assassination attempt, no plot.

Hutchinson's questioning of Detective Superintendent John Sands brought MI5's involvement into the open. Hutchinson had subpoenaed John Ottaway of MI5 to attend court as a witness if required. Sands, a police officer with years of experience in stonewalling defence lawyers, proved effective in skirting around what he knew of MI5's relationship with McMahon. Hutchinson asked Sands if he had heard McMahon say at the Bow Street hearing that he had been giving information to the authorities and had obtained a revolver and cartridges for his own protection in 1935. Sands replied that he had not been in court to hear that, but continued, 'I have seen the shorthand notes and have no reason to doubt it.'

Did Sands know that McMahon had shown his revolver to the MI5 officer? Sands's answer was carefully ambiguous. 'I do not know who that may be.' He said he was aware that an MI5 officer had been subpoenaed to appear, but knew no more than that. Did Sands know that McMahon had dealings with that officer? 'No, I do not.' Hutchinson asked, 'Has he, in fact, been in touch with MI5, the secret part of the War Office, since October 1935?' – 'I can say he has been in touch with MI5. I cannot tell you the date or the value or otherwise of the information.'

There followed an exchange which revealed a glaring example of either police incompetence or of total indifference to the seriousness of what was taking place. Hutchinson asked Sands whether he knew that Inspector Cooper visited McMahon on the Tuesday before the incident, 14 July, and Inspector Clarke had followed up this visit the next evening, the day before the attack. Both were Special Branch officers. Sands said he was aware of their visits.

> Hutchinson: 'Do you know that because of something he told them a watch was kept upon him at the Express Dairy?' – 'I do not know. Inspector Clarke's report states that he called at the Express Dairy on Thursday somewhere about one o'clock.'
> Hutchinson: 'That was because of something McMahon told him?' – 'Because of what happened on July 16.'
> Hutchinson: 'Do you mean after the event?' – 'Yes.'
> Hutchinson: 'I suggest that McMahon told Inspector Clarke that something of this sort was going to occur, and the people concerned in it were going to meet in the Express Dairy. Surely he would not turn up after the event, would he?' – 'I cannot tell you what this man told Inspector Clarke.'
> Hutchinson: 'Did he go to the shop because of something McMahon told him?' – 'He was directed to go there by the Commissioner of Police.'

No comment was made on what Sands had said in reply to Hutchinson's questioning: that the Metropolitan Police commissioner had ordered a Special Branch officer to go to the conspirators' meeting place some time *after* the incident. The police had made no effort to go to the Express Dairy on the day and at the time McMahon had told them the plotters could be found there. It was as if everyone – counsel and witnesses – were averting their gaze, unwilling to see what was before their eyes.

Presentation of the prosecution case – Somervell's outline, witness evidence, Hutchinson's cross-examination – had taken two hours. At its conclusion McMahon's counsel Hutchinson submitted to Mr Justice Greaves-Lord that he believed there was no evidence that justified continuing with the Firearms Act charge, possessing a weapon with intent to endanger life. The only two people close by McMahon on Constitution Hill had both testified that if he had intended endangering the king's life he could easily have pulled the trigger. Instead, said Hutchinson, he threw the revolver in such a way that nobody would be hurt.

The judge said the fact remained that here was 'a man under peculiar circumstances in possession of a revolver, loaded in four chambers'. Perhaps McMahon had been intending, as he told Inspector Kidd at Bow Street Court, to make his protest and then shoot himself in front of the king. That, he suggested, was endangering life. Hutchinson's exasperation leaps from the page: 'But surely the Act does not mean killing himself.' Greaves-Lord said he was not so sure about that, but agreed McMahon had posed no direct threat to the king.

Hutchinson then turned to the second charge, one under the Treason Act – presenting a pistol in the presence of the king with intent to break the peace. He asked the judge's opinion on the interpretation of 'present' in this context. Greaves-Lord said his inclination was to see the word meaning to point at. In his view, there was nothing to show McMahon had pointed the weapon directly at the king. (The London *Evening News* headline on 16 July had been 'Man Aims A Revolver At The King'.) Prosecuting counsel Somervell agreed with the judge, saying that having carefully considered that morning's evidence he no longer felt justified in asking the jury to consider the charge against McMahon of intent to endanger life. On the second charge, he said he placed himself in the judge's hands.

Greaves-Lord turned to the jury, telling them that it would be 'your duty, as I am sure it will be your pleasure, to find a verdict of not guilty against the prisoner on the first two counts of the indictment, leaving, of course, the third for your consideration hereafter.' The jury did as they were instructed. The judge then adjourned proceedings for lunch to be taken. What McMahon had forecast in the letter to his wife on 10 September, four days earlier, had come to pass. 'I understand,' he had written, 'that if I adopt a certain course the chief charges will be dropped.'[42]

8

After lunch, McMahon, the only witness the defence proposed to call, went into the dock to tell his story. Hutchinson took him almost at once to his dealings with the intelligence services of a foreign power and with MI5. If McMahon had made a deal, it evidently did not involve saying nothing about the workings of the security service and Special Branch.

In reply to Hutchinson's questions, McMahon – 'quietly-spoken, quietly-dressed' as the *Daily Mirror* put it – said he had been involved with 'a foreign power', unnamed, since late October 1935 and that their London representatives asked him to undertake 'spy work'. A week or so after his initial contact he reported their request to the 'War Office' (which McMahon used as a synonym for MI5) and he kept his security service contact informed. MI5 never paid him anything for his information, he said, but he did take money from the foreign power. Hutchinson asked McMahon about his relationship with MI5: 'How many times were you in touch – I don't want his name – with the gentleman who was dealing with the matter?' – 'He was in touch with me roughly between 30 and 35 times, probably more.'

McMahon told the court his contact with the foreign power had been arranged by an Englishman who was a member of a 'political body' with the same objects as that power. He was then introduced to a diplomat at the embassy, whom he could name. The judge said he saw no reason the individual's identity should be made public unless it was essential to the case. McMahon wrote on a slip of paper which was passed to the judge, the jury and finally to the Attorney General, Somervell. It was not read out in court. The note, the original of which is retained in the National Archives at Kew, says, 'Mr Fitz Randolph – German'.[43]

The man in question, Henry Sigismund Fitzrandolph, was an American-born diplomat, press attaché at the German Embassy in London from 1933 until the eve of war in 1939. MI5 had a file on Fitzrandolph – PF 42931. An enthusiastic Nazi, he reported directly to the propaganda minister, Joseph Goebbels, in Berlin. He was also involved with the Anglo-German Fellowship, a far-right organisation of influential British individuals who had sympathies with the Nazi regime. The Fellowship had been set up following Edward's 1935 speech to the British Legion in which he had welcomed a visit of former servicemen to Germany and called for closer understanding between the two countries. Not a case of cause and effect, but there was certainly a connection.

McMahon said he had also been introduced to a baron at the embassy, whom he could also name (but was not asked to). He could, if required, describe in detail the embassy interior and the room where discussions took place. He also had the names of other people involved at the embassy. As a number of German names were cross-referenced on McMahon's MI5 personal file – Wuhl RL 82783, Heinz PF 19542, Smazi PF 44568, Fitzrandolph PF 42931, Winter PF 43099 – these were presumably the people he was referring to, Fitzrandolph among them. Ottaway, the MI5 officer handling McMahon throughout, subsequently told Harker, his superior officer, 'McMahon never disclosed that he was working for the Germans.'[44] The cross-references to German contacts in McMahon's file suggest MI5 were well aware of his involvement with individual Germans. McMahon may not have mentioned this directly to Ottaway, but it seems unlikely the officer – experienced and long-serving – really did know nothing about this.

McMahon said he had initially been giving the embassy officials information on German refugees in this country. He had kept MI5 informed of this.

Having worked for them in that way for a little time did they then begin to speak to you about your grievance against the police? – Yes. And against authority? – Yes.

You are an Irishman, are you not? – Irish by birth.

Did they speak to you about the rights and wrongs of Ireland? – Yes.

Did they suggest to you that this was not a very pleasant government here? – Yes.

And their system of government was better? – Yes.

Did they try to inflame you against the British government and the British nation? – Yes.

McMahon was certainly going into significant detail about his contacts at the German Embassy and what they were supposed to have said to him. But was he combining two separate elements to add colour to his story – his certainty that he had become involved in a conspiracy with his knowledge of the interior of the embassy, some of the personnel working there, and other conversations he had had? A compulsion to embellish and exaggerate seemed an essential part of McMahon's nature, one that could sometimes undermine even the truth. And why no mention of the Italian Embassy, which even MI5 could confirm he had dealings with?

Hutchinson now took McMahon to the heart of the matter – the plan to attack the king. His contacts, McMahon told the court, proposed that Edward should be assassinated at the Trooping the Colour ceremony, the annual parade at Horse Guards Parade celebrating the monarch's official birthday, held on 23 June in 1936.

Did they suggest that they might be going to make a sudden coup somewhere? – Yes, sir.

Was the idea that if there was a turmoil going on in this country we should be less likely to interfere in foreign affairs? – Yes.

What did they want you to do at the Trooping the Colour? – I was to shoot the King, and I was to get £150 for doing it.

The conspirators abandoned that plan on the day. They then set about preparing an attack on Edward following his presentation of new colours to six Guards battalions in Hyde Park. Hutchinson asked, 'Did you report this to the War Office?' – 'I did, sir.' Why, Hutchinson wanted to know, was McMahon prepared to undertake a risky enterprise of this kind for such relatively small reward? Desperation, McMahon explained. 'They knew my position and had been giving me money from time to time.' He said he took some of the money they offered but told the authorities what was being planned. 'I asked them to listen to my story and send some responsible person to investigate it.' Hutchinson asked, 'You never had any intention of doing it?' – 'No, sir.'

Hutchinson asked McMahon why he carried a gun. 'I was playing a dangerous game,' McMahon replied. 'I was obtaining money from one power and passing information to the British Government, and I was rather afraid.' Had he told the 'person at the War Office'? 'Yes. I showed him the pistol.' He carried the revolver with the chamber next to the barrel empty because he was afraid the weapon might accidentally discharge in his pocket. He had never fired a gun in his life and really knew nothing about how they worked.

McMahon said that when the plans for the Thursday 16 July attack on Constitution Hill were in place, the plotters told him where he should go on the day. He reported this to his MI5 contact on the Monday before, 13 July. Hutchinson reminded McMahon that the officer had been subpoenaed to appear in court and would be available to testify if required, so the story could be checked. 'Did you tell him all the details?' – 'Not all the details. I merely told him what was going to happen.' Subsequently, McMahon went on, two Special Branch officers visited him, Inspector Cooper on Tuesday 14 July and Inspector Clarke on Wednesday, the day before the attack was due to take place. It had been arranged that McMahon should meet other conspirators at the Express Dairy on the morning of 16 July between eight and nine.

Did you tell that to Inspector Clarke? – Yes. He called another man over to verify it. I merely told him that something was going to happen to the King, and could I keep in touch with some responsible official, as I did not want to give my life for nothing.

You say that the War Office knew more or less the details of the plot, and that Inspector Clarke knew what was to happen next day? – Yes.

Did you think they would have you followed? – I did, definitely.

They did not, in fact? – I don't think so.

On the morning of 16 July one of the plotters told McMahon the meeting place had been changed from the Express Dairy to the corner of Kingsway and Holborn. From that point, McMahon was sure he was under surveillance by the conspirators. The previous evening two of them had dictated the letter he sent to Sir John Simon, the Home Secretary. When he telephoned Simon the next morning from the telephone box three plotters stood by the door listening to what he was saying. McMahon said he later realised that the reason the conspirators insisted he should write the letter and make the call was to give the impression the attack was motivated by his grievance against the police. 'You mean so that if you were captured no suspicion would be thrown on anyone but yourself?' Hutchinson asked. 'Yes,' was McMahon's one word reply.

Hutchinson's questioning moved on to the events on Constitution Hill. McMahon agreed that witnesses that morning had been correct in saying he threw the pistol. 'Why did you do that?' – 'Because I did not want to shoot.' The exchange between the two men, lawyer and defendant, became tense and agitated.

Why did you do that? – Well, sir, I thought when they were walking away ... I was determined not to do the thing they were paying me for. I thought if I got rid of it that way I could make a suggestion someone had knocked it out of my hand.

You mean to the people who were employing you? You hoped to be able to prove to them that you, in fact, would have done it if it had not been knocked out of your hand? – Yes.

Had you ever any intention at all of alarming the King? – No, sir. Rather to save him.

Presentation of the defence case ended, one fact stood out: Hutchinson had not called the MI5 officer, Ottaway, though he mentioned he had been instructed to stand by in case he was required as a witness. There were a number of questions he could have asked, particularly about the warnings from McMahon of long-standing plans for an attack. Had failing to call Ottaway been part of the deal Hutchinson had mentioned to McMahon in Brixton Prison before the trial, in return for which the two most serious charges would be dropped? If so, it was an agreement reached behind McMahon's back, as he would later complain.

9

The Attorney General, Somervell, would give McMahon a rougher ride in the witness box that afternoon. But there was a paradox running through the prosecution case. The two most serious charges had been dropped early in the trial. Somervell, though pressing hard in his cross-examination of McMahon, seemed at the same time to be working to downplay the significance of what had happened on Constitution Hill, to minimise the event's importance. Why was that? One historian who has examined closely the drama of Edward's life in 1936 has no doubt: 'In order to allay panic, the story which was officially released at the time spoke only of a pistol being tossed by a malcontented spectator at the King's horse.'[45]

There was an objective far more important than protecting the British public from the idea that anyone would possibly want to assassinate a beloved monarch. The actual purpose was to protect MI5 and the Metropolitan Police Special Branch. The more trivial the threat could be portrayed as having been, the less questioning there would be about the action – or inaction – of these two organisations, both charged with ensuring Edward's safety.

Somervell concentrated on probing the discrepancies between what McMahon had said at Bow Street and what he was saying now, reading out extracts from the earlier testimony to highlight the contradictions. 'You were telling lies on oath.' – 'I was not telling lies.' Somervell put it to McMahon that he had lied about his letter to the Home Secretary, that he had written to Simon because of his grievance against the police and nobody had dictated it to him. McMahon insisted he had been compelled to write.

> That is what you are telling us now. – My life is in danger. I have nothing to hide. Why should I want to fence with you? I will tell the whole truth.
> You swore to tell the whole truth before the magistrate? – Yes.
> From what you are telling us now you did not carry out your oath. – I did, and I am carrying out my oath.

McMahon said his hope had been that by staying quiet immediately after the incident the organisers of the plot would be arrested. 'There was one of them in this court this morning.'

> Somervell: But why did you not tell us? – I did tell, and that is why the life of the King was endangered because they would not pay any attention to me.
> Somervell: I am going to suggest that this story about the plot is the product of your imagination. – I wish to God it were.
> Somervell: I am suggesting that the action you took in Hyde Park was to draw attention to your own grievances. – It was not, sir. Why should I do such a thing?

Somervell reminded McMahon that he had testified he had not been planning to go to Hyde Park until 'Captain' Faulkner mentioned he was taking his son to the ceremony. 'That is a lie?' he asked. McMahon admitted it was. But he denied demanding payment for information on the proposed attack on the king. His only concern was getting a guarantee his wife would be looked after. Mr Justice Greaves-Lord intervened, giving the impression from what he said and the manner in which he spoke that he had forgotten his role and was acting for the prosecution:

Have you always said you are a loyal subject? Have you always said
both at the police court and otherwise and in the two petitions – one
to King George and one to the present King – that you are a loyal
subject? Do you think it is the act of a loyal subject – knowing of a
plot against his King – to say that he would not disclose it unless he
received money?

McMahon again denied he had asked for money, repeating that his concern had been for his wife's safety. Greaves-Lord asked, 'Did you say that
you would not give information unless you were guaranteed of that?'
– 'No, I did not.' Somervell jumped in. 'You have just told me you did.'
– 'I do not know how to put it into words. I naturally expected my wife
would be looked after if I was deliberately throwing my life away.'

As Somervell's cross-examination proceeded, it became increasingly
obvious that his tactic was to undermine McMahon over small issues
while avoiding as far as he could the crucial point: that McMahon had
warned both MI5 and Special Branch of the plot to kill the king, but
they had done nothing to prevent this. Somervell, however, found he
had no choice but to touch on this aspect of the case, hoping by doing
so to dispose of it quickly. 'Enquiries were made on the purported information you gave in April, and the authorities were satisfied there was
nothing whatever in your story.' – 'That may be their view.' McMahon
now forced the reality of what had been happening into the open:

> The very fact that I was able to do a thing after their knowing of it
> going to happen shows there is no safety guaranteed for the King in
> his own country.
> The only danger to the King came from yourself. – Yes, because of
> the bungling of the officials. I am not pleading for mercy. I do not
> want mercy. I am more safe in prison than outside it. You did not
> want me to come in and give evidence. You wanted to give me a light
> sentence. Why was that offer made to me but to hide the bungling of
> other people?

Somervell replied lamely, 'No one wants to hide anything.' But the final exchange between the two, the Attorney General and McMahon, had shone a light on the central fact. The danger to Edward had come about through the incompetence or indifference of the authorities responsible for the king's security: MI5 and Special Branch. Every effort was once again being made to obscure that.

Questioned for a second time by his defence counsel, Hutchinson, McMahon was agitated, at times almost incoherent. He accused both the police and the prosecution of 'bungling' and making 'a mess of it'. He said he had told the truth throughout. 'As God is my judge, I have nothing to gain in not telling the truth.' Wiping perspiration from his forehead, McMahon told the court, 'I want to go to prison. I want you to give me the heaviest sentence you possibly can. It is only by remaining in prison that I can save my life.' Hutchinson asked from whom he needed protection. 'From the people I have given away.'

Somervell's final speech for the prosecution was perfunctory, writing McMahon off as no more than a liar. McMahon, the Attorney General said, tells one tale one week and another a few weeks later. Somervell decided which one was the truth, telling the jury to believe what the prisoner had told the magistrate at Bow Street in July, that there was no conspiracy. 'One thing is clear – a man who treats the oath in that way is a wholly unreliable person … I ask you to accept the broad story he told at the police court rather than the improbable story he has told today.' McMahon, he said, had been trying to draw attention to his grievance against the police and had chosen to do this by 'throwing a weapon at the head of a procession … an act calculated to cause alarm'.

Hutchinson had a far more difficult task. He had to convince the jury that while McMahon had indeed gone to Hyde Park carrying a loaded revolver and that he had thrown the weapon in the king's direction, his purpose had not been to alarm the king. There was, Hutchinson needed to argue, a reason for McMahon's action that day, one the jury should try to understand. It was true, he told the court, that McMahon had a grievance and that – as the prosecution insisted – was one part of the story. But, he went on:

Why, if this is the true story, has this man not adhered to it? You may think he is muddle-headed, not quite normal, but why on earth, when this man has a perfectly good story that would have enabled him to escape, if not altogether, comparatively lightly – why on earth has he substituted for it a story which I admit is more difficult for you to believe?

Hutchinson admitted what McMahon had told the court was fantastic, but that in itself did not make it untrue. McMahon, he said, had been employed by a foreign power and he had told the authorities about this. He had offered names, all of which could be checked by the 'secret police', and had written down the name of one embassy official. McMahon was an Irishman with a grievance against this country, and Irishmen 'were supposed to have been nurtured in hatred against Great Britain'. Could the plotters, Hutchinson asked, have found a better candidate than such a desperate individual? 'He was a man absolutely down and out. They excited him, pushed and urged him on.'

Hutchinson appealed to the jury's sense of logic: 'Why did he go and tell the Secret Service at the War Office that something was going to happen if it was untrue? If he was going to throw something for a grievance they might have prevented him doing it.' The really alarming aspect of the case, Hutchinson concluded, was that the police had not kept McMahon under observation, despite the danger the king might face. 'Let us hope if this case has done nothing else, it will teach the police that it is worth while to send out one man to watch a man, whether they believe or do not believe the story.'

Summing up, Mr Justice Greaves-Lord said a distinction had to be made between making a protest and causing alarm. 'Does a man who wants merely to make a protest go into a public place with a revolver loaded in four chambers out of five?' he asked. Surely throwing a weapon was calculated to cause alarm. He took up the prosecution's main theme about the different stories McMahon had to tell. 'From the defence at the police court no one could possibly gather any story of the nature as they heard in the witness box today. Not a word about that extraordinary story was said.' It was for the jury to determine whether

McMahon's intention had been to cause alarm or whether he was – as he claimed – attempting to deceive 'those who had employed him' that he had tried to play his part in the plot.

The jury took just ten minutes to find McMahon guilty of unlaw-fully and wilfully producing a revolver with intent to alarm the king. Greaves-Lord said he well understood why the jury had not been misled by McMahon's tale. But the judge left one thing in the air: if McMahon's story was so blatantly absurd why had the prosecution not called Ottaway to refute it, to say what exactly had led MI5 to reject McMahon's claim of a conspiracy as beyond belief? If the authorities were hesitant to put an MI5 officer in the witness box because of a question of security, the court could have been cleared and his evidence given *in camera*. Why the reluctance?

The judge told McMahon, 'I do not want, and I am not going to make you into a sort of fancied hero.' To ensure that did not happen, Greaves-Lord said, he would sentence him to – at this point McMahon turned away and was forced to face the judge by two accompanying prison officers – twelve months' imprisonment, with hard labour. The *Daily Mirror* injected a final piece of colour: 'The sound of his lame foot falling on the stone steps leading to the cells echoed through the silent court room.' But a *Times* leader adopted a more sinister tone. Events had shown, the newspaper declared, 'Not even the King can be put beyond the reach of every conceivable danger.'[46]

10

The writer Compton Mackenzie (who had served as an MI6 officer in Greece during the First World War) noted a suspicion among sections of the public that there was more to the story than had come out in court. He recounted a rumour circulating after McMahon's trial that 'the whole business was deliberately arranged by the authorities to give them an excuse to insist on the King's paying better attention to his personal safety.'[47] Though this was wide of the mark, the signs were there that a natural scepticism alerted some people at least to oddities in the trial and in the behaviour of MI5 and the police. It should be added that Mackenzie had little sympathy with MI5. They kept a file on him following publication in 1932 of his book *Greek Memories*, which revealed awkward secrets about MI6 and MI5 wartime activities. By coincidence, when he was prosecuted under the Official Secrets Act his defence had been led by McMahon's counsel, Hutchinson.

Special Branch and MI5 were equally worried about possible public criticism and reacted at once to the remarks McMahon's counsel had made in his closing speech. They jointly leaked information to the *Daily Express*, with direct quotations intended to give the tale the necessary air of authority. 'I understand', an *Express* reporter wrote, 'that Scotland Yard Special Branch and MI5 – the secret service – investigated McMahon's "plot" before the 16 July incident, and reached the conclusion that McMahon was "imaginative, makes statements that cannot be relied on".' Official buffoons were obviously at work and the leak continued with a combination of a glaring lie and unintentional comedy.

> Scotland Yard officers shadowed him constantly. He had been shadowed for three days when, on the morning of July 16, the detectives posted themselves outside McMahon's house long before the hour at which he usually left home, found that he had left at 6.45am. These and subsequent events in the search for McMahon before his arrest at Constitution Hill shortly before 1pm were afterwards the subject of a Scotland Yard inquiry.[48]

The absurdity of what the authorities were feeding the *Daily Express* reporter showed the extent of their desperation. If the police had been convinced McMahon's past statements were 'imaginative' and unreliable, why were they now trying to claim they had wasted police resources by putting men on his tail for three days? But if it were decided that on this occasion his story was believable, the least that could have been expected was that police officers were outside his home at whatever time he left. The police had not shadowed McMahon and, as Detective Superintendent Sands revealed in his evidence, they had even delayed going to the Express Dairy cafeteria, where McMahon had told them the conspirators were due to meet, until after the attack had taken place.

The *Daily Mirror*, meanwhile, used the reaction of McMahon's wife to squeeze as much human interest from the trial as possible:

'Whatever it means to me I shall stick by my husband.' With that resolution helping her to fight back the tears from her eyes, brunette Rose McMahon heard last night that her husband, George Andrew McMahon, had been sentenced to twelve months' hard labour for producing a pistol with intent to alarm the King.[49]

After McMahon's dramatic outburst from the Old Bailey dock – 'It is only by remaining in prison that I can save my life' – there was no telling how he would respond to his conviction and sentence. Twelve months was, in the circumstances, remarkably lenient. Another Old Bailey judge had, after all, given him double that term in 1933 for defaming police officers. Calling two police sergeants corrupt was, on the face of it, a less alarming act than confronting the monarch with a loaded pistol. Following a meeting with his client in Wandsworth Prison in the evening, solicitor Alfred Kerstein told reporters, 'In view of his assertion in court today that he would be safer in prison, I am not sure that he will want to appeal.' Kerstein added that Mrs McMahon had gone into seclusion to avoid further attention from reporters.[50]

Scotland Yard's appeal in the press for witnesses to the 16 July attack had attracted a wide range of eccentrics, pranksters and even a few people who genuinely believed they had useful information to impart. As McMahon came to trial there had been a further trickle of letters. The most intriguing was from Belfast, addressed to 'Mr Justice Greaves-Lord or Sir D. Somervell'. On 18 September Somervell passed the letter to Harker at MI5. 'I do not suppose it is true, but it would be rather amusing if it was,' Somervell wrote in a covering note. The two-page handwritten letter was dated 14 September, the day of McMahon's trial, and was from D. Gilligan at the Union Hotel, Belfast.[51]

Gilligan offered what he said was 'new information' on the background to the threat McMahon had posed to the king:

I was associated with McMahon as an Irish colleague in London. He had 'Left' political views, and when the Italo-Abyssinian trouble began some members of the Union of Democratic Control (a Left-wing organisation) got into touch with him, and it was decided that if £150 of the subscribers' money were passed to McMahon and the latter handed it to the British Govt. (alleging it was from Italian conspirators) it would inevitably prejudice the Govt. against Italy during the Abyssinian trouble which the U. of Dem. Control was deeply interested in). Italy actually had nothing whatever to do with the £150. No attempt was planned against the King – not even by McMahon. The whole thing was simply a stunt to prejudice the British Govt. against Italy.

Gilligan said he was surprised the prosecution seemed to be taking McMahon's story about his contacts at the Italian Embassy seriously and doubted McMahon had genuinely planned an attack on the king. The entire affair, he said, was partly a Union of Democratic Control 'stunt' and partly a ruse to give McMahon the opportunity to air his grievance against the police and win a notoriety that would help sell his magazine and a book he hoped to write as a follow-up.

Harker replied to Somervell on 22 September, 'I am looking into this but it sounds too good to be true.' He said that the British Union of Fascists and National Socialists had forwarded to the Home Office another letter Gilligan had written the same day, 14 September. MI5 now had a copy.[52] Gilligan's letter to Mosley's BUF was tailored to specifically interest fascists. 'It is dangerous to allow a precedent to be established for this form of agent provocateur! Think of the frame-up against Italy. Do you remember how this same Union of Dem. Control perpetrated a frame-up against you years ago with a false blue pamphlet outside the Albert Hall purporting to be B.U.F. literature?'[53]

The Union for Democratic Control (UDC) had been formed in 1914 as a pressure group opposing secret diplomacy, which the movement's supporters believed had led to the outbreak of war. By 1917 it had become a mass movement, with over 650,000 followers. Many of its prominent activists were Labour or Liberal Party members. By the 1930s support had waned and UDC emphasis was opposition to the Fascist regime in Italy and to Nazi Germany. MI5 had kept a close watch on the UDC since its establishment and suspected the organisation's secretary, Dorothy Woodman, an active Labour Party member, was also a Soviet agent. Harker asked Maxwell Knight, the head of MI5's M Section – which had agents penetrating both the Communist Party and the British Union of Fascists – to 'make discreet enquiries' through a contact in the UDC.[54]

Whatever report, if any, emerged from M Section's enquiries was destroyed in the weeding of McMahon's MI5 file, but Gilligan's accusation against the UDC seemed groundless and no more was heard of it. What was interesting was the concerted attempt still apparently being made, whether officially or not, to distance Italy from the events of 16 July 1936. In July, immediately after the Constitution Hill attack, the Italian Embassy tried to discredit anything McMahon had to say by feeding the Foreign Office the story about a spurious assassination plot against Mussolini. Gilligan appeared to be up to the same trick from a different angle.

11

By his second day in Wandsworth Prison the always unpredictable McMahon had changed his mind about appealing against his conviction. He wrote to his wife from his cell on 15 September:

> I do trust that you were not unduly perturbed by yesterday's unpleasant happening. The blow fell with less severity than I anticipated especially after the Judge's vehement summing up. Naturally I was surprised that he did not give full vent to his ill-concealed bias.

But, McMahon said, he had decided to challenge the trial result, reminding her of his successful appeal in 1933. 'They had their way once before, and they "ate humble pie". They will do so once more than ever, within a short time.' He said the true story had been suppressed in court, but he would be vindicated.[55]

McMahon had obviously discussed appealing with Kerstein, who told a *Daily Mirror* reporter the same day the main ground would be misdirection by Mr Justice Greaves-Lord. The judge, he said, had informed the jury that 'McMahon's story had been told at the Old Bailey for the first time, whereas the evidence was unchallenged that McMahon had told the same story to the War Office several months before.'[56] McMahon continued to claim that his act had not been motivated by his grievance against the police but was an attempt to thwart a conspiracy. The British public, he told his wife, would not tolerate 'a bungling and incompetent administration that will not even exert themselves to try and save their own Sovereign, King Edward'.[57]

However confident McMahon tried to appear when writing to his wife, he must have realised an appeal stood no chance of success. Mr Justice Greaves-Lord had given McMahon a relatively short sentence on the mildest of the three charges he had originally faced. Any ordinary criminal would consider himself lucky to have escaped so lightly. Kerstein shared his doubts, but both continued in what was essentially a time-wasting exercise. Home Office officials suspected McMahon and Kerstein were simply seeking further publicity. On 17 September McMahon wrote to the Home Office from Wandsworth Prison asking for a visit from a 'responsible official' as he had an important matter he wanted to discuss. The Home Office replied telling him to put anything he had for them to consider in writing.

McMahon wrote again on 23 September. His letter suggested he was hoping to by-pass the legal system. In his typically inflated style, McMahon claimed there were 'numerous people who appear most anxious to assist me in my fight to vindicate myself'. But, 'despite all that I would ultimately gain when the full facts became public' he believed it was necessary to do what was right for his country and his wife. 'I know', he wrote – and what he said could only be taken as a veiled threat – 'that considerable "diplomatic" discord may accrue if my true story is published, and after all no matter how turbulent we all may be we nevertheless all seek peace.'[58] Was he bluffing?

McMahon said he was 'prepared to sign a confession which will appease everyone on condition that I am allowed to enter some approved Religious Home where I can be permitted to meet my dear wife'. He would remain there for as long as the authorities demanded, he would pass over all documents he had left in the hands of 'certain custodians', and would cancel any contracts he had entered into with the foreign press or publishers' agents. The final threat must have seemed a clever one to McMahon. Nobody, he said, knew he was writing in this way, not even his legal advisers.

When Carew Robinson, a senior civil servant in the Home Office Criminal Division, sent a copy of the letter over to MI5, Harker at once saw it for what it was. He told Robinson on 25 September he had discussed McMahon's suggestion with his director, Vernon Kell, and his opinion was to have nothing more to do with 'this individual'. Harker concluded, 'Our view is that he is simply out to make trouble, and in the classic words of the Duke of Wellington our answer is "Publish and be damned!"'[59]

Kerstein now took his turn in a ploy he and McMahon had surely worked on together. He wrote to the Home Secretary – still Sir John Simon – on 29 September to say his client had been unable to tell the full story at the Old Bailey about the assassination plot as doing so would have endangered international relations. McMahon had therefore been prevented from putting up a solid defence and he would be unable to put his actual case to the Court of Criminal Appeal. Consequently, Kerstein demanded, McMahon should either be given a free pardon or have the remainder of his sentence remitted.[60]

McMahon would have been flattered to hear about the flurry of meetings involving Robinson of the Home Office, Harker of MI5 and the Director of Public Prosecutions, Sir Edward Atkinson, to discuss his and Kerstein's suggestions. Their conclusion was that as McMahon was seeking leave to appeal the case was *sub judice* and the Home Office was precluded from becoming involved. Carew Robinson had a clear-cut opinion on what McMahon and Kerstein were up to, setting it out in a memorandum:

The Director suggests, and I agree, that we ought not to be drawn into any discussion with Mr Kerstein, and that the less said to him the better. There is reason to believe that McMahon's defence was financed by newspapers, and that Mr Kerstein was expected to conduct it on lines which would provide good 'copy' ... It is not unlikely that Mr Kerstein, expecting that nothing further can be brought out in the Court of Criminal Appeal, is anxious to get the Secretary of State to do or say something which would make sensational reading and round which further stories could be built.[61]

On 16 October a Home Office civil servant wrote to Kerstein to say the Secretary of State was unable to intervene in any way, dismissing both his and McMahon's suggestions. For McMahon, everything now rested on his appeal.

In the midst of these brazen attempts to find a way round the legal system, McMahon wrote to his wife on 3 October: 'I was delighted in many ways through your visit on Sat. but especially the fact that you were your old charming self with that ever-present sparkle in your eyes, acted as a decided tonic.'[62] A fortnight later he said he understood only too well that she was 'suffering even more than I through this unhappy phase of our union, but dearest, do cheer up with that epigramatical thought that circumstances such as we experience at present "Could be much worse".'[63]

McMahon meanwhile told Kerstein that what he thought needed to be stressed in his appeal was that Ottaway had time and time again guaranteed him immunity from prosecution if he continued to co-operate with MI5.[64] Kerstein asked for more information about this. McMahon's reply on 12 October was rambling and ungrammatical but his main points were plain enough. There is a ring of truth about them:

When I was discussing details of the plot with Mr. O. the question of my future welfare was raised. He – Mr O. – said 'that I would be well looked after'. I was not however fully satisfied with this and suggested a written guarantee. Mr. O. then said he would have to see his superiors, two days later, he came to see me, and mentioning his difficulty in getting in touch with the necessary high superior, as the reason for delay then said, 'It's alright "Mac", no matter what happens you will be looked after and protected, only my superiors cannot suggest the advisability of giving anything in writing'. At this I demurred. He then said 'You have my word that my superiors will cover you up'. I then said supposing the persons concerned are arrested, and I, as must of necessity be also arrested. What can I say of your promise? He answered 'Surely old chap you accept my word.' (And I honestly did and yet do accept Mr. O. word) He also emphasised that his superior authority was the highest in this country, meaning I presume that their word carried weight. There was also a suggestion that if the necessity of my arrest arose, I would be secretly conveyed to a safe haven.[65]

MI5's reluctance to commit themselves in writing was understandable, but McMahon, who – as Kell, the director, had acknowledged – had been supplying worthwhile information, was equally justified in expecting an officer's promise would be honoured. Ottaway subsequently gave a careful response when he was asked to comment on McMahon's claim, not quite evasive but not quite to the point. It was true, he agreed, that in April 1936 he had told McMahon, 'every protection by the authorities would be afforded him.' But matters had moved on by July. 'McMahon's story on the 13th July was altogether different to that told me in April, but no promise or assurance was given him on the last occasion.'[66] For any kind of a promise to be given at any time implied McMahon had been seen as a useful informant and not the unreliable eccentric he had been portrayed as in court. McMahon may rightly have assumed that an undertaking once made remained an undertaking, but there must have seemed little point in pursuing the matter.

Setting out on a different tack, McMahon complained to Kerstein that Hutchinson's conduct of his defence at the Old Bailey had been inadequate. The failure to call Ottaway, the MI5 officer central to the case, would surely have been uppermost in his mind. Ottaway had been in a position to confirm much of what McMahon claimed in court, though he may have refused to reveal what he knew on security grounds. 'I have been pondering over many details of my trial,' McMahon wrote on 12 October, 'and despite the fact that I hate to do so, cannot but conclude that Mr St Hutchinson completely ruined my defence.' He said he would prefer that Hutchinson did not represent him in his appeal application. 'I will put forward my own case, and no matter how much I may "muck it up" to use a parlance I cannot do worse than Mr H.'[67]

On 26 October three judges at the Royal Courts of Justice gave their decision on McMahon's request for leave to appeal. He was not represented in court. Lord Chief Justice Hewart, who had ordered McMahon's release from custody in the libel case in 1933, supervised the hearing. McMahon, denied permission to attend and waiting in his cell at Wandsworth Prison for news, may have felt a surge of hope when he found Hewart was involved. He was to be disappointed.

Hewart noted that McMahon 'raises no complaint, naturally enough, of the very lenient sentence which was passed'. McMahon, he said, had admitted throwing the pistol and at Bow Street claimed he was acting on a grievance. At the Old Bailey he continued to admit his action but his defence was new and entirely unrelated to what he had told the magistrate. 'The gist of the story,' Lord Chief Justice Hewart continued, 'was that he had been in touch with some foreign power who wanted him to act as a spy, and he reported that fact to the War Office, and he received money from that power …' This was true, as MI5 would have confirmed if Ottaway had been called to give evidence at the trial. Hewart continued, 'It was, he said, suggested that he should attack His Majesty the King so that he might kill him …' Once again, McMahon had told MI5 this before the 16 July incident and Ottaway could have confirmed at the Old Bailey trial that he, MI5 Director Kell and the Metropolitan Police Special Branch were all aware of the plot.

Not fully aware of the actual course of events in the months and weeks before 16 July – or if he did know, choosing to ignore them – Lord Chief Justice Hewart described McMahon's testimony at the Old Bailey as a 'cock-and-bull story'. He concluded, 'This man has been three times previously convicted of fraud … The application is dismissed.'[68] The implication was that as McMahon had past convictions for fraud, nothing he said could be ever relied on as he was incapable of telling the truth.

V

Afterlives

1

Prison was no new experience for McMahon. In 1927 he had served sixty days at Glasgow's notoriously harsh Barlinnie for embezzlement. He went on in 1933 to do seven weeks of a twelve months' sentence in Wandsworth for criminal libel before the Court of Criminal Appeal ordered his release. He settled into life back in Wandsworth in 1936, despite the disappointment of judges rejecting his request for leave to appeal in October. McMahon was held on the medical wing for a time. The prison doctor reported that while he did not consider the prisoner certifiably insane, he did have concerns that McMahon was 'quite unreliable' and often drifted 'into a state of phantasy whence he emerges with his persecutory ideas woven into a tissue of malicious defamation of others'.[1]

The doctor was probably going too far in taking the police view of events. McMahon had exposed corruption among Notting Hill detectives, had been wrongly imprisoned, and had been denied compensation. He had been sacked from a job, had difficulty securing accommodation for himself and his wife, and had lost access to a free office, all because of continuing police harassment. A sense of persecution on McMahon's part was perhaps understandable in the circumstances.

Once he was confirmed as being at least physically fit, McMahon was given a job in the prison library and passed much of his sentence working there. 'Everyone was very kind to me,' he later said. 'I have no complaints about my treatment.'[2] One connection McMahon made in Wandsworth enabled him to set out a version of his life, as well as giving full expression to his taste for melodrama. A retired army officer and visiting justice of the peace at the prison, Lieutenant Colonel Cecil Bevis, came into contact with McMahon and they spoke regularly during his sentence.

On 1 April 1937 McMahon wrote his long letter to Bevis, setting out what he said was a record of his past – the closest he ever came to an autobiography – and of his hopes on release. He was, McMahon said, writing 'to a gentleman who I know can understand that the truth can often by stated by one who, though wearing a felon's garb and in a prison cell, is still possessed of a soul'.[3]

McMahon portrays himself as a sensitive individual, a constant victim of misunderstanding and the vindictiveness of others. 'I, even now,' he wrote, 'bear no real malice against anyone, because I have gained something which I do not believe I could ever possibly have gained except through this unpleasant phase of my life. I refer to my new belief in God.' The old lag's remorse gambit, with violins in the background. His only wish, he said, was for a peaceful life, perhaps in a religious community abroad. 'I feel that the strain of everyday life is unsuited to my nature.'[4]

> However, dear sir, my real reason for writing to you is that you will please see your way clear to grant me the honour of accepting my avowal that I was not guilty of attempting in any way to alarm H.M. King Edward, and that should anything happen to me in the future you will kindly see that my dear wife will not be denied a chance to exist. She is a most wonderful woman.[5]

McMahon returns again to the 'documents' referred to in the letter he wrote to the Home Office on 23 September 1936 offering a 'confession which will appease everyone'. He asks Bevis whether he can pass these papers to him when he is released from Wandsworth. Having read them, McMahon says, Bevis will be in no doubt there has been a miscarriage of justice. Bevis did not react to this but asked McMahon if he could pass a copy of the letter to MI5, as there were a number of references to the security service. McMahon agreed. Surprisingly, given that it contained McMahon's life story, or a version of it, Bevis told MI5's head, Vernon Kell, 'There is nothing much in the letter but I think it should be, or a copy of it, attached into his dossier.'[6]

After working through McMahon's letter to Bevis, Harker extracted what appeared to him to be the most relevant, and possibly damaging, sections to MI5. He asked Ottaway, the officer who had been dealing with McMahon between October 1935 and July 1936, to comment. Ottaway, who by now had left the service, replied to Harker in a handwritten letter from his home in Essex on 10 June 1937.[7] The first of Harker's worries was whether MI5 should have been aware that McMahon had contact with the German Embassy, a fact which had come out at the Old Bailey trial in September 1936. Ottaway said McMahon had 'never disclosed that he was working for the Germans'. While it is true there are no direct references to German contacts in Ottaway's notes on McMahon's file, there are a number of cross-references to Germans who were certainly of interest to MI5. The possibility of a connection could not be denied.

Next came McMahon's claim that he had desperately wanted to break his contact with the Italian Embassy but that Ottaway had persuaded him to carry on, promising he would be protected. Ottaway agreed with this in his reply to Harker:

> During my contact with him he did express fear in furnishing information to the Italians and that in consequence he was inclined to finish with them, but I assured him everything would be well provided he told me all they wanted and before replying to let me know what his replies were to be.

This response confirmed McMahon had been working as a double agent: learning from the Italians what they wanted to know, informing Ottaway, then passing whatever MI5 thought was suitable to the Italian Embassy. As McMahon persistently claimed, this was indeed a dangerous position for him to be in. The reality contrasted sharply with the impression the authorities had put about that McMahon was an unimportant individual with a petty grievance who had suddenly arrived on the scene one day. Ottaway said McMahon had agreed to continue his work, but he thought McMahon had never told MI5 everything.

Ottaway agreed with McMahon's statement in the letter to Bevis: 'I was in constant contact with MI5 from late 1935.' McMahon wrote, 'I passed over certain papers which were found to be useful.' Ottaway's reply was studiedly ambiguous, intended to cover his own back as much as MI5's. 'Any papers passed to me were apparently of little importance, except to corroborate his statements which I duly reported.' On McMahon's disclosure to him in April 1936 of a plot to shoot the king, Ottaway's response was as bland as he could make it. 'When he told me of the plot to assassinate the King I pointed out to him that it was a matter for the police and that they would be informed.'

What comes across is the concern MI5's senior officers felt about what McMahon might say once he was free to speak. He had no intention of keeping his mouth shut and MI5's vulnerability lay in the fact that so much had been hidden to mislead the public. The Old Bailey trial had been an exercise in minimising the 16 July incident's significance to obscure the extent to which MI5 and Special Branch had known what was about to happen that day. Harker commented on Ottaway's letter to Kell. 'I do not think there is anything more we can now do. If and when the question is raised, we have got a perfectly good answer.'[8] He did not say what precisely 'the question' was, but it did not need much reading between the lines. Kell's brief response, in red ink, was 'Let me know when McMahon comes out of prison.'[9] Harker telephoned the Prison Commission and an official agreed he would inform MI5 a few days before McMahon's release.

As the Prison Commission had promised, an officer contacted MI5 on 6 August 1937 to alert them that McMahon would leave Wandsworth the following week, on Thursday 12 August. McMahon said he wanted to avoid Friday the thirteenth being his first day of liberty and the prison governor had agreed. He was released quietly, with no public announcement, at 6 p.m. to prevent crowds gathering. The *Daily Express*, with whom the McMahons and Kerstein had an exclusive arrangement, splashed the story – written by Lindon Laing – across the following day's front page.[10]

Waiting at the prison gates with Laing and Kerstein for her husband to appear, McMahon's 'brown-eyed, rosy-cheeked wife' told the reporter, 'I shall take him away and nurse him. My poor Jerry! I know what he has suffered in there.' McMahon walked to freedom wearing the black coat and striped trousers he had ordered from Lockwood & Bradley for his performance at the Old Bailey. Laing had choreographed the scene well. Mrs McMahon took a watch from her handbag, strapping it on her husband's wrist; then a ring, which she slipped on his finger. On cue, McMahon smiled. 'Now we are married again.' The happy couple sped from Wandsworth in the *Daily Express* car, holding hands, off to an exclusive interview with Laing.

What he wanted above all, McMahon said, was to vindicate himself. He would write a letter of explanation to the king, something the prison authorities had prevented him from doing. He would go to Scotland to hide away with his wife, to whom, he said, he had caused so much pain and humiliation. 'I know how she has suffered. People used to say, "There is the wife of the man who tried to shoot the King".'

> I never intended to shoot the King. But there was a plot to kill him. My life in London brought me into touch with many strange characters, and it was because of my association with political refugees and others that I carried a revolver … I want to keep out of the under-world of intrigue. But I hope I shall be left alone to go my own way with my wife. I am thinking of going to some other part of the Empire so that I can start a new life.

Shortly after McMahon regained his liberty a rumour began circulating that Edward had given him money to help in his resettlement. When the story reached him, Edward was amused. 'He is about the last man I would help.'[11] It seemed just the kind of tale McMahon himself would enjoy spreading.

A few weeks after his release McMahon wrote to the new Home Secretary, Sir Samuel Hoare, from a hotel in Rothesay. He said he would shortly be returning to London to make arrangements to travel abroad. He reminded Hoare of the fears he had expressed at his Old Bailey trial. He said he believed the plotters against Edward still posed a danger.

> I am a rather sick man and wish to avoid any possible trouble. Will you therefore please allow someone to protect me as in view of certain past happenings I am somewhat afraid, not really for my own safety but that of my dear wife who has already suffered so much.[12]

The Home Office passed the letter to the police. An officer noted in an already bulging file that McMahon's request should not be treated seriously as it was 'a product of the state of egoism'.[13] McMahon showed no sign of leaving the country and in October police recorded that he and his wife were living in a flat at 215 Gloucester Terrace. 'So far as can be discovered McMahon has no fixed employment; he is said to spend much of his time about newspaper offices in Fleet Street.'[14]

2

Edward's life had passed through a dramatic transformation while McMahon was serving his sentence in Wandsworth Prison between September 1936 and August 1937. Having survived in the summer of 1936 what could so easily have been an assassination, the king was on the path that would enable the political and royal establishment to finally remove him from the throne. *The Week*, a privately circulated news sheet produced by the well-informed journalist and Communist sympathiser Claud Cockburn, referred to 'disgruntled former Palace influences' who 'circulate, and allow to circulate, rumours which depict the King as unconstitutional and headstrong. From these aristocratic mileux flow a continual stream of tit-bits to swell the rumours.'[15]

It was one of these 'influences' who planted in the American press a story that George V's widow, Queen Mary, was moving from Buckingham Palace – where Edward as king would live – to Marlborough House in protest over her son's friendship with Mrs Simpson, which then had to be officially denied.[16] In fact, Edward had been reluctant to move from the bachelor comfort of York House at St James's Palace to the vast formality of Buckingham Palace. He later recalled that he never felt he belonged there and, with the benefit of hindsight, 'Somehow I had a feeling that I might not be there very long.'[17]

Whatever tales disgruntled courtiers might be feeding to the press, Edward was more than capable of generating unpopularity on his own account. Following the king's telephone suicide threat on 16 September, Wallis had agreed to join him at Balmoral, the royal holiday home, after their eventful Adriatic and Aegean cruise. On 23 September he drove from the castle to Aberdeen station to pick up Mrs Simpson and her American friends, Herman and Katherine Rogers, on their arrival by train from London. His brother, the Duke of York, meanwhile, was officially opening a new wing at the nearby Aberdeen Royal Infirmary after Edward had declared himself unavailable. A local newspaper highlighted the brothers' contrasting sense of duty. The American news magazine *Time* reported that shortly afterwards angry Aberdeen citizens had chalked streets with the message 'Down with the American Harlot'.[18]

The king and Mrs Simpson entertained his guests at Balmoral with films of the fun the couple and their companions had had on their summer holiday, lounging on the *Nahlin*, strolling through the streets of Athens and Istanbul, surrounded by adoring crowds. As *Time* put it: 'All this was news to most of the assembled Dukes and Duchesses ... for such scenes have been kept from the British newspaper-reading and newsreel-viewing public by a form of British self-censorship.'[19] Not quite. The dukes and duchesses were all too aware of the relationship, but the bulk of the British public were kept in the dark about what was about to explode into a crisis. For popular consumption, Edward's place on the throne was secure and on 1 September 1936 the first postage stamps bearing his head were issued, though as yet no coins. 'Miners and East Enders, however,' one historian comments, 'knew nothing about their monarch's foibles, his pro-Fascist leanings, his calamitous selfishness – or Wallis Simpson.'[20]

But there was nothing to prevent American newspaper and magazine readers from enjoying the spectacle, particularly in view of

Mrs Simpson's heritage, as British politicians knew. The Labour MP Ellen Wilkinson, prominent in the recent Jarrow unemployed march, asked the president of the Board of Trade, Walter Runciman: 'Can he state why in the case of two American magazines of high repute imported into the country within the last few weeks, at least two and sometimes three pages have been torn out? Can he say what is this thing the British public is not allowed to read?' Runciman batted the question aside.[21]

What the British public was denied the chance to read was the build-up to a final confrontation between politicians and the king, but there was still gossip. Wallis wrote to Edward on 14 October that she was upset by incidents she was hearing about and the way his popularity was being undermined:

> I hear you have been hissed in the cinema, that a man in a white tie refused to get up in the theatre when they played God Save the King and that in one place they added and Mrs Simpson. Really David darling if I hurt you to this extent isn't it best for me to steal quietly away.[22]

The next day Alec Hardinge, private secretary to the king, but certainly by now no friend, heard that a date had been set for Mrs Simpson's divorce petition to be heard at Ipswich Assizes: 27 October. Conscious of the implications, he warned the prime minister, Stanley Baldwin, asking whether there was any way he could prevent the hearing. Edward, now back at the palace and worried how the British press would handle the news, looked to the proprietors of the two leading newspaper empires – Lord Beaverbrook, owner of the *Daily Express* and London *Evening Standard*, and Lord Rothermere, of the *Daily Mail* and London *Evening News* – to maintain the silence, seeking their 'aid and understanding'. He summoned Beaverbrook – who had the strange habit of rising from his seat when speaking to Edward on the telephone – on 16 October:

> I told him frankly of my problem. I had no thought of asking him to use his influence on other newspapers publishers for the purpose of hushing up the news of the imminent divorce petition. My one

desire was to protect Wallis from sensational publicity, at least in my own country.

Max heard me out. 'All these reasons,' he said, 'appear satisfactory to me – I shall try to do what you ask.'[23]

Beaverbrook spoke to Rothermere and the censorship by silence continued under their 'gentlemen's agreement' for a few more weeks. Beaverbrook later said he had no idea at the time that the king was contemplating marrying Mrs Simpson, though he would still have acted in the same way. It was a long-standing tradition of the British press not only to ignore royal frailties but to mislead their readers into believing they did not exist.

Despite this silence, the news sheet *The Week* had no doubt that behind the scenes the political establishment was manoeuvring into position for a showdown with Edward, forecasting this on 14 October. *The Week* reported there were plans to detonate 'a social bomb under the King. The ideal method envisaged by those planting the bomb would be for a reference to be made from the pulpit to "the very standards of conduct set to his subjects by the late King".'[24]

Baldwin made his first move on 20 October, seven days before Mrs Simpson's petition was due to come before the court. Meeting Edward at Fort Belvedere, Baldwin said he was receiving letters from British citizens abroad complaining about what they were reading about the king's relationship with Mrs Simpson. He said he himself had seen the reports in the American press. Cabinet minutes record Baldwin's description of his warning to Edward:

... the Prime Minister said that he had then told the King that a con- tinuance of the present state of affairs would sap the public respect for the Throne. If that respect went, nothing could restore the position of the Throne, and on the Throne depended the solidity of the whole Empire, including India.[25]

Then Baldwin came to the actual purpose of his car journey from Downing Street, the divorce petition. 'Must the case really go on?' he asked. The former king's recollection in his memoirs was that he replied, 'I have no right to interfere with the affairs of an individual.' It would be wrong, he said, to try to influence Mrs Simpson's decision on the matter simply because she was his friend.[26] That was a dishonest answer, as even Lord Beaverbrook, one of Edward's staunchest supporters, was to recognise. 'That was a perfectly proper reply provided the King had no feelings towards her except friendship,' Beaverbrook would write. 'If he had deeper feelings, and an intention to marry, it was no reply at all.'[27]

The prime minister told Edward that once the decree nisi had been granted everyone would be asking what was to happen when the divorce became absolute. The press would break its silence and there would be a storm just before the coronation in May. He asked if Mrs Simpson could not at least leave the country for six months. The king did not reply and there for the time being the matter rested. The prime minister's son later wrote of the meeting, 'To Baldwin the King, for all his courtesy and friendliness, was in an exalted frame of mind which nothing could shake.'[28] Six days after this inconclusive discussion the *New York Journal* splashed the story 'King Will Wed Wally' across the front page.

At Ipswich Assizes on 27 October – with police barring access to the public gallery, apart from the judge's wife and her friend – Mr Justice Hawke granted Mrs Simpson a decree nisi, the divorce to be made absolute by application in six months. As Baldwin had feared, this would open the way for Edward and Wallis to marry before his coronation on 12 May 1937. That evening Edward gave Wallis an emerald ring inscribed – signifying the initial letters of their first names – 'WE are ours now, 27.X.36'.

Reporting of the case in the British press was minimal, but there was no holding back the tide of rumour. On 10 November the Chancellor of the Exchequer, Neville Chamberlain, was answering questions in the House of Commons on financial arrangements for Edward's forthcoming coronation. The Independent Labour Party MP John McGovern asked, 'Is it wise to proceed with the expenditure in view of the gambling going on at Lloyd's as to whether or not this Coronation will ever take place?' Chamberlain ignored him.[29]

An American journalist put the matter even more bluntly:

> Mr Baldwin probably has in mind the thought that a woman divorced twice in twenty years might be just naturally restless. The idea of a Queen of England packing off to Reno and then into the movies and selling her memoirs doubtless disturbs him.[30]

3

Edward, as he was soon to realise, was being pressed into a corner. On 13 November he returned to Fort Belvedere from a two-day inspection of the Home Fleet at Portland. He found a disturbing letter from Hardinge, his private secretary, waiting for him. Hardinge was aware that two affidavits were being presented to the king's proctor alleging collusion between Edward and Mrs Simpson over the divorce. This could lead to a re-opening of the case, a public revelation of the real nature of the couple's relationship, and an annulment of the decree nisi. Hardinge mentioned none of this in his letter but warned the king that the press were close to breaking their silence about 'Your Majesty's friendship with Mrs Simpson. It is probably only a matter of days before the outburst begins.'[31] He said the effect of this 'will be calamitous'.

Hardinge advised Edward that the Cabinet were about to meet to discuss developments and that the government's resignation was possible. This, he said:

> … would result in Your Majesty having to find someone else capable of forming a government … I have reason to know that, in view of the present feeling prevalent among members of the House of Commons of all parties, this is hardly within the bounds of possibility. The only alternative is a dissolution and a General Election, in which Your Majesty's personal affairs would be the chief issue …

Only one step, Hardinge suggested, could avoid this dangerous situation and that was for Mrs Simpson to go abroad '*without further delay*'.

Edward interpreted the phrase 'I have reason to know' as a sign that Baldwin had primed Hardinge to write. Shocked and angry, Edward passed the letter to Wallis, who had by now arrived at Fort Belvedere. After reading what Hardinge had to say, she told the king that there seemed no choice – she would have to leave England.

> Almost peremptorily he said, 'You'll do no such thing. I won't have it. This letter is an impertinence.'
>
> 'That may well be. But just the same I think he's being sincere. He's trying to warn you that the government will insist you give me up.'
>
> 'They can't stop me. On the Throne or off it, I'm going to marry you.'[32]

As the crisis of Edward's reign entered its final weeks, he spoke to an old friend from his time at Oxford, Walter Monckton, now a successful barrister and since 1932 legal adviser to the Duchy of Cornwall. 'I am beginning to wonder whether I really am the kind of king they want,' he recalled saying to Monckton. 'Am I not a bit too independent? As you know, my make up is very different from my father. I believe they would prefer someone more like him. Well, there is my brother Bertie.'[33]

The king and Baldwin met again on 16 November, four months to the day since the attack by McMahon on Constitution Hill. For the first time the possibility that Edward and Mrs Simpson would marry was raised. The prime minister told Edward that the British public would not accept a marriage 'for the reason that the wife of the King automatically became Queen'. The discussion went on for a quarter of an hour, Edward conscious of Baldwin's habit of 'imparting emphasis to his discourses by snapping and cracking his fingers with a quick flip of the hand past his right ear'.[34] The king came to the point. 'I am going to marry Mrs Simpson,' he said. 'You are right about opinion in the country, so I shall go.' If there were to be an abdication, Baldwin asked that it should be arranged in such a way as to avoid a constitutional struggle, to ease matters for his successor.

Edward understandably commented to Baldwin that he found it hypocritical for people to raise no objection to Mrs Simpson as a mistress, while they would reject her as his wife.[35] That evening the king told his mother, Queen Mary, and then, over the next day or so, his three brothers, of his determination to abandon the throne. The queen rejected Edward's plea that she should meet Mrs Simpson. Baldwin, meanwhile, was telling the Cabinet what had passed in his meeting with Edward, making it plain that the Duke of York, the king's brother, would be ushered onto the throne. Duff Cooper's recollection was of Baldwin confiding to his ministerial colleagues in Downing Street, 'The King had many good qualities but not those best fitted for his post, whereas the Duke of York would be just like his father.'[36]

His decision apparently made, the king left by train for a two-day visit to the Welsh coalfields, a 'distressed area' of long-term mass unemployment between the wars. 'I was at peace with myself. My spiritual struggle was over. I had passed the climax.'[37] An event was to take place in South Wales that would enshrine the convenient myth of the radical king, driven from the throne by the 'old gang' because of his love for his people. On 19 November, at the abandoned Guest, Keen and Nettlefolds steelworks in Dowlais, workless men all about, an obviously genuinely troubled Edward turned and said, 'These steelworks brought the men here. Something must be done to see that they stay here – working.'[38]

A version of this went down in history as 'Something must be done', to be interpreted as an attack on the national government's policies, a call for determined action against unemployment. But Edward had already decided what was to be done: he was to stand down from the throne, to abandon what influence he had, limited though it was. His words, as he would have known, were meaningless. He had been in the habit of making verbal gestures that no doubt gave him a warm feeling but led to nothing. Once, years before as Prince of Wales he asked one of the tenants in a Glasgow slum, 'What is your rent?' She replied, 'Thirty-one pounds a year.' 'That is far too much.' And that was it. What action did he imagine he was going to take? Seek out the landlord and tell him to reduce the rent? Persuade the government to introduce rent controls? Off-the-cuff statements of this kind were taken up to encourage a myth that Edward was the 'people's king'.

On the king's return from Wales, Esmond Harmsworth, son of the owner of the *Daily Mail*, Lord Rothermere, raised the possibility of a morganatic marriage, with Mrs Simpson becoming wife but not queen. Edward was partly persuaded this was a solution and took the suggestion up with Baldwin at a further meeting on 25 November. The prime minister doubted the House of Commons would accept this, but promised to consult the Cabinet, the other main party leaders and the Dominions prime ministers. Edward said, 'I believe many people would be sorry to see me go.' Baldwin agreed everyone wanted to avoid abdication, 'but that there were things that public opinion would not stand and that they attached most tremendous importance to the integrity and position of the Crown, which were the only things that held the Empire together.'[39] The Cabinet rejected the idea of morganatic marriage on 2 December, followed by the Dominions governments. Only War Secretary Duff Cooper, Edward's friend, dissented and his preference had been to delay a final decision.

Edward was cornered. Cabinet minutes recorded the crucial exchange between Baldwin and the king: 'His Majesty then said, "You want me to go, don't you?" The Prime Minister agreed.'[40] Edward's future entailed abandoning either the Crown or Mrs Simpson. The government had ruled he could not have both. McMahon may have failed to fire the gun on 16 July, but six months later the political establishment was able to manoeuvre the king into leaving the throne by other, less bloody, means. A *Daily Express* reader would echo the official view: 'Isn't it very dreadful that Edward VIII, son of our Beloved King George, should bring Hollywood ideals to Britain? Surely he could have found some sweet British girl.'[41] Just as the Bishop of Chelmsford had suggested in 1917.

It was now time for the press to finally break the conspiracy of silence. The first fracturing came by chance on 2 December, when the influential provincial newspaper the *Yorkshire Post* reported comments at a diocesan conference by Alfred Blunt, Suffragan Bishop of Bradford. Blunt remarked that to do his duty the monarch needed God's grace. 'Some of us wish that he gave more positive signs of such awareness.' Blunt claimed he was not thinking of Edward's private life, about which, as he said immediately after, he really knew nothing. He was more concerned about the king's irregular church attendance. Blunt subsequently admitted his intervention had been intentional. 'I took the risk because of the danger that silence was doing to the Crown and Empire.'[42] But at the time the *Yorkshire Post* assumed, and said, he was referring obliquely to rumours about the relationship between the king and Mrs Simpson published 'of late in the more sensational American newspapers'.[43]

Next day, as Fleet Street finally revealed the story kept hidden from the public for months, Mrs Simpson left London for the Cannes villa of her friends, Herman and Katherine Rogers. Beaverbrook's *Daily Express* and Rothermere's *Daily Mail* not surprisingly backed Edward, but *The Times*, reflecting establishment opinion, denounced the possibility of 'a marriage incompatible with the Throne'.[44]

Having failed so signally to act to protect Edward's life in July 1936, even to the extent of neglecting to warn him at all of the danger he faced, MI5 now proceeded in December to work with determination when it came to eavesdropping on his telephone conversations. On 5 December, as the abdication crisis was reaching its climax but governing circles remained uneasy about the king's next move, Sir Samuel Hoare's office sent a handwritten note marked 'Most Secret' to the head of the General Post Office, which operated the national telephone service:

> The Home Secretary asks me to confirm the information conveyed to you orally with his authority that you will arrange for the interception of telephone communications between Fort Belvedere and Buckingham Palace to certain addresses in London on the one hand and the Continent of Europe on the other hand.[45]

The London addresses included 145 Piccadilly, the home of Edward's brother, the Duke of York, while 'the Continent' was a reference to the villa where Wallis was now waiting until her divorce became absolute. MI5, which ordinarily supervised interception of mail and telephone calls, was central to this exercise. In London, MI5 officer Thomas Robertson – recruited personally by Kell via his son in 1933 through the old-boy network – listened in to Edward's calls to his brother, tapping the line through a junction box by Green Park. What intelligence the eavesdropping gathered remains a mystery, though Robertson claimed to have intercepted the news of the king's final determination to abdicate as he explained his decision in a call to the Duke of York.[46]

Faint-hearted attempts to form a 'King's Party' foundered, as a bizarre combination of the British Union of Fascists, the Communist Party of Great Britain, the arch-Tory Churchill and the newspaper-baron Beaverbrook, each with their different and conflicting motives, protested against the inevitable. 'Our cock won't fight,' said Beaverbrook, describing Edward's unwillingness to slog it out, to Churchill on 5 December. Mosley demanded a 'People's Vote' on whether the king should stay. On 10 December Edward signed the Instrument of Abdication, witnessed by his three brothers Albert, George and Henry. In a covering letter to the speaker of the House of Commons, Edward wrote, 'I take my leave … in the confident hope that the course which I have thought it right to follow is that which is best for the stability of the Throne and Empire and the happiness of my peoples.'[47]

Scotland Yard flooded central London with police, fearing possible riots given the intensity of public feeling. Five thousand demonstrators massed outside Buckingham Palace, among them 500 Mosleyite followers chanting, 'One, two, three, four, five, we want Baldwin dead or alive.' Others gathered at Downing Street with placards reading, 'Sack Baldwin. Stand by the King.'[48]

The prime minister's measured description to the House of Commons that evening of the events leading up to Edward's abdication was well received by government and opposition MPs. But speaking afterwards to a friendly backbencher, Baldwin said, 'You see … the man is mad, MAD. He could see nothing but that woman. He did not realise that any other considerations avail.'[49] Edward's mother, Queen Mary, wrote in her diary at the end of the day, 'The more one thinks of this affair the more regrettable it becomes.'[50]

The Declaration of Abdication Act passed quickly through Parliament, received royal assent, and on 11 December Albert smoothly replaced his brother, taking the name George VI to simulate an uneventful continuation from the reign of George V. The establishment breathed a sigh of relief: a pliable and predictable man with a wife and two children was on the throne. That evening Edward broadcast a final speech – helped in his drafting by Walter Monckton and by Winston Churchill – telling a worldwide audience he had found it impossible 'to carry the heavy burden of responsibility and to discharge my duties as King as I would wish to do without the help and support of the woman I love'.[51]

Edward took on a newly manufactured title, Duke of Windsor, leaving England for the Continent and a life of well-publicised and comfortable unimportance. The British fascist paper *Action* declared in an editorial that 'Baldwin the King-breaker has robbed us of the services of a great Englishman.'[52] British children sang a newly made-up rhyme in the streets and school playgrounds:

'Hark the Herald Angels sing,
Mrs Simpson's pinched our king.'[53]

4

What had failed to take place on 16 July 1936 was achieved five months later: Edward no longer wore the crown. His father, George V, had anticipated this; some around him had wished it; the astrologer Cheiro had foretold it. A biographer of Wallis Simpson described the situation in a dramatic sentence that could hardly be improved upon. Baldwin as prime minister, the writer says, had 'fretted and worried' over the problem of a man he distrusted as king. 'Then Edward had offered him a pistol marked "Abdication" and Baldwin had, thankfully, shot him with it.'[54]

Edward left Portsmouth Harbour on the destroyer HMS *Fury* at two in the morning of 12 December. He had abandoned his throne to be with Wallis – 'So far as I was concerned love had triumphed over the exigencies of politics.'[55] But they remained apart until she was able to apply for the decree absolute, Edward at Baron Eugène de Rothschild's Schloss Enzesfeld in Austria, and Wallis at the Villa Lou Viei in Cannes. Over twenty weeks the couple kept in touch by letter and daily telephone calls. Wallis had no doubt that Edward had been driven from the throne by a conspiracy. Writing on 3 January 1937 she pointed to references to him that Baldwin had made in his Commons speech on the abdication:

> I realize it is put there by the politicians whose game it is to have you forgotten and to build up the puppet they have placed upon the throne. And they can succeed, because just as they had for months an organised campaign to remove you – and how cleverly they worked – so have they one to prove they were right in what they did and the first step is to eliminate you in the minds of the people.[56]

Had she heard the broadcast speech of the Archbishop of Canterbury, Cosmo Lang, given as soon as Edward had left England, she would have found further confirmation that the establishment had damned him. Lang denounced the former king's friends, including – though she was not named – Wallis herself. How strange and sad it was, the archbishop said:

> ... that he should have sought his happiness in a manner inconsistent with the Christian principles of marriage, and within a social circle whose standards and ways of life are alien to all the best instincts and traditions of his people. Let those who belong to this circle know that today they stand rebuked by the judgement of the nation which had loved King Edward.[57]

Lang's speech was criticised by some as a cowardly and mean-minded attack on Edward as an individual now that he had gone, but it fitted the establishment's intention to ensure the former king became as far as possible a non-person. The financial settlement negotiated with his brother, now George VI, guaranteed £10,000 a year, with an additional £11,000 annually from the king personally, on condition that Edward never returned to England without express government permission. The terms were otherwise generous, and Edward had failed to mention to George the substantial savings he had banked from over twenty-five years of Duchy of Cornwall revenues, estimated at 1 million pounds.

There was, naturally, no expectation on anyone's part that Edward would find a way of earning his living, although Wallis was once heard to suggest: 'he was born to be a salesman. He would be an admirable representative of Rolls-Royce. But an ex-King cannot start selling motor cars.'[58] Wallis already had a bleak realisation of their future together as the truth of the situation struck home. 'One realizes now the impossibility of getting the marriage announced in the Court Circular and of the HRH,' she wrote to Edward, referring to his disappointed hope that once they were married she would bear the style Her Royal Highness. 'It is all a great pity,' she went on, 'because I loathe being undignified and also of joining the countless titles that roam around Europe meaning nothing.'[59]

Wallis's divorce was declared absolute on 3 May and the couple reunited the following day at the Château de Candé, south-west of Paris. On 12 May they listened together to George's coronation on the radio, Edward staring into the fireplace through much of the broadcast. A fortnight later he received a letter from his brother with final confirmation that Wallis would not be granted the rank of Her Royal Highness. George wrote that his hands were tied by legal formality and he hoped this would not be taken as an 'insult'. Wallis recalled Edward's anger and he said to Walter Monckton, who had carried the letter from London, 'This is a nice wedding present.'[60]

There was an assumption that the marriage would not last, Wallis would go through her third divorce and – as Edward's brother pointed out to Baldwin – once bestowed, the honorific HRH could not be withdrawn. The fear was then that Wallis would be free to flaunt her title around the world and if Edward were to marry again there would be two women bearing the title Her Royal Highness. The wedding on 3 June was a small and sad affair, ostentatiously boycotted by the British establishment.[61] 'The drawbridges are going up behind me,' Edward had told Wallis when he arrived at the chateau. 'I have taken you into a void.'[62] Edward's mother, Queen Mary, wrote pointedly in her diary, 'Alas! The wedding day in France of David & Mrs Warfield.'[63]

He had chosen his social death. No family member came to the ceremony and Mountbatten, his cousin and oldest friend, withdrew an earlier understanding that he would act as best man, having wisely shifted his allegiance to the new monarch. The ever-loyal 'Fruity' Metcalfe took Mountbatten's place. Wallis was given away by her old friend Herman Rogers, and a maverick Church of England vicar conducted a religious ceremony, Lambeth Palace refusing to authorise the joining together of the couple under church rites. George and Queen Elizabeth sent a telegram of congratulations, Baldwin a friendly letter, Hitler a gift and his good wishes. Edward's mother, Queen Mary, was silent. He wrote to her afterwards, 'I was bitterly hurt and disappointed that you virtually ignored the most important event of my life.'[64]

A brief paragraph in *The Times* on the decision of newsreel distributors not to exhibit film of the wedding in any of the country's cinemas demonstrated, by its very denial, that there had been government interference. 'It is stated that the decision was made independently, without pressure or guidance from the Government or any other authority.'[65]

After a honeymoon in a Carinthian castle, Budapest and Vienna, the couple took a suite at the Hotel Le Meurice, Paris, where they stayed until in late 1938 they leased a house close to the Bois de Boulogne. Their days took on a pattern they would follow for most of their lives: shopping and entertaining, some golf and gardening for the duke. Both, Edward most of all, appeared happy and contented, though he often turned conversations to the possibility of at some point returning to England, to Fort Belvedere in particular. 'One of the Duke's favourite jokes', his official biographer writes, 'was provided by a roll of lavatory paper which, when pulled, played "God Save the King". The duke would lurk outside the lavatory door and bellow, "Stand to attention!" when the unsuspecting guest pulled at the paper.'[66]

Harold Nicolson wrote a cruel entry in his diary, mocking both Edward's acquired Anglo-American accent and his obsession with ensuring the duchess was accorded royal status. The couple were due for dinner with a group at the writer Somerset Maugham's Cap Ferrat villa, along the coast from Nice. They finally appeared and cocktails were served:

> 'Oim sorry we were a little loite,' said the Duke, 'but Her Royal Highness wouldn't drag herself away from the Amurrican orficers.'

He had said it. The three words fell into the circle like three stones into a pool. Her (gasp) Royal (shudder) Highness (and not one eye dared to meet another).[67]

Even off the throne and away from England, Edward retained his capacity to inflict a combination of annoyance and embarrassment on the British political establishment. An example was the visit of the Duke and Duchess of Windsor to Germany in October 1937. Ostensibly a private expedition for – in Edward's words – 'the purpose of studying housing and working conditions', the ten-day tour was milked by the Nazi regime as a golden propaganda exercise. Hitler saw the chance of profiting from what would become a bitter feud between the duke and the king.

The British Foreign Office instructed the embassy in Berlin to ignore the event as far as possible and to extend the couple no official recognition. The ambassador in Paris had no doubt that the duke's hosts would seize every opportunity 'to make HRH even more pro-German than he is already supposed to be in Germany'.[68] The regime ensured Wallis was flattered by treating her as royalty, a Royal Highness. The couple travelled in Hitler's personal train, inspecting factories, housing projects and sports facilities in nine cities, meeting Goebbels, Goering, Himmler and other leading Nazis.

The Times reported, 'His Royal Highness acknowledged with smiles and the National-Socialist salute the greetings of the crowds gathered at his hotel and elsewhere during the day.'[69] Newsreels back in Britain were careful to exclude Edward's enthusiastic Nazi salutes, which he claimed were just an expression of 'good manners'.[70] Was Edward dreaming of a future, a triumphant return to the throne in alliance with Germany, with Wallis by his side? Were pre-abdication fears of the extent of his pro-Nazi sentiments now being confirmed?

The mission's high point was a two-hour meeting with Hitler at his Berchtesgaden outpost on 22 October, twenty minutes of which was a private conversation between Edward and the German leader. Wallis later asked Edward what they had discussed. 'What he's trying to do for Germany and to combat Bolshevism.' Wallis wanted to know what

Hitler had to say about Bolshevism. 'He's against it,' the duke replied.[71] Thirty years later, after a world war and the revelation of the Holocaust, Edward had no qualms about confiding to a friend, the historian Lord Kinross, 'I never thought Hitler was such a bad chap.'[72]

A week or so after the couple's return to Paris, the duke, boosted by his well-managed reception in Germany, revealed a continuing failure to come to terms with his irrelevance now he was no longer a monarch. Speaking at a lunch given by the Anglo-American Press Association, he said:

> I am now a very happily married man, but my wife and I are neither content nor willing to lead a purely inactive life of leisure. We hope and feel that in due course the experiences we gain from our travels will enable us, if given fair treatment, to make some contribution as private individuals towards the solving of some of the vital problems that beset the world today.[73]

On 27 August 1939, with war by now inevitable, Edward sent Hitler a telegram 'as a citizen of the world' asking him to use his influence to find a peaceful solution. Hitler, his troops poised to invade Poland, replied that this depended on Britain. The duke and duchess were at their new villa at Cap d'Antibes with 'Fruity' Metcalfe on 3 September. A little before noon a servant told Edward the British ambassador was on the telephone from Paris. The duke went in to take the call, returning after ten minutes. The duchess recalled: 'Walking straight to the edge of the pool, he said in a quiet voice, "Great Britain has just declared war on Germany, and I am afraid in the end this may open the way for world Communism." Then there came a splash; he had dived into the pool.'[74]

Edward would have no doubt in his own mind what had caused the war, and it was not Germany and Hitler's expansionist dreams that he chose to blame. As he later told a British journalist: 'There'd have been no war if Eden hadn't mishandled Mussolini,' he said. 'It was all his fault.' He added, as an afterthought, 'Together of course with Roosevelt and the Jews.'[75]

The couple sailed back to England on the destroyer HMS *Kelly*, cap-
tained by Edward's old friend Mountbatten. In London, the duke saw
his brother for the first time since the abdication and was given the rank
of major general in the army. With no command or combat experience
to speak of, he returned to France with the same type of inconsequential 'liaison' job he had undertaken as a junior officer in the First World
War. The military authorities were determined to keep Edward far away
from confidential intelligence, certain it would end up with Wallis,
who was staying in Paris. Despite this, the German ambassador in the
Netherlands was able to report back to Berlin information on British
Expeditionary Force preparations in France based on the duke's loose
talk. As the 'phoney war' ended in the summer of 1940 and German
forces advanced rapidly into France, the duke first went with his wife
by chauffeur-driven car to Biarritz, returned to Paris to fill the car with
valuables, and the couple then travelled into neutral Spain, arriving in
Madrid on 23 June.

The duke and duchess were driven on to Portugal, reaching a villa
rented for them in Cascais, along the coast from Lisbon, on 3 July. Here
the newly appointed British prime minister, Churchill, first ordered
Edward to return at once to England, following that command with a
telegram offering an appointment as governor and commander-in-chief
of the Bahamas. 'St Helena, 1940 style,' as the duchess put it, referring to
the scene of Napoleon's exile. The British government was now anxious
to remove the duke from Europe for reasons he claimed not to understand. Edward reluctantly accepted the appointment and the couple
began preparations to leave. But the duke's often-expressed sympathy
with the Nazi regime led to a bizarre plot concocted by Ribbentrop,
the German ambassador in London from 1936 to 1938, a man close to
Wallis, and now the country's foreign minister.

On 11 July Ribbentrop ordered Germany's ambassador in Madrid,
Oswald von Hoyningen-Huene, to come up with a pretext that
would persuade the duke and duchess to return to Spain. Once there,
Ribbentrop said, Edward would be told, 'Germany is determined to
force England to peace by every means of power, and upon this happening would be prepared to pave the way for the granting of any wish

expressed by the Duke, especially with a view to the assumption of the English throne by the Duke and Duchess.' It was also to be whispered into the duke's ear that Churchill was planning to have him assassinated. The ambassador, for his part, had little doubt that the duke's sympathies were with Germany and that he wished to play some part in ending the war. 'The Duke definitely believes', Huene said in a telegram to Ribbentrop on 11 July, 'that continued severe bombing would make England ready for peace.'[76]

Two emissaries visited the duke, one his oldest Spanish friend, Miguel Primo de Rivera, brother of the Spanish fascist leader José Antonio, executed in the Spanish Civil War. He told Edward the Madrid government had an urgent message for him concerning his safety and then asked whether the duke would one day return to the throne. An 'astonished' Edward said this was constitutionally impossible but went on to criticise the king and British policy, which he said he would publicly disavow. Even Edward would have realised that the British constitution would no longer apply in the event of a German occupation of the country. Following this conversation, a German diplomat, Eberhard von Stohrer, sent an optimistic telegram to Ribbentrop in Berlin:

> Politically the Duke has moved further and further away from the King and the present English government. The Duke and Duchess do not fear the King, who is utterly stupid, as much as the clever Queen, who is constantly intriguing against the Duke and particularly the Duchess.

Edward told a second messenger he believed at some time in the future it might be possible for him to act as an 'intermediary' for peace between Britain and Germany should the need arise.[77] The duchess's memory differed over some aspects, though the conclusion was the same – Edward at some point being king once more. In her version Walter Monckton flew to Portugal to tell the duke British intelligence had information that German agents were plotting to kidnap them. When Edward asked whatever for, Monckton said Churchill believed Hitler was planning in the event of a successful invasion to restore the duke to the throne to counter any further resistance.

The duchess wrote, 'David was flabbergasted. "Winston couldn't possibly think that."'[78]

The duke and duchess left Lisbon for the Bahamas on the *Excalibur* on 1 August and arrived in the capital, Nassau, after a sixteen-day Atlantic crossing. 'Of course,' the duke said, relaxing after a welcoming banquet, 'if I'd been King there'd have been no war.'[79] Not for the first time Edward showed his difficulty in recognising the limitations of the monarch's role. But one person had no doubt he was right: Oswald Mosley's wife Diana: 'If the King and my husband had been in power, there would have been no war with Hitler.'[80]

5

The official story of what had taken place on Constitution Hill on 16 July 1936 was simple: a man had produced a pistol in the presence of King Edward VIII with the intention of drawing attention to his grievance against the police. Edward himself had a distorted perception of this when he came to write his autobiography a decade or so after the event:

> By some tortured feat of reasoning this man had convinced himself that the Secretary of State for Home Affairs, Sir John Simon, had conspired to prevent his publishing in London a journal called the *Human Gazette*. Foiled in his efforts to reach the Home Secretary himself, McMahon had resolved to publicize his fancied injustice by causing a public disturbance.[81]

The actual story was far more complex. If McMahon really was simply a disturbed individual whose grievance had pushed him into a relatively harmless protest, one meriting a lenient prison sentence of twelve months, why would MI5 and Special Branch continue to take an interest in him, not just for a year or so, but for over a decade? Why did Special Branch observe his movements, watch his contacts, and why did MI5 devote so much attention to keeping his file up to date, to wondering about his activities when all seemed quiet? It was as if both believed he had been, and still was, a far more serious threat than the authorised version allowed. One Metropolitan Police officer noted on McMahon's file early in 1939 that he was 'a very dangerous blackguard'.[82]

On his release from Wandsworth Prison in August 1937 McMahon returned for a time to relative obscurity. He told the *Daily Express* he intended to write to the Duke of Windsor, the title Edward had acquired on his abdication. 'He knows I never meant him any harm,' McMahon declared to the newspaper's reporter. 'I was prevented from sending a humble note to him on the occasion of his marriage. I had told him that as he himself had been so harshly dealt with it was not for me to complain.'[83]

Much of the information in McMahon's MI5 file about his activities in the years after his release has been destroyed, with bare notes giving only a clue. Colonel Bevis was still, it appears, in touch with McMahon and taking an interest in him, an interest Bevis had no doubt MI5 shared. In December 1937 he sent two letters to Kell, MI5's chief, about McMahon's employment, writing again on the same subject in February and March 1938. The letters are no longer in the file. But McMahon retained MI5's attention and his sources of income remained a puzzle. Was he still in touch with foreign embassies, supplying information on refugees, as he had in the past? If he was, then MI5 and Special Branch appeared to have no record of it. He was certainly no longer in direct contact with them.

In the summer of 1938 Special Branch reported that McMahon had stayed in the Desmond Hotel at 104 Kings Road, Brighton, from 17 to 22 July. Their interest in keeping a watch on him was that McMahon was in Brighton when the king, George VI, was visiting France, the police believing there must be some connection between the two. Assassination was obviously in their mind if not in McMahon's. While every effort had been made in 1936 to play down his action on Constitution Hill, now he appeared to be seen as a potential assassin. A Special Branch officer observed that McMahon was paying twenty-five shillings a day for board and lodging for him and his wife, 'and during licensing hours he could invariably be found in the Grand Hotel buffet – an expensive establishment – spending money freely', McMahon did not at the moment appear to be, the officer noted, 'in a dire financial position'.[84]

His prosperity seemed short-lived and in September 1938 McMahon was writing begging letters from his home at 215 Gloucester Terrace, W2. MI5 attached an example to McMahon's personal file, noting that he was 'sending them out to selected people from whom he may obtain monetary assistance'. Vernon Kell's deputy at MI5, 'Jasper' Harker, passed a copy to the head of the Metropolitan Police Special Branch, Albert Canning, confirming the concern both bodies continued to maintain in McMahon's activities two years on from the attack on the king. In the top left-hand corner of his appeal, McMahon attached a photograph of the Duke of Windsor and on the other one of 'Myself and Wife'. The letter began, 'As you are known as a humanitarian and a lover of justice, I appeal to you to mete out to this plea for justice your humane consideration.'[85]

McMahon ran through the familiar story of the events that had led to 16 July 1936, how he had become 'entangled with alien agents and assisted them with certain missions' but that he had kept MI5 informed. Then he had learned of 'the dastardly plot to harm His Majesty'. He said he had 'dared to reveal' all this in court and because of this 'I was – against all evidence – sent to prison'. In full flow, all taps open, McMahon went on:

> Since my release I have been vainly struggling to obtain vindication and to have the stigma of Attempted Regicide – the most horrible and the worst which a Briton can bear – removed. The Authorities have ignored these pleas. Her Majesty the Queen Mother, His Majesty the King, together with H.R.H. the Duke of Gloucester, and other distinguished personages, have most graciously endeavoured to assist me in this fight for Justice but I am still awaiting results.

Did McMahon really expect anyone to be convinced by this? He finally came to the point: 'I am unable financially to send out a public or a general appeal and am only approaching real humanitarians like I know you to be.' A note at the foot of the page said, 'Published and Printed by

Paramount Service Association', a foretaste of McMahon's future interest in establishing spurious companies. There is nothing to show whether McMahon successfully extracted contributions from any of his targets.

With money a perpetual problem, McMahon was still disputing the bill for his defence with Alfred Kerstein, his solicitor, long after the trial had concluded. He also claimed Kerstein had not passed him payments newspapers had made for interviews. The dispute over costs went to the taxing master at the Royal Courts of Justice to resolve. After a hearing in January 1939, an argument in the street outside the court became so heated that McMahon assaulted Kerstein, threatening he would shoot him. The police obtained a search warrant but found no weapon at McMahon's home. Officers reported McMahon had been happy with the search, saying, 'It will make a good write up and bring me in a bit of money.' The police visit over, he telephoned the *Daily Express* and the story was in next day's paper.[86] The head of the Criminal Investigation Department commented, 'Everybody who knows McMahon is satisfied that he is a border line mental case and a born liar.'[87]

As the quarrel became increasingly bitter, Kerstein asked for police protection when he walked the streets between his office and court for the next hearing. Detective Sergeant Peter Pryke accompanied Kerstein on 28 February. McMahon insisted on talking to Pryke in the court waiting room and then wrote to him the next day, addressing the letter to 'Kerstein's No 1 Bodyguard' and enclosing a photograph of himself and his wife, both looking stylish and respectable.

> Though your presence was rather disturbing on our nerves we did feel that you had to be there as an unpleasant duty. The fact of your being loaned to 'protect' that swindling Jew by your superiors did not in any ways debar you from acting in a courteous and just manner to us.

Pryke wrote in a minute to his senior officer, 'McMahon is a dangerous man and it may be that he had some object in writing to me personally.'[88]

A few days later McMahon turned the tables by telling police he was the one who now required protection at court. Kerstein, he said, intended to plant associates there to annoy him so he lost his temper and was discredited as a witness. Police agreed to his request, and as a satisfied McMahon left Bow Street police station, he promised, spontaneously, to provide information on the activities of the Irish Republican Army.[89] The IRA had recently begun a bombing campaign in England in January 1939, with explosions in London and Manchester. The attacks continued through the year – over 120 in all, with five people killed in a Coventry attack – but no more was heard of McMahon's offer. His dispute over fees with Kerstein was finally settled in June by a payment of £30.

On his release from prison in 1937, McMahon had told the *Daily Express* he was considering leaving the country to start a new life. Almost two years on the *Toronto Daily Star* reported that he intended to travel to Canada for five months to visit relatives. He also claimed to have written a book about Edward VIII called *He Was My King*, to be published in the United States.[90] McMahon said Edward had already agreed to accept a copy. Who else would have given this story to the paper than McMahon himself?

When Scotland Yard became aware of his plans, Inspector John Kelling was despatched to the Canadian High Commission. An immigration officer told Kelling that McMahon's criminal record automatically prohibited him from entering Canada, whether as a tourist or an immigrant. If he attempted entry he would be prevented and returned home. All shipping lines would be informed and would refuse him a ticket to travel. Kelling then contacted the American Embassy, where the immigration section said that in no circumstances would McMahon ever be granted an entry visa. Besides, Kelling noted, 'I have ascertained from the Passport Office that no passport has been issued to McMahon (or Bannigan) and that he is the subject of a "stop".' He added that Special Branch would be informed.[91]

6

Ten days after the outbreak of war in September 1939 McMahon wrote to the War Secretary, Leslie Hore-Belisha, offering his services as an agent for MI5. Given the difficulties in McMahon's brief relationship with the security service, it is hard to know how seriously he expected to be taken. The offer was of course dismissed out of hand, an MI5 officer noting on McMahon's file: 'This man is slightly insane. He should not be employed in any confidential capacity.'[92] Ignoring the rebuff, McMahon wrote a rambling letter to Colonel Hinchley Cook at the War Office on 24 November. He offered as his credential the fact that the private secretary of a prominent Nazi, Julius Streicher, had stayed at McMahon's home in 1938 and talked freely about the regime. McMahon said he had developed a friendship with the man 'which I feel I could now use in the interests of my country to erase my past, and my trouble to your department'. He went on:

> I mention this to prove in some little way that I can prove useful if given a chance, and would if given a trial be found tactful and silent. Irrespective of what your answer may be I shall not hesitate to forward any 'news' that comes my way.[93]

Was McMahon genuine, deluded or playing a surreal game with MI5? It is impossible to tell. Whichever it was, both the police and MI5 seemed unable to ignore him. In January 1940 he sent MI5 copies of anti-Semitic letters attacking the War Secretary, Hore-Belisha, on War Office notepaper, confident they would find them of interest. They were accompanied by a letterhead reading 'The McMahon Publications, Incorporating The Human Gazette – London-Paris-New York', with the address 23 Surrey Street, WC2, just off the Strand. Three company directors were named, McMahon as managing editor, Lieutenant Commander H.B.F. List, RN Rtd. and Colonel F. Matthews Rtd. Did the Lieutenant Commander exist? Matthews certainly did, though his status as a colonel was questionable. A familiar crony from McMahon's past, it was Matthews who had given McMahon some of the materials he was passing to Ottaway of MI5 in 1935.

The first of the letters, dated December 1939, was headed 'Belisha Must Go'. Hore-Belisha was described as a 'rascally Jew' and the writer demanded he be 'hounded' from office:

It has now been established that the Jew has had close contact with the exiled traitor Windsor, for the purpose of assisting in a campaign for the traitor to again assume his relinquished Kingship, which he discarded for a discarded adventuress. Every loyal subject of Our Gracious King George must do his utmost to prevent such an injurious happening.

The second letter, on War Office headed paper, signed 'A Loyal Englishman' and dated New Year's Day 1940, was even more ugly in its anti-Semitism. The writer demanded the mass expulsion of Jews from every public office. 'Only then will our country be a land fit for Englishmen to dwell in ... Jews crucified Christ many years ago, today they are crucifying our fellow countrymen.'[94] Both letters found their way into the national press, MI5 subsequently discovering McMahon had sent them copies. Coincidentally, Prime Minister Neville Chamberlain dismissed Hore-Belisha on 5 January 1940 after he had been involved in a series of arguments with army generals and the king. Anti-Semitism in the military command had undoubtedly played a part in his sacking.

Once Hore-Belisha had been removed, the origin of the letters – which played no part in his dismissal – seemed academic. But rather than ignoring the matter, MI5 opened an investigation. Major Gilbert Lennox interviewed McMahon and produced a five-page typed report at the end of January 1940. Not revealing that he was with MI5, Lennox masqueraded as a member of the War Office press section. Lennox commented on McMahon: 'His condition can be perhaps described as both drunk and daft.' McMahon told Lennox he had 'found' the letters on the desk of a retired army colonel, but refused to name him. Lennox felt convinced McMahon had written the letters himself in the hope of making money by selling them to newspapers. MI5 knew that McMahon had also tried to get the Mosleyite paper *Action* involved, but they had refused to take the bait. Lennox concluded: 'After one interview, I would put him down as a drunkard, a rogue and a mentally unbalanced exhibitionist.'[95]

In April 1940 a letter arrived on the desk of the chief inspector at Albany Street police station, a short walk from 13 Park Crescent, where

McMahon was now working and living as a caretaker. The writing was scrawled and not easy to decipher completely.

> There's a man named McMahon or McMarne. They say he is a care-taker somewhere in Park Crescent ... He seems to have his hand in a few mugs. He is a Nazi in link with chaps in high job. Money plenty. Thick with Pub —L. Lords wri— thems got palls in Army to get information. May be nothing in it. Seems fishy. An observer J Potts.[96]

A detective inspector was despatched to Park Crescent to investigate. He found no evidence that McMahon was engaging in pro-Nazi activities. The officer said in his report he doubted McMahon was 'pro-anything' but just sought 'a little cheap notoriety' and was mentally unstable. 'In any case he is well known to officers of the Special Branch, who keep a close watch upon his activities.'[97] Special Branch's continuing interest in McMahon, the perceived need to keep a 'close watch' on him four years after the Constitution Hill attack, indicated that they, as well as MI5, had seen the incident as far more significant than the official version insisted.

And then, abruptly, McMahon was out of circulation, another bout of petty crime catching up with him. On 24 September 1940 he was convicted at the Old Bailey of assault occasioning actual bodily harm, obtaining £2 – and attempting to obtain a further £100 – by false pretences. The judge sentenced him to terms of fifteen months and six months imprisonment, running consecutively, a longer term than the twelve months he received in 1936 for producing a pistol with intent to alarm the king.

Meanwhile, Vernon Kell, head of MI5, had been dismissed, cast out with no warning after almost forty years' service. Kell had been closely involved throughout McMahon's contact with MI5, particularly in the build-up to the attack on Edward and the confused aftermath. The pressure of war revealed inadequacies in MI5's organisation and Kell was blamed. On 10 June 1940, a month after Churchill replaced Chamberlain as prime minister (and the day Italy declared war on Britain), Kell was summoned to the Treasury by Sir Horace Wilson, head of the civil service. Wilson said it had been decided 'to make certain changes in the controlling staff' of MI5. Kell wrote in his diary, 'I get the sack from Horace Wilson. 1909–1940', underlining the dates.

By the time of Kell's sacking, MI5 had reached, a serving officer was quoted as saying, 'a state which can only be described as chaotic'.[98] At the age of 67, a broken and bitter Kell retired to his Buckinghamshire cottage, did what service he could for the community as a special constable, and died in March 1942. Command of MI5 passed, briefly, to 'Jasper' Harker, the officer who had ordered his subordinate Ottaway to 'drop' McMahon when he first mentioned a conspiracy to kill the king.

7

Routine observation by Special Branch of McMahon's activities showed that, once more out of prison, he was employed as a salesman in the Selfridges grocery department in Oxford Street for a year from August 1942, before moving on to higher-paid work. A sergeant reported, 'During the time he was there several small incidents occurred which made the management think that he was slightly mentally unbalanced', but nobody seems to have made a connection between McMahon the salesman and the perpetrator of the July 1936 incident. To add another layer of mystery, Special Branch understood he was writing a book about the Soviet Union and selling articles to newspapers, both under a *nom de plume*.[99]

McMahon did not come into MI5's orbit again until March 1943, when an officer in F Branch, which dealt with counter-subversion, noted his growing involvement with right-wing fringe politics. As far back as 1931 McMahon had assisted in the Liverpool election campaign of the anti-Irish and anti-immigrant pastor, Harry Longbottom, leader of the Protestant Party. He had also displayed an instinctive anti-Semitism while in dispute with his solicitor, Alfred Kerstein, in 1939 by describing him as a 'swindling Jew'. It was hardly surprising, then, that he would associate himself with the far right. But, given his earlier activities with German and Italian intelligence agents and with political refugees, was it possible that he was still hoping to collect information he could pass on for cash to whoever would pay?

If McMahon was prepared to sell other people's secrets for money, there were also individuals willing to pass on information about him. An informant told MI5 McMahon had joined an organisation called the People's Common Law Parliament and was in contact with a former member of the British Union of Fascists, Florence Hayes. She was known to be working to establish an underground fascist movement.[100] The People's Common Law Parliament (PCLP) had been formed in the mid-1930s and was now attracting former Mosley supporters to its campaign for the release of interned fascists. Hayes had been an organiser of the Bournemouth BUF branch and was held in Holloway Prison with Oswald Mosley and his wife until being released in 1941. In 1942 an MP denounced the PCLP in the House of Commons as 'fascist and defeatist'.

McMahon's MI5 file has an extended series of notes on fascist and PCLP meetings he attended through the spring and summer of 1943. A report from an MI5 officer to Special Branch in April connected McMahon with the anti-Semitic Anglo-Saxon League and made a surprising reference to another familiar figure:

> There is a possibility of the Anglo-Saxon League being taken over by G. A. McMahon and receiving support through him from the People's Common Law Parliament. According to the source of our information the latter organisation has been largely financed by Mrs. Van der Elst, and McMahon has great hopes of obtaining funds from this woman ...[101]

There was no further mention of Mrs Van der Elst's involvement, but MI5's interest intensified. A six-page typed report from MI5 to Special Branch at the end of May 1943 claimed 'reliable sources' had disclosed that former BUF members were now at an advanced stage in setting up a shadow fascist movement. Running parallel would be a legal front, the 'People's Alliance', intended to appeal to fascists and non-fascists, led by none other than McMahon. His plan to take over the Anglo-Saxon

League had, it seemed, foundered. 'He seems to be generally distrusted by ex-members of the British Union who wish to make use of him for the money which he could put up, but exclude him from the organisation of the underground movement.'

MI5 included a detailed People's Alliance programme, with policies on agriculture, industry, social services and finance, all clearly based on Mosley's pre-war book *Tomorrow We Live*. McMahon was said to be co-operating on this project with leading BUF figures who had been released from internment and he was renting an office in Victoria Street from which to operate. 'I think you will agree that the organisation is a potentially dangerous one,' the report concluded.[102]

Surely only McMahon himself, or someone acting on his behalf, would have been the source of these blatantly absurd stories, either directly or indirectly. A note on McMahon's file that MI5 had made enquiries in June about the mysterious Matthews – who had been involved in McMahon's escapades in the past – suggested someone there was beginning to make a connection. But MI5's fascination with McMahon continued and in August 1943 a plaintive sounding minute asked:

> Has [deleted name] heard nothing about McMahon lately? He seems to have fallen out of the picture altogether and I am wondering whether he is running some other organisation than that with which he was formerly associated. I have heard nothing of McMahon from the other informant so presume that he is in London at present.[103]

The reply from another MI5 officer on 17 August was that neither Florence Hayes nor the People's Common Law Parliament had any idea what McMahon was doing or where he had gone. And that, for the time being, was the end of any connection between McMahon and MI5, although the security service maintained a sporadic interest. An officer running through the history of McMahon's recent engagement with fascist politics concluded: 'I should think that he is the sort of man who is perpetually thinking out magnificent schemes, but who has very little ability to execute them.'[104]

8

Edward's five-year term in the Bahamas was not entirely happy, though the couple took what comfort they could and always performed well in public, however reluctant and resentful they felt. The duke did at least have a position of some kind, overseeing a 70,000 population spread across twenty-nine islands. He hoped the post would serve its purpose as a stepping stone to his return to Britain. But later he was to tell Lady Diana Cooper, an old friend, 'It was a bit difficult for me, you see, I'd been King-Emperor and there was I, a third-rate Governor.'[105] The duke and the duchess, when it came to it, hated the Bahamas, the heat, the humidity and the society they felt forced into.

Almost immediately on arrival, the duke proposed holidaying for a few weeks at his Canadian ranch to escape Nassau's August heat.[106] The Colonial Secretary, Lord Lloyd, refused Edward permission to leave his post. Lloyd then turned down his request for a £5,000 refurbishment of Government House, saying the middle of the Battle of Britain was hardly the time to ask for money better devoted to buying a Spitfire. Finally, Lloyd issued a reminder that the duchess should be addressed as Her Grace, not Her Royal Highness.

The duke and duchess tried, in their own way, to ameliorate the poverty of the black population and the squalor in which most were forced to live. Their presence alone encouraged American tourists, boosting the local economy. But, well meaning as they were, their actions were invariably rooted in paternalism, tinged with racism. 'We Southerners always flatter ourselves', the duchess told a visiting writer, 'we know best how to deal with coloured people.'[107] Wallis set up Red Cross clinics, but denied black people service in the canteens, while Edward objected to black police officers patrolling white areas. When a black building contractor was recommended as the best person to act as liaison officer with American contractors constructing two air bases, Edward was aghast. 'We can't have a coloured man for this job. We must have a white man.'[108] He ordered that black visitors to Government House should always enter through the back door, though this had probably always been the practice.

Edward appeared a liberal compared to the 'Bay Street Boys', the white business elite that effectively controlled the Bahamas through the House of Assembly. He insisted on efforts to ensure the black population were well housed, educated and provided with medical care rather than treated simply as a source of cheap labour. He complained to Walter Monckton, 'I am afraid that it will always be a struggle to get Bay Street to devote money to any project that does not directly benefit themselves.'[109] When riots erupted in 1942 as the couple were on a visit to the United States, Edward blamed 'Jews and Communists' but returned to Nassau to recommend wage increases and fairer labour laws, angering the Bay Street Boys. However, he never abandoned his conviction that black Bahamians were incapable of self-government, telling Churchill that 'negroes in the mass are still children both mentally and morally.'[110]

In 1943 Churchill offered Edward a new post, the governorship of Bermuda. 'It was clear now beyond all question', the duchess later wrote, 'that David's family were determined to keep him relegated to the farthermost reaches of the Empire.'[111] He turned this down and in March 1945 resigned from his job in the Bahamas, leaving the islands in May. The couple went first to the United States then, in September, returned to France. Now that the exile of the Duke and Duchess of Windsor safely across the Atlantic had ended, the problem for the political and royal establishment was what should be done with a former monarch.

Edward briefly visited England – without Wallis – meeting his brother the king and his mother on 5 October 1945. Queen Mary said she would never meet Wallis, while George told his brother there could be no place for him in England. George was aware, though Edward was probably not, of the efforts made by British intelligence in recent months to secure papers in Germany, the 'Marburg files', with potentially embarrassing revelations about the duke's wartime conversations with Nazi diplomats.

The French government provided the Windsors with a house – described as a virtual palace – in Paris on the Neuilly side of the Bois de Boulogne at a nominal rent, allowing them to live free from income tax. The couple began a routine of remaining in France from April until after Christmas, holidaying in August with friends in Biarritz or Venice, then staying at a rented flat at the Waldorf Tower in New York, going on to Palm Beach to enjoy friends' houses. There were stories that the Windsors occasionally took money to be displayed as house guests. The Mosleys were neighbours in France and Diana painted a gushing picture in her biography of Wallis. She described 'the rich and beautiful table of the Duchess, with its talk that was always amusing and some-times brilliant, fantastic food and sumptuous wines'.[112] Edward and Oswald were politically close and – according to one of Mosley's sons – talked about a world in which one had remained king and the other had become prime minister. Diana Mosley's sister, Nancy Mitford, wondered why the two couples lived in France rather than Germany, so nostalgic did they seem for the days of the Third Reich.

In the early 1950s the duke and duchess bought a small seventeenth-century mill house, Moulin de la Tuilerie, twenty-five miles from Paris, dividing their time in France between there and the house in the Bois de Boulogne. The couple had the footman, butler, cook, gardener and the paraphernalia of servants Edward had always been accustomed to and the house was filled with furniture from Fort Belvedere. The duch-ess made daily visits to the hairdresser and shopped for clothes, jewellery and furniture, while the duke gardened and played golf. But he remained frustrated at the persistent official refusal to acknowledge the duchess as Her Royal Highness, while for her the life she had taken on began to lose its sparkle. Edward's friend Duff Cooper, now British ambassador to France, sympathised: 'You have all the disadvantages of royalty and none of its advantages.'[113]

In May 1951 Diana Cooper wrote to her son that Wallis had 'selected for her scandal and presumably her lover', a gay beneficiary of the Woolworth fortune, 'Jimmy' Donahue Jr, nineteen years her junior.[114] As the two flaunted their relationship in New York clubs, without Edward, an American newspaper bore the headline, 'She married a King and screwed a Queen.' Edward at first raised no objection: the camp Donahue amused him and was generous with money, paying for a Mediterranean cruise the three enjoyed together, settling restaurant bills, and topping up Wallis's already ample supply of jewellery and furs. There were rumours, too, that the duke himself might be enjoying a fling with Donahue, Wallis playing her part as a cover, though Donahue himself always denied this. These stories coloured the public's view of the 'romance of the century'. Either way, by 1954 the Windsors had tired of Donahue and he was dropped, telling a gossip columnist, 'I've abdicated.'[115]

The routine the Windsors had begun after their return from the Bahamas, the annual progress from France to the United States and back again, continued through their lives – movement, as an acquaintance commented, giving the illusion of activity. Their homes in France mimicked the court life Edward had abandoned for Wallis, with bows, curtsies and kitsch decoration masking the Windsor charade's essential emptiness.[116] A British journalist, Frank Giles, who had first met the couple when they were en route to the Bahamas in 1940, described their regular chums as 'a motley and not very attractive company: blue-rinsed widows of American millionaires, members of French café society, hangers-on of one sort or another'.[117] A monthly magazine in America, where the couple had always been popular, focussed on Edward's everyday existence in the 1950s:

> It is both sad and amusing to see a former King of England reduced by the woman he loves to 'Little Man' – to the rank of a meek husband. What should one do, laugh or cry, when one looks at the ex-Caesar in the role of handbag-carrier, a sort of walking ornament … reverent and filled with domestic fear like any husband after 15 years of sub-missive marriage.[118]

In 1951 Edward published his memoirs, *A King's Story*, co-written with an American journalist, an editor at *Life* magazine, Charles Murphy, who put in the donkey work that gave the book its shape. Interest in the man who had abandoned his throne 'to be with the woman I love' remained strong and the book sold in hundreds of thousands. The £500,000 that Edward made encouraged the duchess to put her name a few years later to an equally lucrative and in some ways more revealing autobiography, *The Heart Has Its Reasons*.

Meanwhile, Edward's immediate family were dying – his brother King George VI in 1952 and his mother Queen Mary a year later. The duke attended both funerals in England without the duchess. 'What a smug, stinking lot my relations are and you've never seen such a seedy worn-out bunch of old hags most of them have become,' he wrote to Wallis after his mother's funeral.[119] In 1953 his niece, Elizabeth, was crowned and neither of the Windsors were invited to the coronation. They watched the ceremony on television, as they had listened on the radio to George VI's in 1937, like any other ordinary person.

As Edward's health declined there were signs of, if not warmth, then at least a thaw in relations with the royal family. On his seventieth birthday in 1964 the queen sent a congratulatory telegram, later visiting him in the London Clinic when he was recovering from an eye operation. In 1966 the duke and the duchess were both invited to the unveiling of a plaque celebrating Queen Mary at Marlborough House in London, the royal family's first public acknowledgement of Wallis, thirty years after the abdication. The queen offered Edward the opportunity to attend the investiture of Prince Charles as Prince of Wales – the first investiture of an heir to the throne since his own in 1910. He declined when the invitation did not explicitly include Wallis.

In the mid-1950s an old acquaintance had met the Duke of Windsor at a friend's house for dinner and found him looking fit and well:

> He chatters and chatters. He pretends to be very busy and happy, but I feel this is false and that he is unoccupied and miserable … Although he must have talked to me for three-quarters of an hour without stopping, there was nothing of any interest at all that he had to say.[120]

Similarly, Frank Giles, the journalist who had known Edward since 1940 and would become editor of the *Sunday Times*, recalled that whenever they occasionally met in Paris, 'He would always embark on some issue of contemporary interest, on which his views would generally lie somewhere between the naïve and the silly.'[121]

Having survived the danger that McMahon's revolver posed in July 1936, Edward had been half-pushed and half-jumped from the throne in December, condemned and condemning himself to a life with barely a pretence of any meaning. He had been born to be king, to be and not to do. The crown removed from his head, Edward became nothing.

9

In November 1945 MI5 intercepted a letter from McMahon to Jeffrey Hamm, a close colleague of the fascist leader Oswald Mosley and a leading figure in the reviving post-war movement. Hamm had been interned in 1940, along with Mosley, had joined the army on release but was discharged in 1944 as a disruptive influence. By 1945 he was leading the British League of Ex-Servicemen and Women, effectively a fascist front organisation pending Mosley's return to active politics in Britain.

McMahon had not abandoned his flirtation with the political right and his addiction to self-aggrandising fantasy continued. In his letter to Hamm, McMahon explained he had been 'thinking how best to assist your most worthy League of ExService people'. He said he had been chairman of the People's Common Law Parliament and had contacts possibly of use to Hamm's League, among them a Vice Admiral Creagh, 'a fighter for justice for the British Serviceman'. There was indeed a Rear Admiral James Creagh, who had retired in 1935 but was still alive, though given McMahon's fondness for collecting and freely dropping names it seemed unlikely the two had ever met. McMahon told Hamm he was considering how to arrange financial assistance for the League, 'and hope to have good news very soon'.[122] MI5 intercepted a further letter to Hamm in September 1947 but as the copy in McMahon's file was destroyed in weeding it is impossible to guess how far his connection with the League had developed.

In March 1948 McMahon stood as an independent candidate for St Marylebone Borough Council in a by-election on a platform of 'Better Treatment for the Aged and Infirm, Clubs and Playgrounds for the Kiddies, Decent Homes for Marylebone People'. His nerve in putting barefaced lies on his election leaflet was remarkable. Neglecting to mention that he had served almost two years in prison from 1940 for assault and obtaining money by false pretences, McMahon claimed, 'I, through disablement was refused entrance to the Services, but served in the Auxiliary Fire Service during the War.' He went on:

> My circle of friends here in this Borough range from the most emi-
> nent to inmates of the Workhouse and Almshouses, they are my
> friends because they know that I am free from Party fetters. My policy
> is Justice for the highly born, the small trader, the homeless, and
> the unfortunate.[123]

McMahon failed to win a seat, but in October he enclosed a copy of his election leaflet in a letter to Sir Oswald Mosley, which was intercepted by MI5. McMahon began badly by misspelling Mosley's name Moseley. He claimed he was publishing a new local journal 'to save our own countrymen and women … from the complete domination of the alien horde which is swamping this borough'. He asked Mosley if he would help by arranging an interview with one of his 'close friends' for publication.

> I already have had the honour of meeting you in the past dark days,
> when to do so was considered, by your enemies, a crime. Thank God,
> those days have now past, and a brighter and more proud moment is
> present. A number of your brave supporters have personal knowledge
> of my activities during the past ten years.[124]

There is no sign Mosley bothered to reply, if he even read the letter. McMahon's communications were so blatantly exaggerated and untrue it is hard to decide whether he was tongue-in-cheek, having a private joke, or actually believed what he was saying. He was often plausible at first glance and in 1949 pushed himself into the position of leader of a group of independent candidates for St Marylebone Borough Council.

McMahon probably had serious hopes of winning a council seat this time, the culmination of his lifelong search for the recognition, rather than the notoriety, that had eluded him. But as so often in his life the enterprise ended in farce. Fifteen non-party candidates stood for council seats on 13 May 1949, including McMahon and his wife. He claimed at the count to be their leader and told a reporter even before votes were tallied that he would be lodging a petition against the conduct of the election. The McMahons were both candidates for Dorset Square and Regent's Park ward and polled 197 and 163 votes. The Conservative candidates won overwhelmingly. McMahon refused to join in the traditional vote of thanks to the returning officer. He claimed there had been irregularities in the election and that he would be asking the High Court to declare it invalid. There is no sign that he ever did. He would, as ever, have been gratified to know that Special Branch were taking an interest and sent a report of the evening's events to MI5.[125]

With his attempt at winning a political position disappointed, McMahon reverted to what he had been in the beginning, what had driven him from Glasgow in the early 1930s – a petty criminal. 'After leaving prison I had not the courage to go home to my people who would have welcomed me, so became a wanderer,' he had written in 1937.[126] He had been convicted and imprisoned in 1940 and now was at the same game again. But he never lost the inner confidence that the world would accept his innocence. Arrested by a detective sergeant on 5 December 1950 and charged with false pretences, McMahon declared, 'I say that these charges are ridiculous and blackmailing.' At the magistrates' court hearing he said with his usual optimism, 'I've only to say that when these charges are brought before a higher court, I shall stand with a complete answer to all. I plead not guilty.'[127]

The trial opened at the Old Bailey on 6 February 1951, a building McMahon was only too familiar with, having made appearances there in 1933, 1936 and 1940. There was even a link with MI5. Prosecution counsel Edward Cussen was a former security service officer. He had interrogated the comic writer P.G. Wodehouse about his ill-advised wartime broadcasts from Nazi Germany. McMahon faced eighteen counts of embezzlement. First, while working for the Artizans, Labourers and General Dwellings Company in Paddington he had pocketed over £70 by making false entries in rent books. A second batch of charges involved a phoney company, Modern Society Publications Ltd (Incorporating Human Gazette and Paramount Service Association). The company's registered office was at 5 New Bridge Street, London EC4 – an accommodation address – and its directors Sir Walter Peacock KCVO and Colonel Frank W. Mathews (Retd) DSO.

Matthews weaves in and out of McMahon's life and had last put in an appearance in 1940 as a director of 'The McMahon Publications, Incorporating the Human Gazette', without the DSO. Peacock was a new addition to McMahon's headed notepaper scams, and was genuine. Peacock (Eton and Cambridge) had worked for Edward, Prince of Wales, as treasurer from 1910 to 1915, and as Keeper of the Records of the Duchy of Cornwall, retiring in 1930. McMahon wrote to Peacock in 1938, telling him he was a journalist. McMahon's ability to present a plausible front still worked, and the two met occasionally over the next few years. In 1949 McMahon told Peacock – now approaching 80 years of age – that he was setting up a newspaper with Colonel Matthews and that they had £20,000 capital available for the project. Peacock told police that, believing everything was above board, he had agreed to act as a director of the proposed company.

As Peacock and Matthews were not prosecuted, the police presumably accepted neither was involved in McMahon's next step, selling shares in a company that had never actually come into existence. McMahon set up all the paraphernalia of printed letterhead, incorporation documents and share certificates, but the business was a sham. Claiming that Modern Society Publications produced books and owned land, McMahon persuaded four people to give him a total of £1,600 for worthless shares he was unloading. He borrowed £70 from a fifth person who said she could not afford to invest. McMahon, not surprisingly, never repaid her, an old habit. When McMahon's bank account was examined he was found to have spent five shillings every week trying his luck on the football pools, paid by cheque.

McMahon's barrister could find nothing to say in mitigation, but read a letter to the court from Princess Elizabeth in which she thanked him for a wedding present he sent in 1947 'on behalf of the children of Marylebone'. On 9 February 1951 the Old Bailey judge sentenced him to three years. As he left the dock McMahon, unselfconsciously defiant to the end, shouted, 'Is this British justice?'[128]

McMahon was of no further public interest. MI5's registry added a cutting from *The Times* of 10 February 1951 reporting his Old Bailey appearance and sentence to his file. At that point the man who had first aroused MI5's interest by writing to the *Daily Worker* in 1933, eighteen years before, ceased to exist officially. Jerome Bannigan, alias George Andrew McMahon, returned to the obscurity he had struggled throughout his life to escape.

10

As in life, so in death: much is known about the manner and time of Edward's death, little about McMahon's beyond the bare details on his death certificate. But John Ottaway was the first to die. Ottaway, the MI5 officer to whom McMahon had brought news of the conspiracy to kill the king in April 1936, died in 1954 in the seaside town of Bournemouth, after a long and tranquil retirement. McMahon was next, dying on 28 February 1970 in Springfield Hospital, Tooting, South London. There had always been some question about his date of birth, which the registrar noted on the death certificate as 'about 1900'. His marriage certificate in 1933 had said that when the ceremony took place he was 30 years old, which would have made him 67 in 1970. A doctor certified the cause of death as bronchopneumonia, combined with cerebral haemorrhage and hypertension.

Given the frequency with which McMahon had been described as mentally unstable, it was no surprise he should end his days in Springfield, recorded on the death certificate as his 'usual address'. This suggested he had been an in-patient for some time. The hospital had opened in 1840 as the Surrey County Pauper Lunatic Asylum. By the mid-twentieth century, a history of the hospital observes, many of the patients were admitted suffering the effects of poverty and alcoholism, an end McMahon might himself have foretold. Registering his death on 3 March 1970, McMahon's widow, Rose, described his occupation as 'journalist', as he would so much have wished. Whether he was cremated or buried, where, and who was at the funeral service to mourn his passing will never be known.

Edward's death followed McMahon's by two years. As the duke lay dying in the bedroom of the couple's Paris home in May 1972 his niece Queen Elizabeth, Prince Philip and the Prince of Wales visited him, a final reconciliation of a kind. He died of throat cancer nine days later at 2.25 a.m. on 28 May, aged 77. His obituary in *The Times* was headed 'King who gave up a throne to marry the woman he loved', which is how he lives in the public memory. The title Duke of Windsor, created in the specific circumstances of the abdication in 1936, died with him. His body was flown from France and lay in state at St George's Chapel, Windsor. The duchess returned to England two days later, was met at Heathrow by one of Edward's oldest friends, now Earl Mountbatten of Burma, and driven to Buckingham Palace, where she stayed until after the funeral.

On 5 June the duke was interred in a plot in the royal burial ground at Frogmore, the Georgian house by Windsor Castle, the resting place of Queen Victoria, his grandmother. There were few mourners outside the immediate family: Queen Elizabeth, Prince Philip, the Prince of Wales, Princess Anne, Princess Margaret, and the Queen Mother, widow of Edward's brother. In 1986 the duchess – for whom Edward had abandoned his throne and country exactly half a century earlier – took her place beside the duke.

VI

Bungling or Collusion?

1

The *Annual Register* for 1936 provides an example of the construction of official history. The publication claimed to offer an objective account and analysis of the year's news. Coverage of the incident on Constitution Hill briefly outlined the events of the day and then concluded:

> On being interrogated, the prisoner, a journalist named George Macmahon [*sic*], said that he had had no intention of shooting, but merely desired to call attention to a grievance which he had against the Home Office on the ground of false imprisonment which he had suffered. He was committed for trial, and was eventually found guilty of attempting to frighten the King and sentenced to twelve months' imprisonment.[1]

There was no reference to the actual evidence given at the Old Bailey trial, no mention of McMahon's previous involvement with MI5 and Special Branch, nothing about his relationship with foreign embassies or his revelation to the security authorities of a wider conspiracy to assassinate the king months before the event. He was simply a loner with a grievance, a man with a grudge, precisely the story the authorities had been working so strenuously to persuade the public to believe.

Muddle-headed, a drunk, a petty criminal, these things McMahon undoubtedly was, but there is no disputing the clarity with which he described events preceding the 16 July 1936 attack. 'Assume that I, since last April,' he wrote to Lieutenant Colonel Cecil Bevis from Wandsworth Prison in the weeks before his release in August 1937:

> Assume that I ... warned you of certain happenings affecting say, your business. I outlined certain facts, and you actually knew me to be in a position to get these facts, would you totally ignore the disaster I was warning you against? That is what the officials concerned did. They knew I was in a position to obtain these facts about the plot against H. M. They had already been supplied with definite proofs of my con-nections with the Embassies ... They allowed me to retain a loaded revolver. They encouraged me to continue my dangerous work ... Again assume that my story about this plot against our revered ex-King was false, that although they could not dispute the authenticity of my other informations, my past life was a black one, that I was har-bouring a grievance against the police or even H. M., why was I not arrested from April to July?'[2]

The questions McMahon asked Bevis to consider carry as much weight now as on the day he posed them. Why did MI5 and the Metropolitan Police Special Branch allow him to walk the streets of London carrying a revolver? Why did they do nothing to prevent him standing with a loaded weapon on Constitution Hill waiting for Edward to pass by on horse-back? The two bodies charged with ensuring the security of the state and the monarch's safety bungled so badly that senior officers of both should have been dismissed for incompetence or they were so indifferent to the threat they knew Edward faced they effectively colluded in a conspiracy to murder.

2

When McMahon first told Ottaway, his MI5 handler, in April 1936 that he had become involved in a conspiracy to assassinate the king, Ottaway's response was to pass him to Special Branch. The police interrogated McMahon and dismissed his story. As the Special Branch report of the interview was subsequently destroyed it is not possible to say why that was. MI5's reaction to the report was to drop McMahon as an inform-ant, both Kell and his deputy Harker telling Ottaway to break contact. When McMahon brought the news in July 1936 that the attack was now imminent, Ottaway again sent him to Special Branch. Police actions over the next few days verged on the farcical. Neither they nor MI5 warned Edward of the danger he could be facing, nor were the police on duty on Constitution Hill on 16 July alerted to the possibility of an attack.

The official line, shared by MI5, the police, the courts and the press was that there was no conspiracy, that McMahon was simply making it up. Mr Justice Greaves-Lord at the Old Bailey declared he did not believe McMahon and that he fully understood why the jury had rejected the tale. Hearing McMahon's appeal, Mr Justice Hewart described it as a 'cock-and-bull story'. *The Times* said McMahon's claim was a 'melo-dramatic superstructure'.[3] But there is every sign McMahon genuinely thought he had become entangled in a plot. Attorney General Somervell put it to him at his trial: 'I am going to suggest that this story about a plot is the product of your imagination.' An anguished McMahon responded, 'I wish to God it were.'

It may have appeared reasonable for Special Branch and MI5 to doubt the truth of what McMahon was saying, though he had shown himself to be a reliable informant in the recent past. He never gave a full descrip-tion of the conspirators, saying no more to Special Branch than that a 'Bill', a 'Tom' and a 'George Thompson' were implicated. But he did pro-vide both MI5 and Special Branch with precise details of where some or all of those involved would be found on the morning of the attack: the Express Dairy on Edgware Road, where he had been instructed to meet the plotters. A Special Branch officer gave McMahon the impression he would be followed there. Not only did they fail to track him, or even plant an officer at the premises, but the Metropolitan Police commissioner took the ludicrous step of despatching an officer to the scene an hour *after* the attack on Constitution Hill, clearly hoping to cover up the force's incompetence.

If McMahon did honestly believe there was a plot, who could the conspirators have been? On the face of it, as he was acting as an informant for both the Italian and German embassies there is good reason to suspect the involvement of one, or even both, of these. He implied as much at the Old Bailey when he wrote down the name 'Fitz Randolph', a German diplomat on whom MI5 were already keeping a file. McMahon's connection with the Italian Embassy, the military attaché in particular, was also well known to MI5. But it is difficult to see what motive Germany or Italy would have had for Edward's murder and what either would have achieved by it. Neither was yet prepared for war with Britain, which proof of their participation in his assassination would surely have provoked. The truth was, both powers had a greater interest in Edward remaining king. His sympathies with these regimes, their anti-communism and their authoritarianism – and with their friend in Britain, the fascist leader Oswald Mosley – was certainly no secret.

It was also unlikely that Communists – who were mentioned as suspects at one point – would embroil themselves in a plot of this kind. At this very moment the Soviet Union, fearing the threat from Nazi Germany, was working to build an alliance with France (the two signed a mutual-defence pact in March 1935) and then with Britain against Hitler. Involvement in the assassination of the British king would shatter any hope of success in that aim. British Communists had even been ordered by Moscow to tone down their criticisms of the monarchy.

McMahon claimed during his Old Bailey trial that he had done all he could to keep MI5 informed, trusting they would act on what he was saying to ensure the plot did not succeed, playing along with the conspirators in order to prevent the murder. If not the German or Italian Embassies, or the Communists, who is left? Who would have lured McMahon into believing there was a plot against Edward and pressurising him into participation? They would hardly have been complete strangers to him. Could it have been one or more of the odd cast of characters who passed through McMahon's life?

There was 'Colonel' Matthews, the man who supplied McMahon with the original information he passed to the Italian military attaché (where the story began) in 1935, an individual who seemed to appear at significant moments and then disappear. MI5 certainly found Matthews of interest and kept a file on him. Was he involved as an instigator, a participant or even an amused observer of McMahon's confusion? This will never be known, but he later complained to McMahon that police had turned up to question him about the attack. And what of 'Captain' Faulkner, the man whose office McMahon had visited, drunk and desperate, with a gun and whom he had by chance arranged to meet on the morning of the attack? Why that very day? By the strangest of coincidences, Faulkner was planning to go to Hyde Park, ostensibly to watch Edward present colours to the Guards. Faulkner's part in events will always remain a mystery.

Then there is Violet Van der Elst, the anti-hanging campaigner, with whom McMahon had clashed vehemently in the course of the previous year. During the November 1935 Putney election campaign, he had threatened to blackmail her and then to shoot her. In April 1936 he sued her in court for money he swore she owed him. Given that, why, immediately after the 16 July attack, did she deny ever having met McMahon, and insisted she did not know him? What did she feel she needed to hide?

One of the many people who wrote to the police after the incident, 'Britisher', made some interesting connections. He claimed Mrs Van der Elst was not only linked with McMahon but also his abortionist friend, the struck-off Dr Starkie. 'Strangely enough each one of these men have applied to Mrs Van der Elst for money or presenting schemes to her.'[4] 'Britisher' found it significant that Starkie had refugees, people with no passports, regularly staying at his house and suspected that he and others were involved in drugs or the 'white slave trade'. After what seems a cursory investigation, the police rejected the suggestion that Mrs Van der Elst had been directly connected with McMahon's attack on the king. Was it possible, though, that she, Matthews and Faulkner

– or a combination of them – had set up the story of a plot to make life difficult for McMahon?

Refugees appear a common factor. After his release from prison, McMahon told a *Daily Express* reporter, 'I never intended to shoot the King. But there was a plot to kill him. My life in London brought me into touch with many strange characters … with political refugees and others.' Was this a clue to the identity of the conspirators? McMahon revealed to the reporter he had been spying on these refugees, passing information on them to the German Embassy. 'It was detestable work. But I had to get money somehow.'[5] Was the 'conspiracy' not one mounted against Edward directly but against McMahon, as revenge?

A fantasist, a man who sees the world in terms of dodges and deceptions, a petty criminal who engages in fraud and embezzlement, can be equally susceptible to the fantasies of others. Had some of the refugees become aware of what McMahon was doing, passing their secrets on to the German Embassy, and decided to play their own game with him, egged on by others who had their own difficulties with McMahon? A busybody and blabbermouth like McMahon would hardly have been able to keep to himself that he was 'working' for MI5. What better trick for refugees he had informed on than to turn the tables on both him and the German Embassy and to feed him a story about a plot to kill the king and to promise McMahon – always scrabbling for money – £150?

McMahon had given them enough to work on and made it obvious what buttons they could press: his sense that the Home Office was denying him the compensation he was due for wrongful imprisonment; disappointment over the failure of his magazine and his belief that police harassment was responsible; and what his defence barrister Hutchinson called 'the rights and wrongs of Ireland'. While they had no actual intention of assassinating the king, they could be sure he would pass the story of a conspiracy to MI5, set the cat among the pigeons, embarrass and discredit the German Embassy and ensure McMahon an uncomfortable time in the process.

At first, in April 1936, McMahon was told all he had to do was supply the necessary weapon, a small task for a man who had no trouble securing arms. But in July the demand became more serious – he was to carry out the shooting. Confused and afraid about what he had become mixed up in, he tried to warn MI5 and Special Branch the attack was about to take place. If his sole interest had been money – the £1,000 Ottaway, McMahon's MI5 handler, claimed he had demanded in April – he surely would not have continued to insist there was a conspiracy when MI5 refused any payment. He would have moved on to some other scheme. Equally, if his motivation were simple attention-seeking, why would he have persisted when MI5 and Special Branch had firmly dismissed his story in April? McMahon fully believed what he was saying and when neither showed any concern or even interest, all that was left was to pretend to be prepared to fire the shot in the hope of sabotaging the assassination.

McMahon's actions on 16 July were not those of a man intent only on drawing attention to his long-running grievance. His incoherent telephone call to the Home Secretary, his thought of simply return-ing home, the inevitable recourse to a drink in a pub, wondering whether suicide was a way out, writing what he believed might be a final message to his wife ('May, I love you'), throwing the revolver to give the impression he had really tried, all were acts of a desperately frightened man, one convinced he had fallen into a plot to murder, trapped with no escape. 'I want you to give me the heaviest sentence you possibly can. It is only by remaining in prison that I can save my life,' he said at the Old Bailey. Who was he afraid of? 'The people I have given away.'

3

MI5 and Special Branch would know none of this. Conspiracy, pre-tend conspiracy or no conspiracy, how they handled the question of the weapon McMahon carried is symptomatic of their lackadaisi-cal attitude throughout. The revolver is at the centre of the story. In its absence the incident on Constitution Hill would have been trivial, a brief interruption to the progress of a royal procession. For McMahon to act with a loaded pistol in his hand raised the stakes dramatically.

At his meeting with Ottaway in December 1935 McMahon had produced a gun. As with much relevant and no doubt revealing material, Ottaway's report on their conversation was removed from McMahon's MI5 file and destroyed during weeding. Ottaway's only comment to McMahon was that he needed a licence from the police to carry a weapon. It is true that MI5 had no law-enforcement role; that was for the police. But Ottaway had been a police officer for almost thirty years before joining MI5, a senior detective for much of the time. In that context his casual attitude towards McMahon's law-breaking can only be described as bewildering. Why did he not at least mention this to one of the Special Branch officers with whom he was regularly in contact?

One obvious answer is that McMahon had shown himself to be a valuable informant to MI5 and it was in Ottaway's interest to keep him in circulation and out of trouble. When McMahon told Ottaway he was concerned for his safety and wanted to end his contacts with the Italian Embassy, the MI5 officer reassured him all would be well provided he did as he was told. As the organisation's director, Vernon Kell, said of the information McMahon brought, 'Some of it was undoubtedly accurate.'[6] McMahon would also have had his use as a conduit for MI5 to feed misinformation to the Italians.

When McMahon told his MI5 handler in July 1936 an attack on Edward was imminent, Ottaway appears not even to have taken the simple precaution of asking whether McMahon still had a revolver. Ottaway lamely told the Home Office later he assumed McMahon had disposed of the weapon, hoping to cover his back. When two Special Branch officers questioned McMahon in July, neither raised the matter with him despite the fact that they were dealing with what McMahon said was an assassination in which he would be a participant. How different the police response would be two years on, in January 1939. When McMahon threatened to shoot his solicitor in a dispute over money, the police obtained a warrant from a magistrate the same day and ransacked McMahon's Bayswater flat searching for the weapon. But what had MI5 and Special Branch done in April and July 1936 when McMahon said he was part of a plot to kill the king and an MI5 officer not only knew he possessed a gun but had seen it? Nothing.

Deputy director Harker subsequently excused MI5's inactivity by saying it was not their role to investigate matters of this kind, although the section Ottaway headed existed precisely to conduct what MI5's official historian calls 'shadowing suspects and making "confidential" enquiries'.[7] It was true that MI5 were drastically short of personnel. Taking over responsibility for monitoring Communist activities in 1931 and now the menace posed by Fascist and Nazi sympathisers, intensified pressure on the security service. But a threat to the king's life – a threat to national security if ever there were one – merited more than passing interest.

When a distraught McMahon told Ottaway on 13 July an attack was imminent, MI5 gave the impression of perhaps taking McMahon seriously enough for the director, Kell, to go over to New Scotland Yard with Ottaway the next day for a meeting with Assistant Commissioner Kendal, the officer directing Special Branch. There is no record of what they discussed but responsibility for what followed was now in the hands of the Metropolitan Police. What happened proved so laughably incompetent the police gave every sign of complete indifference to the importance of what was taking place.

There was, first, the failure by police to follow McMahon to the conspirators' meeting at the Express Dairy. The fact that the meeting place was changed to the corner of Kingsway and Holborn at the last minute made no difference – had police been tailing him and remained alert, McMahon would have led them to the alternative venue. What actually happened was embarrassing in its stupidity. McMahon was expecting to be followed by an officer and, as he told the court at his trial – and as the police were forced to admit – he was not.

As the trial proceeded at the Old Bailey, senior Scotland Yard officers would have been dismayed at the extent to which their incompetence was being revealed, layer by layer. They hurried to cover themselves by using a tame reporter to plant a story in the next day's *Daily Express*. The police tale was blatantly, almost stupidly self-contradictory. MI5 and Special Branch, the report went, had thoroughly investigated McMahon's story and concluded he was 'imaginative' and made statements 'that could not be relied on'. But having dismissed his credibility as an informant (and, as he said, a participant), the police then – they claimed – decided he would be 'shadowed constantly' for three days.

'Detectives', the story continued, posted themselves outside his house early on the morning of 16 July, only to find he had confused them by leaving at 6.45 a.m. McMahon's landlady had said he left home at 7.15 a.m. and McMahon himself said it was about 7.45 a.m. But even if the police story about timings had been true, basic intelligence would suggest they should have proceeded directly to the Express Dairy, where McMahon had said he was meeting the plotters. In fact, no officer went to the cafeteria until well after the incident had taken place. 'Do you mean after the event?' McMahon's defence counsel asked in disbelief at the trial. Detective Superintendent Sands – who headed the investigation – confirmed he meant exactly that. 'He was directed to go there by the Commissioner of Police.'

The authorities having failed to act on McMahon's information, the commissioner, Sir Philip Game, appeared to imagine that an officer turning up hours later was effective policework. The truth was, he believed it would cover up the failure to deploy officers to the scene earlier. Surprisingly, no one in court thought the absurdity worthy of further attention and there was no comment in the press. The story planted in the *Daily Express* was clearly untrue, a lie told by senior officers at Scotland Yard in the hope – successful as it turned out – of concealing the extent of their ineptitude.

If Scotland Yard had taken the threat as seriously as they claimed to the *Daily Express* – keeping a close watch on McMahon for three days – a sensible action for MI5 and Special Branch would surely have been to caution Edward and his staff of the danger he faced in the Hyde Park ceremony or the procession back. They did not. Even the police on duty in Hyde Park and on the route to Buckingham Palace had no idea that a gunman intent on killing the king might be at large. As Edward's description of the incident in his autobiography *A King's Story* shows, he had no warning. In the evening after the attack, well before the police had conducted more than a cursory investigation, the Home Secretary gave St James's Palace a conveniently distorted version of McMahon's actions and their cause.

4

What was happening, and what had been taking place since the afternoon of 16 July 1936, was a sustained effort at concealment. Once the authorities realised the fatal consequences that had only fortuitously been avoided and the extent to which their failure to act laid them open to criticism, the cover up began. MI5 distanced themselves, hoping their involvement could remain hidden; the police simply lied. The final phase of the charade came at the Old Bailey. If McMahon had been charged and tried for illegal possession of a weapon in 1935 he would have faced a sentence of six months. In 1951 the Old Bailey judge gave him three years for embezzlement and false pretences, serious offences no doubt, but hardly life-threatening. For 'wilfully producing a pistol with intent to alarm the King' in 1936 he received a sentence of twelve months. Why the leniency?

What stood out in the course of McMahon's trial was the effort made by everyone concerned to minimise the significance of his actions. This was obviously not out of any sympathy with McMahon. The objective was to keep what MI5 and Special Branch knew before the attack out of the picture, to downplay the extent of their failures. Quite simply, a person determined to kill the king in that place at that time would have had no trouble in succeeding.

When McMahon appeared at Bow Street in August he had been silent about his contacts with MI5 and Special Branch, though he told his wife that the Old Bailey trial would see him 'divulge all'. The authorities were anxious he should not and when he was on remand in Brixton Prison they offered a deal via his solicitor Alfred Kerstein and barrister St John

Hutchinson: the less he said, the less serious would be the charges he faced and, consequently, the less time he would spend in prison.

The prosecution's intention to narrow the incident down was confirmed when the Attorney General, Sir Donald Somervell, told the Old Bailey jury that the evidence he intended to present would begin from 15 July. Limiting the timescale of the issues in this way would avoid embarrassment for MI5 and Special Branch. There would be no mention of McMahon's previous contacts with Ottaway, no mention if possible of his warning of an assassination plot, no mention of Special Branch dismissing what he had to say out of hand. There were good reasons for wanting to keep all this hidden. Would McMahon co-operate? Once the trial began there was a strong impression that the prosecution, defence and the judge had choreographed proceedings between themselves, with McMahon and the jury as onlookers.

McMahon initially faced three charges. The gravest of these were unlawfully possessing a firearm and ammunition with intent to endanger life, and presenting at or near the person of the king a revolver with intent to break the public peace. The third, and lesser, charge was that of unlawfully and wilfully producing a revolver with intent to alarm the king. By lunchtime on 14 September, the midpoint of the trial, Mr Justice Greaves-Lord, with Somervell and Hutchinson concurring, had instructed the jury to find McMahon not guilty on the two more serious charges under the Firearms Act and the Treason Act.

When Special Constable Dick went into the box to give his evidence he gave every impression of a man ordered by his superiors to see his part in the events of 16 July in a new light. On the day of the incident, and for a few days after, Dick was hailed as the hero who had saved Edward's life by forcing a loaded revolver from the assassin's hand. But now, questioned by defence counsel Hutchinson, he was less certain that McMahon had actually been holding the pistol when he struck. Other officers agreed. An interesting game was taking place. The line now was that McMahon had thrown the weapon, though not for the reason the prisoner himself said. The defence pushed this to undermine any idea that he had gone to Constitution Hill intent on assassination, and the prosecution because it played down the fact that MI5 and Special

Branch had bungled and allowed McMahon to confront the king with a loaded gun.

When Somervell cross-examined McMahon, he asked why he was telling a different story from the one he had told at Bow Street. In his final speech to the jury he said McMahon could not be believed because he was a liar, telling different tales in different courts, but then went on to say the story McMahon had told at Bow Street in August had been the truth. But Somervell had been impelled as part of the logic of his argument to refer – reluctantly – to McMahon's disclosure to MI5 in April of a plot. He said there was no substance to what McMahon had said. The exchange was revealing and worth repeating:

> Somervell: Enquiries were made on the purported information you gave in April, and the authorities were satisfied there was nothing whatever in your story.
> McMahon: That may be their view. The very fact that I was able to do a thing after their knowing of it going to happen shows there is no safety guaranteed for the King in his own country.
> Somervell: The only danger to the King came from yourself.
> McMahon: Yes, because of the bungling of the officials … You wanted to give me a light sentence. The offer was made to me, if I pleaded guilty, I would get off with a light sentence. Why was that offer made to me but to hide the bungling of other people?
> Somervell: No one wants to hide anything.[8]

This revealed what much effort had been trying to suppress: the danger to Edward's life had arisen from the incompetence or indifference of MI5 and Special Branch. If, as everyone was suggesting in court, McMahon's purpose had been merely to make a protest about his grievance against the police, why had he told MI5 in April there was a plot against the king's life, repeated this in July, and gone to Constitution Hill with a loaded pistol, which he then threw in Edward's direction? If McMahon's intention had simply been to draw attention to himself he could have thrown anything – a newspaper, a packet of cigarettes, a hat. There had clearly been something more involved, something the court, the police and MI5 wanted to prevent coming to light.

Why did defence counsel Hutchinson not call Ottaway, McMahon's MI5 handler, as a witness? He had after all subpoenaed him. The difference of intentions between McMahon and his barrister seems to be the explanation, as McMahon later complained. McMahon wanted to tell his story; Hutchinson was working to secure the best outcome for his client. This was served as far as Hutchinson was concerned by minimising McMahon's offence, an objective the prosecution conveniently shared. This was easier done by keeping Ottaway and MI5 out of the picture as far as possible. And why had prosecuting counsel Somervell declined to call Ottaway to refute McMahon's conspiracy story? The answer is obvious – the fear that under oath Ottaway would have confirmed what McMahon had been claiming, and much more: that he had been a useful informant, that he had told Ottaway he carried a weapon, that he had been consistent in his belief that there was a plot, and that MI5 – and with them Special Branch – had by their inaction enabled the plot to proceed.

When it came to passing sentence, the judge treated McMahon's story about his contact with MI5 as a fantasy: 'I can well understand the jury not being misled by the story which you have told today.' But the story had never been tested, simply dismissed. Twelve months, albeit with hard labour, for being a few yards from the king wielding a loaded revolver was lenient for a reason: to show that all was well, nothing serious had taken place. There is a point when incompetence of such magnitude effectively becomes collusion. Persistent bungling over the course of months leads to one conclusion – that the authorities were prepared to allow what McMahon was trying to warn them about, a plot to murder the king, to proceed. Why this indifference to the threat against Edward?

5

What is remarkable about the entire affair is that there was one group of people with a genuine wish to see Edward removed from the throne:

not the Italian or German governments, not the Communists, not even the shadowy figures and refugees who played with McMahon, but the British political and royal establishment. Looking back over the events of 1936, a well-informed contemporary commentator had no doubt that Britain's elite was convinced the man who came to the throne in January 1936 was unfit to wear the crown and that his time on the throne would be short-lived: 'Edward VIII was to be a mere interlude, a brief departure from historical continuity.'[9] Baldwin, the prime minister, revealed the depth of the establishment's relief when George VI finally replaced Edward at the abdication, declaring that 'more than any of his brothers he resembles in character and mind his father'.[10]

Edward's father, George, had made it plain a number of times that his son on the throne would be disastrous for the institution of monarchy. He had said as much to the Archbishop of Canterbury, to the head of Edward's household Admiral Lionel Halsey, to his wife, Queen Mary, and to the prime minister, Stanley Baldwin. In 1928 he told his son Albert – more as hope than prophecy – 'You'll see, your brother will never become King.'[11] As gossip spread in the highest political and royal circles no one could be in any doubt about George's opinion of his heir. There was also the astonishing conversation between Edward's private secretary and Baldwin when both agreed the state's interests would be best served if the Prince of Wales were killed in a riding accident and never achieved the crown.

But Edward did succeed and once on the throne concerns about his ability to manage the role's demands were confirmed. A damning official indictment of the new monarch came only a month into his reign when the leading figures in Britain's administrative elite met to discuss their fears that the king's slack attitude was enabling Wallis Simpson to pass confidential information to the German ambassador. The compelling reasons to have Edward removed from the throne by any means possible were adding up: doubts about his ability to perform the essential tasks of a constitutional monarch; the moral paradox of the head of the Church of England insisting on continuing a relationship with a once-divorced and twice-married woman; and the threat posed to national security by the combination of Edward's political sympathies and Wallis Simpson's influence over him.

6

If Edward had died on 16 July 1936 how changed would Britain's future have been? His brother Albert, Duke of York, would have succeeded to the throne as George VI. George would have been followed in due course by his daughter Elizabeth. To that extent, nothing would have changed. But one thing would have been different: how Edward lived on in popular and official memory. Not as the king who abandoned his throne for a twice-divorced American, instead a tragic hero senselessly killed by a man acting on a petty grudge. Spared the long, disheartening years as Duke of Windsor, his fascist sympathies, his idleness and ageing-playboy life forgotten, Edward would be mourned as the 'People's King', the 'Lost King for a New Age', 'the modern turn the monarchy could have taken': the headlines and the book titles write themselves.

If Edward had been assassinated that day and if McMahon not been killed on the spot by the crowd, kicked and trampled to death, or shot by the police or a soldier, he would have been arrested and taken to court. At his trial he would in all likelihood have been declared not guilty by reason of insanity to avoid the need for any mention of his contacts with MI5 and Special Branch and his forecast that the deed was planned. Confined in Broadmoor Hospital, where he would have been held until he died, his story of a plot would have been rejected and derided as the ravings of a man driven insane by an obsessive grievance. But the questions would echo down the years, refusing to go away: 'Was McMahon really acting alone?', 'Who wanted the king removed?', 'What did MI5 and the police really know?', 'Was there a conspiracy reaching to the very top of the establishment?'

Select Bibliography

This bibliography is confined to books, archive files and newspapers that were particularly helpful or interesting. Other sources proving useful are cited in the endnotes. Works on every aspect of Edward Windsor's life fill shelf after shelf and new interpretations of his story appear every year; on Jerome Bannigan, alias George Andrew Campbell McMahon, there is nothing. The 'man in the brown suit' is, like most of us, almost invisible. What facts there are on him have had to be mined from scattered newspaper reports and references hidden in MI5 and the Metropolitan Police files.

The National Archives of the United Kingdom (TNA):
    CAB 23/85: Cabinet minutes and conclusions, 1936.
    CRIM 1/861: Witness depositions at Bow Street Magistrates' Court, 1936.
    CRIM 1/2117: Central Criminal Court, McMahon, 1936 to 1951.
    KV 2/1505(1), KV 2/1505(2) and KV 2/1506: MI5 personal files on McMahon.
    MEPO 3/1713: Metropolitan Police file on 16 July 1936 incident.
    MEPO 10/35: Office of the Commissioner correspondence on Duke of Windsor and Mrs Simpson.

Andrew, Christopher, *The Defence of the Realm: The Authorized History of MI5* (Allen Lane, 2009)
Bloch, Michael (ed.), *Wallis and Edward Letters 1931–1937* (Summit Books, 1986)
Bloch, Michael, *The Reign & Abdication of Edward VIII* (Bantam Press, 1990)
Bloch, Michael, *The Secret File of the Duke of Windsor* (Harper & Row, 1988)
Blythe, Ronald, *The Age of Illusion: England in the Twenties and Thirties 1919–40*, (Penguin, 1964)
Bolitho, Hector, *King Edward VIII: His Life and Reign* (Eyre & Spottiswood, 1937)
Brendon, Piers, *Edward VIII: The Uncrowned King* (Penguin, 2018)
Brendon, Piers and Whitehead, Phillip, *The Windsors: A Dynasty Revealed* (Hodder & Stoughton, 1994)

Donaldson, Frances, *Edward VIII* (J. P. Lippincott, 1975)

Dorrill, Stephen, *Blackshirt: Sir Oswald Mosley and British Fascism* (Penguin, 2007)

Godfrey, Rupert (ed.), *Letters from a Prince: Edward, Prince of Wales to Mrs Freda Dudley Ward: March 1918–January 1921* (Warner Books, 1999)

Griffiths, Richard, *Fellow Travellers of the Right: British Enthusiasts for Nazi Germany 1933–39* (Oxford University Press, 1983)

Hart-Davis, Duff (ed.), *In Royal Service: Letters & Journals of Sir Alan Lascelles 1920–1936, Volume II* (Hamish Hamilton, 1989)

Higham, Charles, *Mrs Simpson: Secret Lives of the Duchess of Windsor* (Pan Books, 2004)

Kell, Constance, *A Secret Well Kept: The Untold Story of Sir Vernon Kell, Founder of MI5* (Conway, 2017)

Martin, Kingsley, *The Magic of Monarchy* (Thomas Nelson & Sons, 1937)

Phillips, Adrian, *The King Who Had To Go: Edward VIII, Mrs Simpson and the Hidden Politics of the Abdication Crisis* (Biteback Publishing, 2018)

Pincher, Chapman, *Treachery, Betrayals, Blunders and Cover-ups: Six Decades of Espionage* (Mainstream, 2012)

Prochaska, Frank, *The Republic of Britain 1760 to 2000* (Allen Lane, 2000)

Quinlan, Kevin, *The Secret War Between the Wars: MI5 in the 1920s and 1930s* (Boydell Press, 2014)

Vickers, Hugo, *Behind Closed Doors: The Tragic, Untold Story of Wallis Simpson* (Arrow Books, 2012)

Williams, Susan, *The People's King: The True Story of the Abdication* (Allen Lane, 2003)

Windsor, Duchess of, *The Heart Has Its Reasons: The Memoirs of the Duchess of Windsor* (David McKay Company, 1956)

Windsor, Duke of, *A King's Story: The Memoirs of H.R.H. the Duke of Windsor K.G.* (Cassell, 1951)

Ziegler, Philip: *King Edward VIII* (Collins, 1990)

Daily Express

Daily Herald

Daily Mirror

Daily Telegraph

The Times

Notes

PROLOGUE

1   *The Latest Decalogue*, in *Poems of Arthur Hugh Clough*, Macmillan, 1890, p.184.

2   *The Annual Register 1936*, Longmans, Green & Co., 1937, p.64.

3   Philip Ziegler, *King Edward VIII*, Collins, 1990, p.264.

4   Michael Bloch (ed.), *Wallis and Edward Letters 1931–1937*, Summit Books, 1986, p.227.

5   André Breton, *Manifestoes of Surrealism*, University of Michigan Press, Ann Arbor, 1972, p.125.

6   New Burlington Galleries, *International Surrealist Exhibition*, 1936, p.13.

ONE   Two Men: Edward and George

1   Letter to Sir Godfrey Thomas, 25 December 1919, quoted in Piers Brendon and Phillip Whitehead, *The Windsors: A Dynasty Revealed*, Hodder & Stoughton, 1994, p.36.

2   *The Times*, 29 June 1894.

3   Duke of Windsor, *A King's Story: The Memoirs of H.R.H. the Duke of Windsor K.G.*, Cassell, 1951, p.2.

4   Alexander, Grand Duke of Russia, *Twilight of Royalty*, Ray Long & Richard R. Smith, Inc., 1932, p.185.

5   Diana Mosley, *A Life of Contrasts*, Gibson Square, 2009, p.217.

6   Harold Nicholson 20 March 1953 diary entry, quoted in Ziegler, p.15.

7   J. Bryan III and Charles J.V. Murphy, *The Windsor Story*, William Morrow & Company, 1979, p.8.

8   Michael Bloch, *The Secret File of the Duke of Windsor*, Corgi, 1989, p.237.

9   Colin Cross (ed.), *Life with Lloyd George: The Diary of A. J. Sylvester 1931–45*, Macmillan, 1975, p.193.

10 Diary note 13 January 1936, Stanley Olson (ed.), *Harold Nicolson Diaries and Letters 1930–1964*, Penguin Books, 1985, p.355.

11 Hector Bolitho, *King Edward VIII: His Life and Reign*, Eyre & Spottiswood, 1937, p.45.

12 Duke of Windsor, *A King's Story*, p.100.

13 Lord Cecil letter to wife, 9 May 1916, quoted in Ziegler, p.72.

14 J.M. Barrie, *Peter Pan*, Dover Publications Inc., 2000, p.49.

15 Edward to Bryan Godfrey-Faussett, quoted in *Daily Telegraph*, 4 December 2008.

16 Duke of Windsor, *A King's Story*, pp.116, 118.

17 Duke of Windsor, *A King's Story*, p.117.

18 Duke of Windsor, *A King's Story*, p.118, Edward to George, 22 September 1915.

19 Charles Carlton, *Royal Warriors: A Military History of the British Monarchy*, Routledge, 2014, p.158. There were suggestions that 'In those four years I found my manhood' was Edward's private joke about having lost his virginity in France.

20 *The Times*, 17 July 1936.

21 *Action*, 23 July 1936.

22 Rupert Godfrey (ed.), *Letters from a Prince: Edward, Prince of Wales to Mrs Freda Dudley Ward: March 1918–January 1921*, Warner Books, 1999, p.13, Edward to Freda Dudley Ward, 1 April 1918.

23 Compton Mackenzie, *The Windsor Tapestry; Being a Study of the Life, Heritage and Abdication of H.R.H. the Duke of Windsor*, Rich & Cowan, 1938, p.211.

24 Frank Prochaska, *The Republic of Britain 1760 to 2000*, Allen Lane, 2000, p.159.

25 Prochaska, *The Republic of Britain 1760 to 2000*, p.174.

26 *The Times*, 12 November 1918.

27 Prochaska, *The Republic of Britain 1760 to 2000*, p.170.

28 Godfrey, *Letters*, pp.211, 245. Letters 15 and 27 September 1919.

29 Duke of Windsor, *A King's Story*, p.132.

30 Bolitho, *King Edward VIII: His Life and Reign*, p.95.

31 Brendon and Whitehead, *The Windsors*, p.36.

32 Frances Donaldson, *Edward VIII: A Biography of the Duke of Windsor*, J.B. Lippincott, 1975, p.96.

33 Godfrey, *Letters*, p.346, Edward to Freda Dudley Ward, 18 April 1920.

34 Godfrey, *Letters*, p.342, Edward to Freda Dudley Ward, 20 March 1920.

35 *New York Times*, 8 June 2003, quoting Edward to Freda Dudley Ward, 5 August 1922.

36 Bryan and Murphy, *The Windsor Story*, p.69.

37 Ziegler, *King Edward VIII*, p.137.

38 Duke of Windsor, *A King's Story*, p.171, Edward to George, 16 December 1921.

39 Godfrey, *Letters*, pp.324, 443–4, Edward to Freda Dudley Ward, 27 March 1920, 22 July 1920.

40 Godfrey, *Letters*, p.476, Edward to Freda Dudley Ward, 9 September 1920.

41 Quoted in Ziegler, *King Edward VIII*, p.111.

42 Duke of Windsor, *A King's Story*, p.213.

43   Michael Foot, *Aneurin Bevan: A Biography, Volume 1: 1897–1945*, Faber & Faber, 2008, p.239.

44   A typical speech, one on sportsmanship and the British race, can be heard at www.youtube.com/watch?v=iL9iTLJOMpE.

45   Alistair Cooke, *Six Men*, Penguin Books, 2008, p.37.

46   *The Times*, 16 June 1926.

47   *Nottingham Journal*, 30 January 1927. In the 1940s Edward would throw away $100,000 in a futile effort to find oil on his Calgary ranch to supplement his income.

48   Letter 28 February 1922, quoted in Ziegler, *King Edward VIII*, p.171.

49   Hugo Vickers, *Behind Closed Doors: The Tragic, Untold Story of Wallis Simpson*, Arrow Books, 2012, p.276.

50   21 February 1916 diary entry, quoted in Ziegler, *King Edward VIII*, p.89.

51   Donaldson, *Edward VIII*, p.74.

52   *Literary Digest*, 19 December 1936.

53   Brendon and Whitehead, *The Windsors*, p.38.

54   The National Archives of the United Kingdom (hereafter TNA), KV 2/1506, Note 148, 23 October 1943.

55   Quoted in *The Times*, 1 August 1936.

56   TNA, KV 2/1505(1), Item 88B, McMahon letter to Bevis, 1 April 1937, p.1. Hereafter 1 April 1937 letter.

57   *The Times*, 15 September 1936.

58   TNA, KV 2/1505(1), Item 105A, A.S.T. Godfrey minute, 21 September 1939.

59   TNA, 3/1713, Note 53, Chief Constable CID to Assistant Commissioner Crime, 30 January 1939.

60   TNA, MEPO 3/1713, Item 3A, Chief Inspector John Sands report, 20 July 1936.

61   *Mid-Ulster Mail*, 1 August 1936.

62   TNA, KV 2/1505(1), 1 April 1937 letter, p.1.

63   *Aberdeen Press and Journal*, 18 July 1936.

64   *Derry Journal*, 20 July 1936.

65   TNA, KV 2/1505(1), 1 April 1937 letter, p.1.

66   *The Times*, 23 July 1936.

67   TNA, MEPO 3/1713, Item 3A, Chief Inspector John Sands report, 20 July 1936.

68   *Derry Journal*, 20 July 1936.

69   TNA, KV 2/1505(1), 1 April 1937 letter, p.1.

70   TNA, KV 2/1505(1), 1 April 1937 letter, p.1.

71   TNA, KV 2/1505(1), 1 April 1937 letter, p.2.

72   *Aberdeen Press and Journal*, 18 July 1936.

73   TNA, KV2 1505(2), Item 87A, Bevis letter to Kell, 24 May 1937.

74   TNA, KV 2/1505(1), 1 April 1937 letter, p.2.

75   TNA, KV 2/1505(1), 1 April 1937 letter, p.3.

76   The section on the case and trial is compiled from reports in *Nottingham Evening Post*, 30 March 1933; *The Times*, 7 April and 13 May 1933; *Yorkshire Post*, 12 and 13 May 1933; *Leeds Mercury*, 13 May 1933; TNA, KV 2/1505(1), 1 April 1937 letter, p.3.

77   TNA, KV 2/1505(2), 1 April 1937 letter, p.9.

78   TNA, MEPO 3/1713, Item 24F, letter 3, McMahon to Mrs L. Waddle, 7 August 1936.

79   *Daily Mirror*, 15 September 1936.

80   TNA, MEPO 3/1713, Item 24F, letter 16, McMahon letter to his wife, 5 September 1936.

81   TNA, KV 2/1505(1), 1 April 1937 letter, p.4.

82   *The Times*, 4 July 1933.

TWO   Prelude to Assassination

1   MI5 has undergone a number of name changes in the course of its history, but for convenience MI5 will be used throughout.

2   R.G. Grant, *MI5, MI6: Britain's Security and Intelligence Services*, Gallery Books, 1989, p.13.

3   Nicholas Hiley, 'Entering the Lists: MI5's Great Spy Round-up of August 1914', *Intelligence and National Security*, Vol. 21, No. 1, February 2006.

4   Christopher Andrew, *The Defence of the Realm: The Authorized History of MI5*, Allen Lane, 2009, p.133.

5   Constance Kell, *A Secret Well Kept: The Untold Story of Sir Vernon Kell, Founder of MI5*, Conway, 2017, p.176.

6   Kevin Quinlan, *The Secret War Between the Wars: MI5 in the 1920s and 1930s*, Boydell Press, 2014, p.181.

7   Quoted in Andrew, *The Defence of the Realm*, p.128.

8   John Costello, *Mask of Treachery*, Collins, 1988, p.348.

9   Chapman Pincher, *Treachery, Betrayals, Blunders and Cover-ups: Six Decades of Espionage*, Mainstream, 2012, p.67. A further ironic twist is that Blunt, while still with MI5, was despatched to Germany in 1945 to gather – and help keep hidden – documents exposing connections between the Duke and Duchess of Windsor and the Nazis.

10   TNA, KV 2/1505(1), 1 April 1937 letter, p.4.

11   Text of 14 August 1934 petition in *The Times*, 1 August 1936.

12   TNA, KV 2/1505(1), 1 April 1937 letter, p.5.

13   TNA, KV 2/1505(1), 1 April 1937 letter, p.5.

14   TNA, MEPO 3/1713, Item 16D, Mrs Violet Van der Elst statement to police, no date.

15   TNA, KV 2/1505(2), 1 April 1937 letter, p.9.

16   *Daily Mirror*, 24 April 1935.

17   TNA, KV 2/1505, Note 6, 29 September 1935.

18   TNA, MEPO 3/1713, Item 16, William Osborne statement to police, 17 July 1936; Item 16G, Lionel Howes statement to police, 17 July 1936.
19   TNA, MEPO 3/1713, Item 16D, Mrs Violet Van der Elst statement to police, no date.
20   *The Times*, 8 April 1936; *Wandsworth Borough News*, 9 April 1936.
21   Claud Cockburn, *The Devil's Decade*, Sidgwick & Jackson, 1973, p.198. MI5 had a file on Cockburn.
22   Diana Vreeland, *D.V.*, Weidenfeld & Nicholson, 1984, p.70.
23   'He ... spent the remainder of the evening in the successful seduction of a Mrs Barnes, wife of the local Commissioner. He told me so himself next morning.' Hart-Davis, *In Royal Service*, p.109.
24   Edward to Freda Dudley Ward, 5 August 1922, quoted in Ziegler, *King Edward VIII*, p.164.
25   Kingsley Martin, *The Magic of Monarchy*, Thomas Nelson & Sons, 1937, pp.23–4.
26   Duchess of Windsor, *The Heart Has Its Reasons: The Memoirs of the Duchess of Windsor*, David McKay Company, 1956, p.206.
27   13 August 1934, Aird diary entry, quoted in Ziegler, *King Edward VIII*, p.202.
28   Edward continued throughout his life to deny he had sex with Wallis before her divorce; he sued one writer for saying so in 1937 and subsequently threatened action against another who made a similar claim.
29   Kenneth Rose, *George V*, Weidenfeld & Nicolson, 1983, p.392.
30   Nicolson, *Diaries*, 13 January 1936 entry, p.89.
31   John Gunther, *Inside Europe*, Hamish Hamilton, 1938, p.252.
32   Christopher Wilson, *Dancing with the Devil: The Windsors and Jimmy Donahue*, St Martin's Press, 2001, p.201.
33   Piers Brendon, *Edward VIII: The Uncrowned King*, Penguin Books, 2018, p.47.
34   TNA, MEPO 10/35/1, Office of the Commissioner Papers, Special Branch report to Commissioner, 3 July 1935.
35   TNA, MEPO 10/35/1, Office of the Commissioner Papers, Special Branch report to Commissioner, 17 October 1935.
36   Private information, cited in Brendon and Whitehead, *The Windsors*, p.62.
37   Robert Beaken, *Cosmo Lang: Archbishop in War and Crisis*, I.B. Tauris, 2012, p.80.
38   Mabel Airlie, *Thatched with Gold: The Memoirs of Mabel, Countess of Airlie*, Hutchinson, 1962, p.197.
39   Thomas Jones, *A Diary with Letters*, Oxford University Press, 1954, p.291.
40   Keith Middlemas and John Barnes, *Baldwin: A Biography*, Weidenfeld & Nicolson, 1969, p.976.
41   William Shawcross, *Queen Elizabeth The Queen Mother: The Official Biography*, Macmillan, 2009, p.308.
42   Bryan and Murphy, *The Windsor Story*, p.69.
43   *The Times*, 4 May 1935.
44   Hart-Davis, *In Royal Service*, p.50.
45   Graham Payne and Sheridan Morley, *The Noël Coward Diaries*, Weidenfeld & Nicolson, 1982, p.520.

46 Kenneth Young (ed.), *The Diaries of Sir Robert Bruce Lockhart, 1915–1938, Volume 1*, Macmillan, 1973, p.262.

47 Charles Higham, *Mrs Simpson: Secret Lives of the Duchess of Windsor*, Pan Books, 2004, p.84.

48 The family practising the Nazi salute is at: www.youtube.com/watch?v=OB0YAVF-eOI.

49 Quoted in Stephen Dorrill, *Blackshirt: Sir Oswald Mosley and British Fascism*, Penguin, 2007, p.294.

50 TNA, MEPO 10/35, Office of the Commissioner Papers, Special Branch report to Metropolitan Police Commissioner, 25 March 1935.

51 Oswald Mosley, *Fascism: 100 Questions Asked and Answered*, BUF Publications, 1936, p.8.

52 *The Times*, 12 June 1935.

53 Kell, *A Secret Well Kept*, pp.164–5.

54 Robert Rhodes James (ed.), *'Chips': The Diaries of Sir Henry Channon*, Phoenix Press, 2003, pp.35–6.

55 Bloch, *Secret File*, p.113.

56 Donaldson, *Edward VIII*, p.208.

57 Donaldson, *Edward VIII*, p.206.

58 Deborah Cadbury, *Princes at War: The British Royal Family's Private Battle in the Second World War*, Bloomsbury, 2016, p.61.

59 Denis Mack Smith, *Mussolini*, Phoenix Press, 1981, p.200.

60 Roberto Olla, *Il Duce and His Women*, Alma Books, 2011, p.42.

61 Mosley, *Contrasts*, p.190.

62 Godfrey, *Letters*, p.77, Edward to Freda Dudley Ward, 26 July 1918.

63 Duke of Windsor, *A King's Story*, p.296.

64 Hart-Davis, *In Royal Service*, p.120.

65 *Time*, 29 April 1929.

66 Quoted in Bryan and Murphy, *The Windsor Story*, pp.77–8.

67 A writer on secrecy and the British state has commented on what is allowed to remain in the small selection of MI5 files passed to the National Archives for public consumption. 'They present a carefully sculpted image of the history of British intelligence: MI5 fully grasps the importance of the politics of archives.' Ian Cobain, *The History Thieves: Secrets, Lies and the Shaping of a Modern Nation*, Portobello Books, 2016, p.234.

68 TNA, KV 2/1505(1), Note 6, 25 September 1935; Note 9, 10 October 1935.

69 TNA, KV 2/1505(2), Item 43A, Kell to Sir Russell Scott, 21 July 1936.

70 TNA, KV 2/1505(1), Note 10, 12 October 1935; Note 11, 15 October 1935.

71 Andrew, *The Defence of the Realm*, p.128.

72 TNA, KV 2/1505(1), Note 13, 18 October 1935 'Report herewith Re interview with McMahon'. The attachment (13A) is marked 'Destroyed' but a copy appears in another section of the file, presumably retained in error by an inattentive weeder. See KV 2/1505(1), addition to Item 116A.

73 George W. Baer, *Test Case: Italy, Ethiopia, and the League of Nations*, Hoover Institution Press, 1976, p.80.

74 TNA, MEPO 3/1713, Item 24F, letter 7, Matthews to McMahon, 17 August 1936.
75 TNA, KV 2/1505(1), Note 14, 18 October 1935.
76 TNA, KV 2/1505(1), Note 15, 22 October 1935.
77 *The Times*, 19 May 1936.
78 TNA, KV 2/1505(2), Item 43A, Kell to Sir Russell Scott, 21 July 1936.
79 TNA, KV 2/1505(1), Note 17, 30 November 1935; KV 2/1505(1), Note 18, 12 December 1935.
80 TNA, KV 2/1505(2), Item 49A, Ottaway to Kell, 22 July 1936.
81 *Daily Express*, 13 August 1937.
82 TNA, KV2/1505(1), Item 89A, Ottaway to Harker, 10 June 1937.
83 Andrew, *The Defence of the Realm*, p.196.
84 Quoted in Charmian Brinson and Richard Dove, *A Matter of Intelligence: MI5 and the Surveillance of Anti-Nazi Refugees 1933–50*, Manchester University Press, 2014, p.51. Hereafter Brinson and Dove.
85 Brinson and Dove, pp.16–19.
86 TNA, KV 2/1505(1), Item 89A, Ottaway to Harker, 10 June 1937.
87 TNA, KV 2/1505(1), written in margin of Note 37, 6 May 1936.
88 TNA, MEPO 3/1713, letter in folder GR 201/MR/1703B.
89 An intriguing coincidence is that some of the work McMahon's solicitor Alfred Kerstein conducted involved refugees. See, for example, the case of a Berlin businessman resisting deportation because he had faced death threats in Germany from Nazi stormtroopers, *Daily Herald*, 11 May 1937.
90 *The Times*, 13 December 1935.
91 TNA, KV 2/1505(1), Note 25, 7 February 1936.
92 TNA, MEPO 3/1713, Item 16h, Inspector Arthur interview with Dorothea Maritch, 24 July 1936.
93 Text of petition from *The Times*, 1 August 1936.
94 TNA, KV 2/1505(1), Note 31, 17 April 1936.
95 TNA, KV 2/1505(2), Item 43A, Kell to Scott, 21 July 1936.
96 TNA, KV 2/1505(2), Item 85A, Ottaway report, 27 October 1936.
97 TNA, KV 2/1505(2), Item 49A, 'Mr Ottaway's statement', undated, attached to file 22 July 1936.
98 *Daily Telegraph*, 15 September 1936.
99 TNA, MEPO 3/1713, Item 24F, letter 27, McMahon to Kerstein, 12 October 1936.
100 TNA, KV 2/1505(1), Note 33, 21 April 1936.
101 TNA, KV 2/1505(1), Note 37, 6 May 1936.
102 TNA, KV 2/1505(2), Item 43A, Kell to Scott, 21 July 1936.
103 TNA, KV 2/1505(1), Note 38, 13 June 1936, S7b to Kell.
104 *The Times*, 1 August 1936.
105 TNA, KV 2/1505(2), Item 49A, 'Mr Ottaway's statement', undated, attached to file 22 July 1936.
106 TNA, KV 2/1505(2), Item 49A, 'Mr Ottaway's statement'.
107 *The Times*, 25 July 1936, Mary Blencowe's evidence at Bow Street Court.
108 *The Times*, 25 July 1936, text of McMahon letter to Sir John Simon.

THREE   'The Dastardly Attempt'

1   Cockburn, *The Devil's Decade*, p.197.

2   Middlemas and Barnes, *Baldwin*, p.976.

3   Chips, *Diaries*, p.53.

4   Duke of Windsor, *A King's Story*, p.277.

5   Juliet Gardiner, *The Thirties: An Intimate History*, Harper Press, 2010, p.377.

6   *The Times*, 21 January 1936.

7   Duchess of Windsor, *The Heart Has Its Reasons*, p.212.

8   20 January 1936 diary entry, John Julius Norwich (ed.), *The Duff Cooper Diaries*, Phoenix Press, 2006, p.226.

9   Donaldson, *Edward VIII*, p.192.

10   Duke of Windsor, *A King's Story*, p.192.

11   Robert Self, *Neville Chamberlain: A Biography*, Routledge, 2016, p.256.

12   A.J.P. Taylor, *English History 1914–1945*, Oxford University Press, 1990 ed., p.398.

13   Middlemas and Barnes, *Baldwin*, p.978.

14   Duke of Windsor, *A King's Story*, p.287.

15   Duke of Windsor, *A King's Story*, p.288.

16   Michael Bloch, *The Reign & Abdication of Edward VIII*, Bantam Press, 1990, p.10.

17   Sarah Bradford, *George VI*, Penguin Books, 2002, p.172.

18   *Daily Express*, 20 July 1936.

19   Shawcross, *Queen Elizabeth The Queen Mother*, p.355. Deeside was a reference to Balmoral, where the royal family traditionally spent the summer.

20   Geoffrey Bocca, *The Woman Who Would be Queen: A Biography of the Duchess of Windsor*, Rinehart & Co., 1954, p.60.

21   Wigram's 15 February 1936 memorandum in Royal Archives, quoted in Ziegler, *King Edward VIII*, p.274.

22   Davidson Papers, quoted in Anne Sebba, *That Woman: The Life of Wallis Simpson, Duchess of Windsor*, Phoenix Press, 2011, p.125.

23   Wigram's 15 February 1936 memorandum in Royal Archives, quoted in Ziegler, *King Edward VIII*, p.274.

24   Shawcross, *Queen Elizabeth The Queen Mother*, p.359.

25   Beaken, *Cosmo Lang*, p.79.

26   Bloch, *Letters*, p.192.

27   Lord Birkenhead, *Walter Monckton: The Life of Lord Monckton of Brenchley*, Weidenfeld & Nicolson, 1969, p.128.

28   Chips, *Diaries*, p.60.

29   Duke of Windsor, *A King's Story*, p.260.

30   Janet Flanner, quoted in Bocca, *The Woman Who Would be Queen*, p.62.

31   *The Literary Digest*, 21 March 1936.

32   Donaldson, *Edward VIII*, p.212.

33   TNA, CAB 23/86/10, Cabinet minutes, 27 November 1936.

34   Bloch, *Reign & Abdication*, p.31.

35   *The Times*, 11 December 1936.

36 *Daily Worker*, 29 June 1936.
37 Nicolson, *Diaries*, 16 July 1936 entry, p.101.
38 TNA, KV 2/1505(2), Item 79A, Home Office minute, 8 October 1936.
39 *Daily Telegraph*, 15 September 1936, McMahon's evidence at the Old Bailey.
40 *The Times*, 1 August 1936.
41 *Daily Telegraph*, 15 September 1936.
42 TNA, MEPO 3/1713, Statement of Goldwin Lloyd Faulkner, 20 July 1936.
43 TNA, MEPO 3/1713, Item 3A, Chief Inspector John Sands report, 20 July 1936.
44 TNA, MEPO 3/1713, Statement of Goldwin Lloyd Faulkner, 20 July 1936.
45 *London Gazette*, 22 December 1915; TNA, AIR76/158/39.
46 *Daily Express*, 1 August 1936, McMahon responding to questions from his solicitor.
47 *The Times*, 1 August 1936; *Daily Express*, 1 August 1936.
48 *Daily Express*, 15 September 1936.
49 Duke of Windsor, *A King's Story*, p.109.
50 *The Times*, 17 July 1936.
51 For a British Movietone News report on the Hyde Park ceremony and the aftermath, see www.youtube.com/watch?v=2fMeDW2kR84.
52 Ian Hernon, *Assassin! 200 Years of British Political Murder*, Pluto Press, 2007, p.150.
53 *Daily Mirror*, 17 July 1936.
54 *Yorkshire Post*, 17 July 1936.
55 *The Times*, 17 July 1936.
56 *Yorkshire Post*, 17 July 1936.
57 *Daily Mirror*, 17 July 1936.
58 *Daily Express*, 17 July 1936.
59 Duke of Windsor, *A King's Story*, p.298.
60 Ziegler, *King Edward VIII*, p.264.
61 Stefano Papi and Alexandra Rhodes, *Famous Jewelry Collectors*, Thames & Hudson, 2004, p.118.
62 *Daily Herald*, 25 July 1936.
63 *The Times*, 25 July 1936.
64 *Daily Mirror*, 17 July 1936.
65 Bloch, *Reign & Abdication*, p.21, 'Paris Papers: Sir John Simon to King Edward VIII, 16 July 1936' from the unpublished archives of the Duke and Duchess of Windsor.
66 Duke of Windsor, *A King's Story*, p.299.
67 *Daily Express*, 17 July 1936.
68 *Daily Express*, 17 July 1936.
69 TNA, MEPO 3/1713, Item 3A, Chief Inspector John Sands report, 20 July 1936.
70 *Daily Mirror*, 17 July 1936.
71 Quoted in *Northern Whig*, 18 July 1936.
72 TNA, CAB/23/85/7, Cabinet minutes, 22 July 1936.

73   *Daily Express*, 17 July 1936; *Londonderry Sentinel*, 18 July 1936.
74   TNA, MEPO 3/1713, Item 24F, letter 4, McMahon to Patrick Bannigan, 7 August 1936.
75   *Daily Express*, 18 July 1936.
76   *Daily Express*, 18 July 1936.
77   *The Times*, 17 September 1936.
78   *Daily Express*, 18 July 1936.
79   TNA, MEPO 3/1713, Item 3A, Chief Inspector John Sands report, 20 July 1936.
80   TNA, MEPO 3/1713, Item 3A, Chief Inspector John Sands report, 20 July 1936.
81   TNA, MEPO 3/1713, letters in folder GR 201/MR/1703B for the written responses to Scotland Yard's appeal.
82   *Daily Express*, 17 July 1936.
83   TNA, MEPO 3/1713, Item 1B, Chief Constable CID Howell to Supt. C1, cc Sands.
84   TNA, MEPO 3/1713, Item 2A, Ashenden's statement; Item 2C, CID report.
85   TNA, MEPO 3/1713, Item 2C, Sands note.
86   TNA, MEPO 3/1713, Item 24F, letter 7, F. Matthews to McMahon, 17 August 1936.
87   TNA, MEPO 3/1713, letter in folder GR 201/MR/1703B.
88   TNA, MEPO 3/1713, Item 16A, Sands memo to C.C. (CID), 3 September 1936.
89   TNA, MEPO 3/1713, Item 16C, Home Office copy of statement by J.M. Williams, 17 July 1936.
90   TNA, MEPO 3/1713, Item 16G, Statement of Lionel Howes, 17 July 1936.
91   TNA, MEPO 3/1713, Item 16F, Statement of Reginald Clifton, 17 July 1936.
92   TNA, MEPO 3/1713, Item 16A, Sands memo to C.C. (CID), 3 September 1936.
93   TNA, MEPO 3/1713, Item 16D, Mrs Violet Van der Elst statement to police, undated.
94   TNA, KV 2/1505(2), Item 55A, Superintendent Channing report, 22 July 1936.
95   *The Times*, 23 July 1936.
96   *The Times*, 30 July 1936.
97   Bloch, *Letters*, p.226.
98   Duchess of Windsor, *The Heart Has Its Reasons*, p.214.

FOUR   McMahon's Trials

1   TNA, CRIM 1/861, H. A. Grierson report to Bow Street Police Court, 23 July 1936.
2   *Daily Express*, 18 July 1936.
3   *The Times*, 20 August 1936.
4   TNA, KV 2/1505(1), Notes 52 and 53.
5   TNA, KV 2/1505(2), Item 43A, Kell to Scott, 21 July 1936.
6   TNA, KV 2/1505(2), Item 43A, Kell to Scott, 21 July 1936.
7   TNA, KV 2/1505(2), Item 44A, Harker note on telephone message from Kerstein, 21 July 1936.
8   TNA, KV 2/1505(2), Item 46A, Harker note re action taken in connection with McMahon's solicitors, 22 July 1936.
9   TNA, KV 2/1505(2), Item 48A, DPP note of interview with Attorney General; Item 47A, Harker note on meeting with Attorney General, 22 July 1936.
10   TNA, KV 2/1505(2), Item 49A, Ottaway statement on dealings with McMahon, 22 July 1936.
11   TNA, KV 2/1505(2), Item 51A, Harker note re interview with Kerstein, 23 July 1936.
12   TNA, KV 2/1505(2), Item 51A, Harker note re interview with Kerstein, 23 July 1936.
13   TNA, KV 2/1505(2), Item 51A, Harker note re interview with Kerstein, 23 July 1936.
14   TNA, KV 2/1505(2), 1 April 1937 letter, p.7.
15   *Sydney Morning Herald*, 25 July 1936.
16   All court exchanges are from *The Times*, *Daily Herald* and *Daily Express*, 25 July 1936.
17   CRIM 1/861, Grierson to Bow Street Police Court, 31 July 1936.
18   All court exchanges are from *The Times*, *Daily Mirror* and *Daily Express*, 1 August 1936.
19   TNA, MEPO 3/1713, Item 24F, letter 1, McMahon to Rev. H. Miller, 1 August 1936.
20   Donaldson, *Edward VIII*, p.226.
21   Bloch, *Letters*, p.227.
22   *Daily Mirror*, 1 August 1936.
23   Duke of Windsor, *A King's Story*, p.306.
24   Duchess of Winchester, *The Heart Has Its Reasons*, p.221.
25   Bolitho, *King Edward VIII: His Life and Reign*, p.262.
26   Higham, *Mrs Simpson*, p.161.
27   Bloch, *Letters*, p.230.
28   Andrew Morton, *Wallis in Love: The Untold True Passion of the Duchess of Windsor*, Michael O'Mara Books, 2018, p.205.
29   Brendon and Whitehead, *The Windsors*, p.74.
30   Bloch, *Letters*, p.234.

31 Ziegler, *King Edward VIII*, p.287; Bloch, *Letters*, p.237.
32 TNA, MEPO 3/1713, Item 24F, letter 16, McMahon to wife, 5 September 1936.
33 TNA, MEPO 3/1713, Item 24F, letter 4, McMahon to Patrick Bannigan, 7 August 1936.
34 TNA, MEPO 3/1713, Item 24F, letter 6, McMahon to Papal Nuncio, 12 August 1936.
35 TNA, MEPO 3/1713, Item 24F, letter 12, McMahon to W.L. Davie 22 August 1936.
36 TNA, MEPO 3/1713, Item 24F, letters 13 and 16, McMahon to wife 24 August and 5 September 1936.
37 TNA, MEPO 3/1713, Item 24F, letter 8, McMahon to Lockwood & Bradley, 19 August 1936.
38 TNA, MEPO 3/1713, Item 24F, letter 13, McMahon to wife, 24 August 1936.
39 TNA, MEPO 3/1713, Item 20A, Criminal Investigation Department report, 11 September 1936.
40 TNA, MEPO 3/1317, Item 24F, letter 20, McMahon to wife, 10 September 1936.
41 This section is compiled from trial reports in 15 September 1936 editions of *The Times*, *Daily Telegraph*, *Daily Express* and *Daily Mirror*.
42 TNA, MEPO 3/1317, Item 24F, letter 20, McMahon to wife, 10 September 1936.
43 TNA, MEPO 3/1713, Exhibit 11 in trial documents.
44 TNA, KV 2/1505(1), Item 89A, Ottaway to Harker, 10 June 1937.
45 Bloch, *Reign & Abdication*, pp.20–1.
46 *Daily Mirror*, 15 September 1936; *The Times*, 15 September 1936.
47 Mackenzie, *The Windsor Tapestry*, p.415.
48 *Daily Express*, 15 September 1936.
49 *Daily Mirror*, 15 September 1936.
50 *Birmingham Gazette*, 15 September 1936.
51 TNA, KV 2/1505(2) Item 68A, Somervell to Harker, 18 September 1936; attached letter from Gilligan, 14 September 1936.
52 TNA, KV 2/1505(2) Item 70A, Harker to Somervell, 22 September 1936.
53 TNA, KV 2/1505(2) Item 69A, British Union of Fascists to Home Secretary, 16 September 1936, with attached Gilligan letter.
54 TNA, KV 2/1505(1), Note 71, 24 September 1936.
55 TNA, MEPO 3/1713, Item 24F, letter 23, McMahon to wife, 15 September 1936.
56 *Daily Mirror*, 16 September 1936.
57 TNA, MEPO 3/1713, Item 24F, letter 23, McMahon to wife, 15 September 1936.
58 TNA, KV 2/1505(2), Item 72A, copy of McMahon letter to the Home Office, 23 September 1936.
59 TNA, KV 2/1505(2), Item 74A, Harker to Robinson, 25 September 1936.

60 TNA, KV 2/1505(2) Item 79A, summary of Kerstein letter in Home Office memorandum, 8 October 1936.

61 TNA, KV 2/1505(2) Item 79A, Carew Robinson memorandum, 8 October 1936.

62 TNA, MEPO 3/1713, Item 24F, letter 24, McMahon to wife, 3 October 1936.

63 TNA, MEPO 3/1713, Item 24F, letter 30, McMahon to wife, 20 October 1936.

64 TNA, MEPO 3/1713, Item 24F, letter 25, McMahon to Kerstein, 3 October 1936.

65 TNA, MEPO 3/1713, Item 24F, letter 27, McMahon to Kerstein, 12 October 1936.

66 TNA, KV 2/1505(2), Item 85A, Ottaway report, 27 October 1936.

67 TNA, MEPO 3/1713, Item 24F, letter 27, McMahon to Kerstein, 12 October 1936.

68 *The Times*, 27 October 1936.

FIVE   Afterlives

1 TNA, MEPO 3/1713, Item 39A, note on McMahon, 15 September 1937.

2 *Daily Express*, 13 August 1937.

3 TNA, KV 2/1505(2), 1 April 1937 letter, p.10.

4 TNA, KV 2/1505(1), 1 April 1937 letter, pp.6, 8.

5 TNA, KV 2/1505(2), 1 April 1937 letter, p.9.

6 TNA, KV 2/1505(2), Item 87A, Bevis to Kell, 24 May 1937.

7 TNA, KV 2/1505(1), Item 89A, Ottaway letter to Harker, 10 June 1937.

8 TNA, KV 2/15052(1), Note 90, Harker to Kell, 18 June 1937.

9 TNA, KV 2/15052(1), Note 91, Kell to Harker, 18 June 1937.

10 *Daily Express*, 13 August 1937.

11 Ziegler, *King Edward VIII*, p.264.

12 TNA, MEPO 3/1713, Item 34A. McMahon to Home Secretary, no date.

13 TNA, MEPO 3/1713, Item 39A, note on file, 15 September 1937.

14 TNA, MEPO 3/1713, Item 41A, Inspector Robert Cooper note on file, 14 October 1937.

15 *The Week*, 28 October 1936.

16 TNA, MEPO 10/65, Item 28, cutting from *New York Sunday News*, 27 September 1936.

17 Duke of Windsor, *A King's Story*, p.314.

18 *Time*, 23 November 1936.

19 *Time*, 5 October 1936.

20 Prochaska, *The Republic of Britain 1760 to 2000*, p.190.

21 *The Times*, 18 November 1936.

22 Bloch, *Letters*, p.24, Wallis to Edward, 14 October 1936.

23 Duke of Windsor, *A King's Story*, p.315.

24   *The Week*, 14 October 1936, quoted in Cockburn, *The Devil's Decade*, p.206. The newsletter's circulation rose sharply when it was recognised as a good source of news on the relationship.

25   TNA, CAB 23/86, 27 November 1936.

26   Duke of Windsor, *A King's Story*, p.318.

27   Lord Beaverbrook, *The Abdication of King Edward VIII*, Atheneum, 1966, p.47.

28   A.W. Baldwin, *My Father: The True Story*, George Allen & Unwin, 1955, p.299.

29   *The Times*, 11 November 1936.

30   United Feature Syndicate, quoted in *The Literary Digest*, 19 December 1936.

31   Text of Hardinge's letter in *The Times*, 29 November 1955. Hardinge wrote in an article that his opinion in 1936 had been that the effect of Wallis marrying Edward and becoming queen would be 'a popular explosion that would not only weaken, but in all probability destroy, the monarchy'.

32   Duchess of Windsor, *The Heart Has Its Reasons*, p.236.

33   Duke of Windsor, *A King's Story*, p.319.

34   Duke of Windsor, *A King's Story*, p.331.

35   TNA, CAB 23/86/10, Cabinet minutes, 25 November 1936.

36   Cooper, quoted in Shawcross, *Queen Elizabeth The Queen Mother*, p.372.

37   Duke of Windsor, *A King's Story*, p.336.

38   W.F. Deedes, *Words and Deedes: Selected Journalism 1931–2006*, Pan Books, 2006, p.542. Deedes was on the scene as a reporter for the *Morning Post*.

39   TNA, CAB 23/86/10, Cabinet minutes, 25 November 1936.

40   TNA, CAB 23/86/13, Cabinet minutes, 4 December 1936.

41   Letter in *Daily Express*, quoted in Martin, *The Magic of Monarchy*, p.66.

42   Beaken, *Cosmo Lang*, p.111.

43   *Yorkshire Post*, 2 December 1936, quoted in Donaldson, *Edward VIII*, p.283.

44   *The Times*, 3 December 1936.

45   *Independent*, 23 May 2013; *Daily Mirror*, 23 May 2013.

46   Geoffrey Elliott, *Gentleman Spymaster: How Lt Col Tommy 'Tar' Robertson Double-crossed the Nazis*, Methuen, 2011.

47   *Annual Register 1936*, p.106.

48   Dorrill, *Blackshirt*, p.406.

49   Nicolson, *Diaries*, 10 December 1936 entry, p.108.

50   James Pope-Hennessy, *Queen Mary 1867–1953*, Alfred A. Knopf, 1960, p.579.

51   A recording of the speech can be heard at www.youtube.com/watch?v=wBn06A-sdok.

52   *Action*, 2 January 1937.

53   Iona and Peter Opie, *The Lore and Language of Schoolchildren*, Oxford University Press, 1959, p.6.

54   Bocca, *The Woman Who Would be Queen*, p.132.

55   Duke of Windsor, *A King's Story*, p.415.

56   Bloch, *Letters*, Wallis to Edward, 3 January 1937, p.288.

57   *The Times*, 14 December 1936.

58   Nicolson, *Diaries*, 28 May 1947 entry, p.323.

59   Bloch, *Letters*, Wallis to Edward, 3 January 1937, p.288.

60 Donaldson, *Edward VIII*, p.344.
61 There is a newsreel of the day at www.youtube.com/watch?v=ui2L67tX9lw.
62 Duchess of Windsor, *The Heart Has Its Reasons*, p.281.
63 Quoted in Pope-Hennessy, p.585.
64 Ziegler, *King Edward VIII*, p.360.
65 *The Times*, 7 June 1937.
66 Ziegler, *King Edward VIII*, p.370.
67 Nicolson, *Diaries*, 5 August 1938 entry, p.129.
68 Ziegler, *King Edward VIII*, p.390.
69 *The Times*, 12 October 1937.
70 There is a short newsreel of the visit: www.youtube.com/watch?v=atXRw_G-uTw.
71 Duchess of Windsor, *The Heart Has Its Reasons*, p.318.
72 Bryan and Murphy, *The Windsor Story*, p.392.
73 *The Times*, 28 October 1937.
74 Duchess of Windsor, *The Heart Has Its Reasons*, p.311.
75 Frank Giles, *Sundry Times*, John Murray, 1986, p.131.
76 Cadbury, *Princes at War*, p.177.
77 Bloch, *Secret Life*, pp.166–8.
78 Duchess of Windsor, *The Heart Has Its Reasons*, p.335.
79 Higham, *Mrs Simpson*, p.343.
80 Dorrill, *Blackshirt*, p.406.
81 Duke of Windsor, *A King's Story*, p.299.
82 TNA, MEPO 3/1713, Note 55, 31 January 1939.
83 *Daily Express*, 13 August 1937.
84 TNA, MEPO 3/1713, Note 51, Special Branch report, 29 July 1938.
85 TNA, KV 2/1505(1), Item 102A, McMahon letter, September 1938.
86 TNA, MEPO 3/1713, Item 53B, Detective Inspector J. Hatton report, 28 January 1939.
87 TNA, MEPO 3/1713, note 54, 30 January 1939.
88 TNA, MEPO 3/1713, Item 60A, McMahon to Pryke, 1 March 1939; Item 60C, Pryke report, 2 March 1939.
89 TNA, MEPO 3/1713. Item 60D, Bow Street Divisional Detective Inspector to Assistant Chief Constable, 10 March 1939.
90 TNA, MEPO 3/1713. Item 58B, extract from *Toronto Daily Star*.
91 TNA, MEPO 3/1713, Item 60E, Inspector J. Kelling report, 23 March 1939.
92 TNA, KV 2/1505(1), Item 105A, A.S.T. Godfrey note to M.I.1a, 21 September 1939.
93 TNA, KV 2/1505(1), McMahon to Cook, 24 November 1939.
94 TNA, KV 2/1505(1) Item 116A, letters in file.
95 TNA, KV 2/1505(1) Major G. Lennox report to O.A. Harker, 11 January 1940. Lennox later handled Louis de Wohl, an astrologer hired by MI5 to cast horoscopes of Nazi leaders to try to determine what astrological advice they were being given.

96   TNA, MEPO 3/1713, Item 69A, Letter to Chief Inspector, postmarked 29 April 1940.
97   TNA, MEPO 3/1713, Item 69A, Detective Inspector Arthur Thorpe report, 9 May 1940.
98   Andrew, *The Defence of the Realm*, pp.227, 237.
99   TNA, KV 2/1506, Special Branch report, 10 October 1943.
100   TNA, KV 2/1505(1), Note 122, G. Shipley, F.3.c.3 to F.3.b.1, 15 March 1943.
101   TNA, KV 2/1505(1), Item 128A, T.M. Shelford F.3.c.3 to Deputy Assistant Commissioner Special Branch, 13 April 1943.
102   TNA, KV 2/1505(1), Item 137A, 'Underground Fascist Activities', T.M. Shelford F.3.c.3 to Deputy Assistant Commissioner Special Branch, 30 May 1943.
103   TNA, KV 2/1506, Item 145A, F.3.c.3, 8 August 1943.
104   TNA, KV 2/1506, Note 148, G. Shipley, 23 October 1943.
105   4 October 1950 letter, Diana Cooper: *Darling Monster: The Letters of Lady Diana Cooper to her Son John Julian Norwich 1939–1952*, Vintage, 2014, p.430.
106   A short newsreel of the new governor taking his oath of office shows the duchess to one side ostentatiously fanning herself: www.youtube.com/watch?v=oGE1nhREXdE.
107   Brendon, *Edward VIII*, p.84.
108   Donaldson, *Edward VIII*, p.410.
109   Ziegler, *King Edward VIII*, p.450.
110   Brendon, *Edward VIII*, p.85.
111   Duchess of Windsor, *The Heart Has Its Reasons*, p.347.
112   Diana Mosley, *Duchess of Windsor*, Gibson Square Books, 2012, p.169.
113   Mosley, *Duchess of Windsor*, p.183.
114   Cooper, *Letters*, p.442.
115   Wilson, *Dancing with the Devil*, p.219.
116   The couple make observations about their lives in a fifty-minute television interview in 1970: www.youtube.com/watch?v=w8u7Ntic5fo.
117   Giles, *Sundry Times*, p.131.
118   *Coronet*, November 1953.
119   Wilson, *Dancing with the Devil*, p.196.
120   Nicolson, *Diaries*, 9 November 1955 entry, p.371.
121   Giles, *Sundry Times*, p.132.
122   TNA, KV 2/1506, Item 150A, McMahon to Hamm, no date.
123   TNA, KV 2/1506, Item 154A, McMahon election leaflet attached to intercepted letter to Mosley.
124   TNA, KV 2/1506, Item 154A, McMahon to Mosley, 2 October 1948.
125   TNA, KV 2/1505, Item 156A, Special Branch report, 23 May 1949.
126   TNA, KV 2/1505(1), 1 April 1937 letter, p.2.
127   TNA, CRIM 1/2117 Part 1.
128   *The Times*, 10 February 1951; *Mid-Ulster Mail*, 17 February 1951.

SIX Bungling or Collusion?

1   *Annual Register 1936*, p.64.
2   TNA, KV 2/1505(2), 1 April 1937 letter, p.7.
3   *The Times*, 16 September 1936.
4   TNA, MEPO 3/1713, letter in folder GR 201/MR/1703B.
5   *Daily Express*, 13 August 1937.
6   TNA, KV 2/1505(2), Item 43A, Kell to Sir Russell Scott, 21 July 1936.
7   Andrew, *The Defence of the Realm*, p.128.
8   *Daily Telegraph*, 15 September 1936.
9   Martin, *The Magic of Monarchy*, p.68.
10 Quoted in Robert Lacey, *Majesty: Elizabeth II and the House of Windsor*, Hutchinson, 1977, p.109.
11 Shawcross, *Queen Elizabeth The Queen Mother*, p.308.

Index

If you enjoyed this title from The History Press …

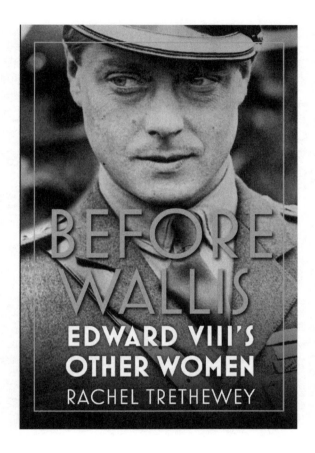

978 0 7509 8560 4

If you enjoyed this title from The History Press ...

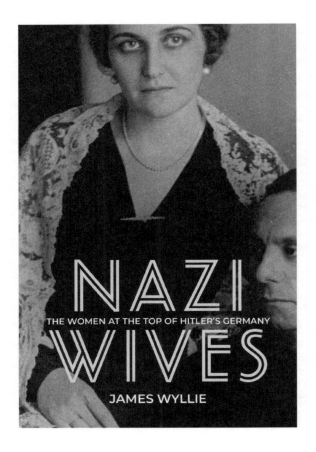

978 0 7509 9122 3